FIRST LADIES
OF THE UNITED STATES

FIRST LADIES
OF THE UNITED STATES

A Biographical Dictionary

ROBERT P. WATSON

LYNNE
RIENNER
PUBLISHERS

BOULDER
LONDON

Published in the United States of America in 2001 by
Lynne Rienner Publishers, Inc.
1800 30th Street, Boulder, Colorado 80301
www.rienner.com

and in the United Kingdom by
Lynne Rienner Publishers, Inc.
3 Henrietta Street, Covent Garden, London WC2E 8LU

Library of Congress Cataloging-in-Publication Data
Watson, Robert P., 1962–
    First ladies of the United States : a biographical dictionary / Robert P. Watson.
        p. cm.
    Includes bibliographical references (p.) and index.
    ISBN 1-55587-907-1 (alk. paper)
    1. Presidents' spouses—United States—Biography—Dictionaries. I. Title.
    E176.2.W369 2001
                                                            00-028068

British Cataloguing in Publication Data
A Cataloguing in Publication record for this book
is available from the British Library.

Printed and bound in the United States of America

The paper used in this publication meets the requirements
of the American National Standard for Permanence of
Paper for Printed Library Materials Z39.48-1984.

5 4 3 2 1

Contents

v

Preface

Although most first ladies of the United States were well known during their time in office, history has largely forgotten them and their many contributions to both the presidency and the nation. A closer consideration of the first ladies offers insights into an important facet of U.S. history and reveals the lives of a group of gifted and intriguing women. This book's goal is to provide the reader with a concise yet thorough profile of those individuals.

The book is organized chronologically according to the time of service of each first lady, beginning with Martha Washington. The main body of the book contains biographies of each presidential spouse who served in the White House during her husband's presidency.

Technically, the term "first lady" refers to the wife of a president; however, this definition is not as clear-cut as it would initially appear. Another consideration in defining a first lady pertains to those women who functioned as official hostesses for bachelor or widower presidents. Without a spouse available to serve as first lady, presidents typically turned to a daughter or niece. These hostesses are also profiled in the main body of the text in chronological order of service.

Five wives of men who would later become president died before their husbands' inaugurations: Martha Jefferson, Rachel Jackson, Hannah Van Buren, Ellen Arthur, and Alice Roosevelt. With the exception of Alice Roosevelt (who had been married only a few years at the time of her death), these women had a major part in their husbands' political careers. Their biographies appear in Appendixes 5 through 8.

The appendixes also include compilations of interesting facts on the first ladies. Comprehensive indexes follow.

*   *   *

This book would not have been possible without the support and valuable contributions of my wife, Claudia Pavone Watson. I also wish to acknowledge my wife and family for the boundless patience they demonstrated during the long hours it took to complete the project. I dedicate the book to them: Claudia, Nancy, Wendy, Bob, Linda, Julio, Celeste, Gustavo, Lisa, and Alessandro.

It is a pleasure to again publish a book with Lynne Rienner Publishers, and I thank Lynne Rienner and Dan Eades for their confidence and interest in my work. I am also indebted to the work of Leanne Anderson, Shena Redmond, and Alice Colwell. Thank you for making the production of this book an enjoyable experience. Aloha!

—*Robert P. Watson*

FIRST LADIES
OF THE UNITED STATES

Introduction:
Powers Behind the Presidency

A White House Institution

She is one of the most popular and recognizable figures in the world. In fact, public opinion research reveals that she is more widely known than members of Congress or even the vice president. Yet we know little about many of her predecessors, especially those who served prior to the twentieth century. She often tops Gallup's annual poll to determine America's most admired women. Yet we don't know what she has done, aside from being married to the president, to evoke such admiration. She is one of the most powerful individuals in the country. Yet she is unelected, unappointed, and unpaid for her service. Who is this intriguing individual? She is, of course, the first lady.

The first lady is worth our attention if for no other reason than that she has been a part of the presidency since the country's founding. Indeed, the existence of the first ladyship even predates the White House. During the inaugural presidency of George Washington, the White House was under construction, and the Washingtons served from a temporary capital, first in New York City, then in Philadelphia. Abigail Adams, wife of the second president, was the first spouse actually to reside in the White House. She and President John Adams moved into the newly completed building in 1800, with only four months remaining in his term. But the "President's House," as George Washington deemed it, was not the grand structure it is today. Far from it. Only six rooms in the building were completed, and little thought was given in the original design of the Executive Mansion to such concerns as practicality and livability. Abigail was forced to hang laundry in the East Room and had a difficult time keeping the building warm

1

and dry in the winter. The president's home was minimally staffed, and early occupants were forced to pay for entertainment and staff support out of their own pockets.

Only two bachelors have been elected to the presidency: James Buchanan and Grover Cleveland. While president, however, Cleveland married Frances Folsom, a woman less than half his age. Five spouses died before their husbands took office: Martha Jefferson, Rachel Jackson, Hannah Van Buren, Ellen Arthur, and Alice Roosevelt. Even though these women did not preside over the White House, they deserve our consideration (see Appendixes 5–8 for their biographies) because they were influential forces in their husbands' lives and careers. Rachel and Andrew Jackson had been married over thirty-seven years before her untimely death during the interim between Jackson's election and his inauguration. Ellen and Chester Arthur had been married twenty years when she died, just before Arthur was selected as vice president. Three first ladies died while living in the White House: Letitia Tyler, Caroline Harrison, and Ellen Wilson. All three appear to have had close relationships with their husbands throughout their married lives, including the period in the White House, and had participated in public life with their husbands. These widower presidents would later remarry; John Tyler and Woodrow Wilson did so while still in office. In total, first ladies served in thirty-seven of the first forty-two presidencies. The institution of the first lady has certainly been a part of the American presidency for most of the nation's history.

Most first ladies outlived their husbands, but only two presidential widows would later remarry—Frances Cleveland and Jacqueline Kennedy, both of whom were younger than their first husbands. Martha Washington and Dolley Madison were widows when they married their second husbands, men who would become president. Both brought children from their previous unions into their presidential marriages, as did Florence Harding. Two eventual first ladies were divorcées when they married their second husbands: Florence Kling (Harding) and Betty Bloomer (Ford).

The presidential wives' service also predates the use of the title "first lady." The first presidential spouses were known by a variety of titles: Martha Washington was widely known as "Lady Washington," and Dolley Madison was occasionally called "Lady Presidentress." Jacqueline Kennedy so disliked the title "first lady" that she forbade her staff from using it. Others like Rosalynn Carter tended to forgo the formality, preferring to be called simply "Mrs. Carter" or "Rosalynn."

The exact date of origin of the title remains unclear but might be traced to the woman who helped make the office popular. While delivering the eulogy at Dolley Madison's funeral in 1849, President Zachary Taylor spoke of her as "our first lady for a half-century." The term did not immediately catch on but would appear again from time to time over the ensuing decades. In the late 1850s, Harriet Lane, Buchanan's niece, was nicknamed the "Democratic queen," yet newspapers of the day also referred to her as the "lady of the White House." (A few years later, during the Civil War, the wife of President Jefferson Davis was referred to by journalists as the "first lady of the Confederacy.") During the late 1870s, newspapers described Lucy Hayes as "the first lady of the land," in reference to a nationwide tour she completed with her husband. It was not until the twentieth century that the term became commonplace, appearing in dictionaries and encyclopedias. In the early part of the twentieth century, two popular plays were staged, one about Dolley Madison, called *The First Lady of the Land* (1911), and the other titled simply *First Lady* (1935). By the end of the century, the term was so accepted that it was extended to prominent women in the arts and even in the business world. Today the title is used internationally, even for female spouses of male governors and mayors. The prospect of a female president in the twenty-first century would bring further change, not only to the nature of the office but the title as well. It is uncertain what title, if any, might emerge. Perhaps "first gentleman"? Or maybe "first spouse" or "presidential spouse"?

The Second Toughest Job in the Country

Presidential wives have made many important contributions to their spouses' lives and presidencies. In so doing, they helped shape the very course of U.S. history. First ladies have participated in all facets of the presidency, and not surprisingly, many a president found his wife's presence, service, and counsel to be invaluable to his own success in the White House.

Although no distinct job description existed for first ladies, the office evolved to encompass the management of the social affairs of the White House. In many ways, the first lady has become the nation's de facto social hostess. She is expected to preside over functions as diverse as formal state dinners for visiting dignitaries to afternoon receptions for women's social clubs to the annual children's Easter-egg roll on the White House lawn. First ladies oversee a large, bustling domestic staff and plan the menus, seating arrangements, and entertainment for a wide variety of events that demand careful attention to detail and protocol.

First ladies have also acted as the chief preservationist, archivist, and tour guide of the White House. Not surprisingly, the wear and tear on the building has required many first ladies to supervise renovations and restorations of its furniture, rooms, and historical pieces. First ladies have acquired official china sets for the White House; refurbished damaged walls, drapes, and floors; and sought historic furnishings and portraits to establish authentic period collections. In part because of the efforts of first ladies, the White House remains a living museum of U.S. history open to the public. First ladies such as Pat Nixon have also been behind efforts to make the White House accessible to non-English speakers and the physically handicapped. Many first ladies have used the White House as a cultural center by showcasing famous entertainers and performers.

A more recent addition to the responsibilities of the presidential spouses includes the role of campaigner. First ladies now routinely function as presidential booster, spokesperson, and surrogate, traveling, appearing on behalf of the president, and even serving as his political adviser. Because of the nature of politics and society in the United States, the wives of politicians must appear in public with their husbands and, at a minimum, give the impression of supporting his campaign and political office. Nowhere in U.S. politics has this been more prevalent than with the candidates for president and first lady. Spouses spend many months making campaign appearances with their husbands. Nor does the campaigning stop after the election.

First ladies are often active in the operations of public policy and politics. It is not uncommon for them to assist the president in making staffing and political appointments, participating on presidential task forces, attending cabinet meetings, and speaking at political rallies. Eleanor Roosevelt, for example, encouraged her husband to appoint the first female to head a cabinet agency and spoke on his behalf at the 1940 Democratic National Convention. And in the nineteenth century, one finds wives such as Sarah Polk editing her husband's speeches and advising him on appointments and policy issues.

The first lady's duties have also extended to her own social activism and advocacy. More recent first ladies have been identified with a particular social cause or "pet project." For instance, Lady Bird Johnson became a visible advocate of conservation and beautification programs during her husband's presidency, Nancy Reagan led the well-known "Just Say No" antidrug campaign, and Barbara Bush crusaded for adult literacy, which was a successful component of the Bush presidency. The public has grown to expect first ladies to champion social issues and perform a wide array of functions within and beyond the White House.

Ironically, first ladies often are subject to criticism for their political activism even if this activism is in response to public expectations. Indeed, the American public has yet to determine what it wants in a first lady or how much involvement it prefers for the president's wife. First ladies have been condemned simultaneously for being too active and too passive, old-fashioned and frumpy yet excessive and uppity, and for having too many socials or not enough. Martha Washington was thought to be too old and Julia Tyler too young. Betty Ford was too outspoken and Pat Nixon too reserved for segments of the American public. So prevalent is public criticism that it would seem to be the only thing all first ladies have in common besides being married to the president.

The most common basis for public condemnation is that a first lady is too powerful. This complaint dates back to the second first lady, when Abigail Adams came under attack from her husband's political enemies. Because of Abigail's perceived influence, the president's opponents resorted to calling Mrs. Adams "Her Majesty" and "Madame President." Eleanor Roosevelt was also accused of having too much power. In the 1980s, Nancy Reagan was vilified as "Queen Nancy" and the "Dragon Lady" for her apparent say within the Reagan administration, and Hillary Clinton was rebuked by her husband's critics for almost everything she did and even things she did not do.

The criticism first ladies have faced has come not only from the president's political foes but also from the press and larger public. At times the attacks have transcended all notions of decency and have been highly personal and painful. For example, political satirists of the day depicted Margaret Taylor as something of a hick who smoked corncob pipes, and insensitive cartoonists drew Eleanor Roosevelt with oversized buck teeth. Incredibly, even First Lady Ida McKinley's epilepsy and Julia Grant's crossed left eye were sources of ridicule.

A first lady's actions, even when performed under noble circumstances, invite controversy. Lou Hoover and Eleanor Roosevelt were attacked in the southern press for inviting African American guests into the White House. Betty Ford was ambushed by the media for her frank views on social problems like abortion and teen drug use. Although some first ladies endured hostility and public scrutiny better than others, most persevered. First ladies can take solace in that, despite the criticism they receive, most have been enormously popular. Recent public opinion polls show that the president's spouse often enjoys higher approval ratings than the president. Since it was first conducted in the 1940s, the annual Gallup poll of the country's most admired women has been dominated by first ladies.

The President's Partner

Of course, it is not only in the public limelight that the first lady exercises her influence. Presidential spouses have apparently wielded considerable power behind the scenes too. This "pillow" influence is hard to gauge but certainly has the potential to be profound. The first lady is, after all, the president's wife, and of all the presidential aides and advisers, none knows the commander in chief as well or has as much access to him as she. The first lady is family, and the majority of first ladies have been the presidents' most trusted confidantes. Many presidential marriages involved a shared interest in the husband's career. As opposed to a single-income family or dual-career family, first families often lead what can be described as "co-career marriages," in which the wife is an intimate part of the political career. White House wives have subordinated their own careers and interests to that of the "team." Even first ladies reluctant to participate in politics or public service have often found they are forced into a political role, or at least the symbolic and social roles associated with being a political wife. A total of twenty-seven presidential couples were married at least twenty years *before* entering the White House; many were together even longer. First couples such as Andrew and Eliza Johnson, Benjamin and Caroline Harrison, the Eisenhowers, and the Carters all spent more than three decades together before the husband's presidency; the Bushes, Washingtons, John and Abigail Adams, and William and Anna Harrison were married more than forty years.

Several presidential spouses have been so intimately concerned with all facets of the public office that they can best be described as "presidential partners." Abigail Adams, Sarah Polk, Helen Taft, Florence Harding, Eleanor Roosevelt, Rosalynn Carter, Nancy Reagan, and Hillary Clinton were all full partners in the presidency.

Because the Constitution is silent concerning the first lady and relatively few legal parameters exist regarding the duties of the office, first ladies have had a minimum of formal guidelines. This does not mean they have been free to function in a manner they alone determine. In formulating their approach to the office, first ladies must take into account the fickle winds of public opinion, major events of the day, and of course the president's preferences. There is also historical precedent to consider, as the actions of all previous first ladies continue to frame the nature of the office. Still, the institution allows for a significant degree of discretion depending on the lady's own talents and vision.

The first lady emerged in the twentieth century as an institution of the White House and the U.S. political system. Although many early first ladies were active and wielded political influence, the Office of the First Lady is a twentieth-century development, dating to the first lady-ship of Edith Roosevelt (1901–1909). In response to the overwhelming amount of mail the first lady receives, Edith requested the assistance of an aide. Isabella Hagner James, a clerk in the Department of War, was reassigned to her and became the first permanent, nondomestic staffer working directly for the first lady. In recent times, the staff has grown to roughly twenty employees, who serve the first lady in such capacities as press relations, scheduling and advance planning, correspondence, and special projects.

The first lady's staff offices are usually located in the East Wing, opposite the presidential offices in the West Wing of the White House. This has led some political observers to comment that whereas the West Wing is the brain of the American body politic, the East Wing contains the heart. With the advent of a presidential partnership, however, the two wings have joined. First Lady Hillary Rodham Clinton relocated her office to the West Wing, symbolically and physically completing the union of the Office of the President and Office of the First Lady.

Historically, marriage was one of the few avenues to political power available for women. And although women have made significant progress in all sectors of American society and today serve in nearly every public office except the presidency, the position of political spouse—especially presidential spouse—remains a conduit to political power.

Serving Their Country

The first ladies represent a somewhat diverse group of intriguing women. We may study them not only to benefit our understanding of the presidency and the history of the country but because they are fascinating individuals in their own right. They have served without pay, often at great personal expense. The White House is an intimidating place for any new resident, yet several presidential spouses had little training to prepare them for its challenges and others were barely out of their teens when thrust into the national spotlight. The trials and tribulations of the White House are difficult even for those in peak physical condition, yet several first ladies were in poor health and others were well into their later years when they arrived, often far beyond the average life expectancies for the time. There are other, grimmer challenges of serving the nation in this capacity: The husbands of Mary Lincoln, Lucretia Garfield, Ida McKinley, and Jacqueline Kennedy were assassinated while in office, and those of Anna Harrison, Margaret Taylor, Florence Harding, and Eleanor Roosevelt suffered from poor health and died before completing their full terms. Eliza Johnson, Pat Nixon, and Hillary Clinton endured the ugly and highly public turmoil surrounding the attempted impeachment of their husbands.

Still, first ladies have persevered. As a group, they have generally been a capable lot, and considering the nature of their responsibilities, they have discharged their duties as well as if not better than the presidents. But they have served largely without proper recognition, and their stories deserve to be told. The significance of the first ladyship as a powerful and important public office is apparent, and study of the first ladies has relevance for the fields of presidential scholarship, U.S. history, and women's studies. It is time to recognize the first ladies' accomplishments and for them to assume their proper place in American history.

1

Martha Dandridge Custis Washington

Born: June 2, 1731; Williamsburg, Virginia
Died: May 22, 1802; Mount Vernon, Virginia
President: George Washington (1732–1799), First President
Husband's Presidential Term: 1789–1797 (Federalist)
Marriage: First: June 1749 to Colonel Daniel Parke Custis, New Kent
    County, Virginia (widowed 1757). Second: January 6, 1759, to
    George Washington, New Kent County, Virginia
Children: Daniel (1751–1754); Frances (1753–1757); John "Jacky"
    (1754 or 1755–1781); Martha "Patsy" (1756 or 1757–1773)

Early Years

Martha Dandridge was born on June 2, 1731, to John and Frances
Dandridge at the family's home near Williamsburg, Virginia. Martha's
father had emigrated from England and found success in the colonies,
establishing a thriving tobacco plantation. He also served as county
clerk. The Dandridges quickly emerged as members of Virginia's gentry
class, although they were not privy to the highest echelons of Tidewater
Virginia society. Nevertheless, Martha was born into privilege and comfort.

Martha was the first of eight children, the youngest born when she was twenty-five. As the oldest child in a large plantation family, she developed maternal and domestic skills at an early age by tending to her younger siblings and helping to run the busy Dandridge household. Her education was typical for daughters of prominent eighteenth-century families; she was taught the skills of domesticity, including sewing and homemaking, to balance the graces of social refinement, such as etiquette, music, and dancing. Martha grew up in a household where politics was often the topic of conversation among her father's guests. She also gained valuable experience in social hostessing.

As Martha matured, she developed a matronly, orderly demeanor, which would remain throughout her life. As a young woman and later as the president's wife, Martha showed little interest in the latest fashions or society life. Even though a plain dresser, she nevertheless carried herself with classical elegance. She was frugal as well: Later in life, despite her great wealth and interest in music and music lessons for her children and grandchildren, Martha opted to handcopy musical scores rather than buy new ones.

At age seventeen Martha Dandridge married Daniel Parke Custis, twenty years her senior and heir to the vast Custis family plantation. The wedding took place in the Custis family home (known as "the White House"). John Custis, the family patriarch and an eccentric, wealthy, and domineering man, opposed the wedding in part because he felt Martha and the Dandridges were not affluent enough for the Custis family's standards. Shortly after the wedding, however, John Custis died, leaving his fortune to Daniel.

The apparently happy marriage produced four children: Daniel Parke, born in 1751, Frances Parke (1753), John or "Jacky" Parke (1754), and Martha or "Patsy" Parke (1756). But Martha's firstborn died in 1754, followed by her father two years later and her husband and second child only a year after that. She was left a widow at age twenty-six, with two infant children.

Martha endured these tragedies and began to oversee the management of the Custis plantation. She seems to have been a shrewd businesswoman and successfully dealt with a lawsuit regarding her late husband's property as well as the lawyers and merchants involved in the plantation business. She had become the owner of an estate of approximately 17,000 choice acres (and over 100 slaves) near Williamsburg, the center of power in the colony, and was one of the wealthiest women in Virginia.

Marriage to George Washington

The young widow George Washington met in March 1758 was roughly five feet tall and had a quiet, gentle manner. Those who knew Martha described her as a pleasant individual. Her portraits, such as the famous miniature painted by Charles Wilson Peale in 1776, which Washington placed in an oval pendant and wore until his death, show a woman with dark hair; it would later turn gray-white and was usually pulled up. Her expression was always calm, her features soft and plump. In her engravings she often wore a pearl necklace and a large, white, loose-fitting bonnet. Martha's description of herself as "an old-fashioned Virginia housekeeper" mirrors her appearance in surviving portraits and engravings.

George Washington was a very ambitious man, especially in his youth. A colonel in the Virginia militia, he longed to become a high-ranking British officer, a position that continually eluded him. He was also attracted to the lifestyle of aristocratic gentlemen. Martha was in many ways a good catch for him, and through their marriage on January 6, 1759, he became enormously wealthy and gained access to Virginia society. He also instantly acquired a family, which would be important to the image-conscious and traditional Washington, as he and Martha never had children of their own. This would cause tensions in the marriage. Both wanted to have children, and he even suggested that his wife's "old age" (twenty-seven at marriage) might be the problem. Martha's family was not fully supportive of her choice, but she wanted a father for her children. For his part, George had been hesitant to marry, believing that one should have money before taking a wife.

Nevertheless, the marriage was a solid one. What the Washingtons lacked in passion for each other they more than made up for in respect. Over the course of the marriage, they become close partners, for they shared many personality traits and had much in common. Both preferred a rigid schedule in their lives. They were early risers and also retired early. They ate breakfast together each morning (and ate the same menu every day) and often read newspapers together after dinner. Both valued family life and were highly conscious of their image and reputation in the community. They avoided vices like the infidelity, financial imprudence, and excessive social festivities that were so prevalent among the aristocratic class. These commonalities helped develop a deep dependence and admiration between "Patsy" and "the General" (she sometimes called him "Pappa") that not only continued through the Revolutionary War and inaugural presidency but were strengthened by those challenges. Indeed, Martha was a major source of support and assistance for her husband during those years.

Family Life

Martha Washington was exceedingly ordinary in many ways. Her first love was spending time with her children and grandchildren, and she was always happiest when at home and when there was order and familiarity in her life. She preferred the simple life over that of the city, and although she enjoyed going to museums, the theater, ventriloquist shows, and waxworks while in the capital city, she counted the days during her husband's presidency until she could return to private life. She was outright bored and bothered by much of the pomp and ceremony surrounding the presidency. In her own words, she dismissed presidential affairs as "empty ceremonies of etiquette," feeling that much of the formality of the office was fake and unnecessary. Her days were typically filled with chores, as well as spinning, sewing, and reading. A devoted Episcopalian, Martha also regularly attended church and observed the Sabbath.

The Washington family home was in the Tidewater region of Virginia, not far from Williamsburg, the capital of the colony. After renting his brother's home, the plantation estate known as Mount Vernon, Washington inherited the place when the brother and later his wife died. The proximity to Williamsburg provided access to the economic, political, and social base of power in the region, and he and Martha quickly emerged as leading citizens. The Washingtons received many prominent visitors at their spacious plantation home. They had so many and the plantation business grew so successful that he renovated and enlarged Mount Vernon several times. As hostess, Martha was quite popular and excelled at accommodating her guests, something that further aided her husband's career. After the Revolutionary period, the family rarely dined alone; George recorded in his diary on July 30, 1785, that he "dined with only Mrs. Washington which I believe is the first instance of it since my retirement from public life." They owned slaves, and Martha had servants and cooks to help with household matters and the steady flow of visitors. It was a busy household and a happy home.

Martha's children often accompanied the parents on regular visits to friends and relatives in the area. Daughter Patsy appears to have been well adjusted, but she suffered from severe seizures, most likely epilepsy, that left her weak and sickly; she died of one at the dinner table on June 19, 1773, at the age of seventeen. Washington recorded in his diary that her death "has almost reduced my poor Wife to the lowest ebb of Misery."

Her son Jacky was a continuing source of trouble for his parents. He was careless with money, lazy, and irresponsible, abandoning his studies at King's College. Jacky married Eleanor Calvert, from a wealthy Maryland family, in February 1774; he was the only one of Martha's four children to live to adulthood. While visiting his father in camp at the close of the Revolutionary War, however, Jacky contracted a fever and died at the age of twenty-six.

After his death, Martha insisted on obtaining custody of two of her four grandchildren. The two eldest—Elizabeth "Betsy" Parke (1776–1832) and Martha "Patsy" Parke (1777–1854)—continued to live with their mother and new stepfather, but the younger two moved to Mount Vernon. This was a common practice of the time, and the grandparents certainly had the means to provide for the children. "Nelly" and "Little Wash" became the focus of much of Martha's life, and she revived a habit of being tough on girls but spoiling the boys, which she had practiced on her own children.

In the 1770s, Martha was increasingly concerned about the prospects of war. Although she had faced ugly accusations of being a Tory and newspapers even labeled her a British loyalist, she refuted these charges and solidly supported the colonial cause. Her fears were realized on June 19, 1775, when her husband was appointed commander in chief of the Continental army. But Martha was not alone in her uncertainty about the future. After the announcement, Washington wrote letters to his wife and friends in which he appears hesitant and uncertain of himself and the task ahead. Writing to his brother John Augustine the day after his selection, he stated, "[I] bid adieu to you, and to every kind of domestic ease, for awhile. I am Embarked on a wide Ocean, boundless in its prospect & from whence, perhaps, no safe harbour is to be found. I have been called upon by the unanimous Voice of the Colonies to take the Command of the Continental Army. An honour I neither sought after, nor desired, as I am thoroughly convinced, that it requires greater Abilities, and much more experience, than I am Master of."

Although the two had become very close by the outbreak of war, Washington did not consult with Martha about his decision to be commander in chief. When he wrote that he had accepted the duty, his tone was almost apologetic. Martha did not want her husband to participate in the conflict, as she longed for a peaceful, comfortable retirement together at Mount Vernon. But she supported him and understood his sense of duty and ambition. During this difficult time, George looked to his wife for strength. In a letter to Martha on June 18, 1775, as he was preparing for war, he says, "Believe me my dear Patsy . . . that I should enjoy more real happiness and felicity in one month with you, at home, than I have the most distant prospect of reaping abroad, if my stay was to be seven times seven years."

The Revolutionary War made the couple instant celebrities in the colonies. She realized this, and although she was hesitant to lose her private life and unenthusiastic about public life, she responded with skill, devotion, and selflessness. As early as 1777, on a visit to Williamsburg Martha was greeted with a thirteen-cannon salute. In a typical and telling gesture, she was nonchalant about the event, writing her sister that it was merely "great pomp" and that the event was "as if I had been a very great some body."

Each winter the fighting abated as the two armies settled in to weather the cold. During these winter encampments, Martha visited her husband at his headquarters. On her first visit, in December 1775, she was shocked by the wretched conditions she found but appears to have had a calming influence not only on her husband but on the troops as well. With morale low, supplies equally sparse, and the winters brutally cold, Martha succeeded in lifting spirits and re-creating a sense of home for George and his officers and troops during her visits. Martha became a kind of mother to the militia; one of the regiments at Valley Forge even adopted the name "Lady Washington's Dragoon." More than boosting morale, she sewed uniforms, nursed the sick and wounded, and hosted the officers and their wives for dinner. She organized sick wards and encouraged women to contribute by making uniforms and bandages, and even began to wear clothing made in the colonies in a symbolic gesture of support. She also succeeded in prompting wives of the colonies' governors to collect money and organize war relief efforts. While in camp, Martha performed clerical work for the general, copied his correspondence, and even discussed details of the war with him. Her letters at the time reveal that she understood the events occurring. He even entrusted her with military secrets. After the war Martha continued to help veterans wherever and whenever possible, giving them money when they were in need, intervening on behalf of a pardon when they ran afoul of the law, and building public support for veterans.

Presidency

The period after the Revolutionary War was a happy time in Martha Washington's life. Back at her beloved Mount Vernon with her family, Martha wanted only to now "grow old in solitude and tranquility together." That would not be the case, of course, as the general was unanimously selected to be the new nation's first president.

Washington preceded Martha to the temporary capital in New York City. In May 1789, along with her grandchildren (George "Little Wash," eight, and Nelly, ten), nephew Robert Lewis, and a family friend who provided the carriage and horses, she departed Virginia for New York. Almost sixty, she was hesitant about both the long trip and the challenges awaiting her. The journey proved both strenuous and historic. The party had trouble crossing the Potomac and Patuxent Rivers because of bad weather and high water and subsequently experienced delays. Yet Martha pushed the group onward, declining offers of extended lodging with friends along the way. Their progress was followed closely by the press, possibly marking the first time in the country that newspaper reports centered on a woman. The trip was also celebrated with much fanfare, as people lined the streets in each town through which the entourage passed in order to glimpse the president's wife. In town after town she was welcomed by political leaders, thirteen-cannon salutes, military escorts, parades, parties, fireworks, and crowds cheering, "Long live Lady Washington!" and "God bless Lady Washington!" When she attempted to go shopping in Philadelphia, she was followed by curious reporters and residents and even protective soldiers.

Such popular enthusiasm for Martha made it clear from the beginning that the wife of the president would fulfill a highly public and ceremonial role. Martha realized this. Despite her natural reserve, she warmly acknowledged the crowds and even gave a short speech while standing in her carriage to thank the troops who escorted her and those who had turned out to see her. It was Martha's first and only public speech as the president's wife.

The last leg of the trip took her through Elizabethtown, New Jersey, where she was greeted by the governor and a military escort. With flags unfurled, a boat took her from New Jersey to New York City; she was welcomed by the governor of New York and a parade in her honor. Arriving at the home of old friends Dr. and Mrs. James McHenry, she changed into appropriate dress and attended a reception in her honor, the first official duty of the presidential spouse. By her second full day in New York, she was presiding over social events.

Both Martha and the president were concerned about the roles they would occupy, for of course there were no precedents to follow. Moreover, the situation in the new country was highly sensitive, as it still faced foreign threats and internal disunity. The powers of Europe considered the former colonies upstarts and believed the new experiment in democracy was doomed to failure. The Washingtons had to address both the American populace and the European nations in blending a democratic concern for simplicity with a sense of importance and ceremony in the social affairs of state. The new government could not be too regal, lest it risk being criticized by its citizenry for aping the courts of Europe, but it had to inspire legitimacy and establish a certain amount of formality at this critical and uncertain point. Martha appears to have achieved a sensitive balance between simplicity and sophistication in her social affairs and official protocol.

The Washingtons' social calendar included Martha's Friday evening drawing room socials, which were open to both men and women. Guests were presented to Martha, then to Abigail Adams, wife of the vice president, who was seated next to her. Martha also held afternoon receptions on Tuesdays and Fridays for social calls, but these were limited to Tuesday afternoons in the later years in office. State dinners were held at 3:00 P.M., and the Washingtons hosted Friday night receptions when Congress was in session. Gala birthday parties were given in George Washington's honor each February. For certain events, Martha had engravings made of herself, with "Lady Washington" next to her likeness, which were then sent to guests, although she worried about how the engravings would be received. To assist her with the social affairs of state, Martha relied on a relative, Polly Lear, wife of Tobias Lear, the president's chief aide and longtime family aide; a small staff of chefs and stewards; and Samuel Fraunces Lewis, a tavern owner who helped arrange dinners.

Martha set precedents for all future first ladies, and she established the custom of opening the presidential residence to the public on New Year's Day, a tradition upheld until 1933. The couple had been married thirty years when he took the oath of office, and Martha had been at his side throughout his public career, longer than any of his aides or cabinet members; she was the president's trusted partner. Her exact role in and contribution to his presidency cannot be measured, but it appears to have been significant. During his bouts with severe illness in 1789 and 1790, Martha nursed the president and calmed an anxious country. Even though she did not particularly enjoy the presidential years, she rose to the occasion and fulfilled her duties graciously with tact and stoicism.

Legacy

The quiet, private retirement the Washingtons longed for eluded them even after the presidency, as they had become national idols and received a steady stream of visitors. Martha was occupied with her grandchildren and was delighted with Nelly's marriage in February 1799 and the birth of a great-granddaughter that November. Two weeks later, however, George Washington caught cold after riding in bad weather. The cold advanced, and he died on December 14.

The death of her beloved husband took much out of Martha. As she had always done, she responded to her sense of duty, greeting the many mourners, sending remembrances and locks of the president's hair to the public, and planning his funeral and state burial. But she had little interest in life thereafter. Perhaps in a final effort to recapture her elusive privacy, Martha burned nearly all of the correspondence between herself and her husband.

Martha Washington was an effective if reluctant public figure who demonstrated remarkable grace, strength, and skill during her long life in the public eye. If history records George Washington as the father of his country, then Martha equally deserves the title "mother of her country," for she originated the office of first lady. Lady Washington was the most admired woman in the colonies from the Revolution and presidential years until her death. She died of "severe fever" on May 22, 1802. An obituary in the *Alexandria Advertiser and Commercial Intelligencer* described her as a most "worthy partner" for the nation's beloved father.

Bibliography

Bourne, Miriam Anne. *First Family: George Washington and His Intimate Relations*. New York: Norton, 1982.

Moore, Charles. *The Family Life of George Washington*. Boston: Little, Brown, 1926.

Thane, Elswyth. *Washington's Lady.* New York: Dodd, Mead, 1960.
Watson, Robert P. *Martha Washington.* New York: Longman Publishers, 2001.
Wharton, Anne Hollingsworth. *Martha Washington.* New York: Scribner's, 1897.

2

Abigail Smith Adams

Born: November 11, 1744; Weymouth, Massachusetts
Died: October 28, 1818; Quincy, Massachusetts
President: John Adams (1735–1826), Second President
Husband's Presidential Term: 1797–1801 (Federalist)
Marriage: October 25, 1764; Weymouth, Massachusetts
Children: Abigail Amelia (1765–1813); John Quincy (1767–1848); Susanna (1768–1770); Charles (1770–1800); Thomas Boylston (1772–1832)

Early Years

Abigail Adams was the second daughter of one of the colonies' leading families and was descended from the Quincys, a wealthy, respected Massachusetts family, on her mother's side. She also came from a long line of Congregationalist ministers and political activists. Her family brought her up in the stern, disciplined tradition of the New England church. This upbringing seems to have stuck with Abigail, as she led a very disciplined life and expected the same from others.

As was typical for young women of the day, Abigail did not formally attend school, but she was educated in a home that placed considerable value on learning. Abigail had an unquenchable thirst for knowledge and love of reading and became arguably one of the best-read women of her time. Abigail was also a prolific writer in her youth and throughout her life. She wrote countless letters to a variety of acquaintances; through these we know much about Abigail's character and opinions on the matters of the day. We know, for instance, that she was very intelligent, tough, and opinionated; her pen names, such as "Diana" and "Portia," reflect her interest in literature.

Marriage

John Adams was attracted to this witty, bright young woman. The two started courting in 1761 when she was seventeen and he was a twenty-six-year-old lawyer educated at Harvard. They shared a love of reading and intellectual conversation, something that would define their long lives together. Abigail's family initially opposed her marriage to John Adams on the grounds that he was not good enough for their daughter: His family was not nearly as affluent as the Quincy family and he had a reputation for a bad temper. Her father seems to have eventually relaxed his opposition, for the two were married in October 1764. John Adams, like George Washington before him, seems to have married up socially.

John and Abigail lived on his farm in Braintree, Massachusetts (later renamed Quincy in honor of Abigail's mother's family), and also in Boston. Adams's law practice grew, and he became a traveling circuit judge, which often took him away from home. During these absences Abigail took care of their growing family and ran the farm. She disliked the separations, but because both had a strong sense of civic duty, they put public service ahead of personal feeling. Moreover (and thankfully for history), the long absences produced an abundance of letters in which they discussed many facets of their marriage and family, as well as politics.

Theirs was one of the most solid marriages in the history of the presidency. John and Abigail viewed it as a true union of individuals and ideas and lived their married life as a partnership. They agreed on most issues and had a deep, genuine respect for each other, something that grew even stronger over time and with each separation. Abigail enjoyed her husband's success and later followed her son John Quincy's career with pleasure.

Adams saw his wife as an intellectual equal—no small statement considering that he was one of the intellectual giants of his day and that women did not hold equal status with men in their lifetime. Abigail was a trailblazer in this and many other matters. At the time of their marriage, for example, they owned two slaves, but Abigail, much more enlightened on the slavery issue than Martha Washington, saw to it that both were taught to read and write and then were granted their freedom.

Abigail was her husband's most trusted counsel; he often solicited and nearly always took her advice. Although her political opinions were similar to his, she was also an independent, progressive thinker. This is perhaps best revealed in a famous letter she wrote Adams while he was in Philadelphia serving in the Continental Congress: "In the new code of laws which I suppose it will be necessary for you to make, I desire you would remember the ladies and be more generous and favorable to them than your ancestors. Do not put unlimited power into the hands of husbands. Remember, all men would be tyrants if they could. If particular care and attention is not paid to the ladies, we are determined to foment a rebellion, and will not hold ourselves bound by any laws in which we have no voice or representation."

She was passionate, outspoken, and ahead of her time on the issue of women's rights; she even jokingly referred to herself as "Mrs. Delegate" during the period of the Continental Congress. She believed in women's abilities and thought they were capable of performing many activities closed to them by the social strictures of the time. She believed strongly in women's legal rights, such as the right to own property even if the woman was married, and she recognized the need for a legal system that would protect women against abusive husbands. Although an advocate of education for women, she appears not to have encouraged women to attempt to vote or hold office. But she did enjoy and support Mary Wollstonecraft, an early champion of women's liberation, and believed that women needed more female heroes and leaders. John Adams, though not necessarily an advocate of women's rights, seems to have been influenced by his wife's opinions, unlike many of his counterparts in the eighteenth century. He believed that behind every great man was a great woman. Certainly his own experiences, as well as those of men he knew such as George Washington, helped shape such views.

Family Life

Abigail had five children; her first, also named Abigail, was born in 1765. Her second child was born in 1767 and named for his father; like his father, he would also become president. Abigail had one more daughter, Susanna, who died in infancy, and two additional sons. On the morning of June 17, 1775, cannon bursts signaled the outbreak of the Revolutionary War. Abigail took seven-year-old John Quincy to the top of a nearby hill and watched the Battle of Bunker Hill, the first of many interruptions to a peaceful family life.

From 1774 to 1783, much of the couple's married life was spent apart. Adams served in both Continental Congresses and as an envoy seeking foreign aid during the Revolutionary War; later, he was a delegate to the Federal Constitutional Convention. His growing prestige during the war secured several diplomatic postings for him in Europe. When he departed for France in 1777 he took young John Quincy with him, while Abigail stayed home. Although she missed her son and husband, even calling her situation a sort of "widowhood," she supported the decision and again resolved herself to the call of duty.

These long separations—six years—and calls to public service seemed to strengthen their fondness for each other. Abigail kept occupied in raising their children and managing family affairs. She also functioned as her husband's political eyes and ears during his absences. While Adams served in Philadelphia or overseas, he relied on Abigail to keep him abreast of events and politics in Massachusetts and the new nation. Her regular letters provided a wealth of information and analysis on the political situation at home, and as her husband's political partner, she was also his sounding board. The two debated his decisions, and she helped him write speeches, while seeing that his actions were favorably reported in the newspapers. Today she would be credited for strategically leaking items to reporters and courting friendly journalists. For instance, early in the war, Abigail felt that Adams should attempt to obtain financial support from the Netherlands. Although he was reluctant, she continued to make her case, even taking it up with Thomas Jefferson, and the Dutch finally offered loans to the colonies beginning in 1782. The downside to her advisory role was that it attracted negative attention and public criticism.

Abigail eventually recaptured some semblance of family life with her husband by joining him in Europe. In June 1784 she departed for London aboard the ship *Active*. The transatlantic voyage was long and difficult: The ship was filthy and poorly kept, and Abigail was often violently seasick. In her typical manner, however, she reprimanded the crew for being lax and took it upon herself to clean the entire ship and even to cook meals. The inquisitive Abigail even succeeded in having the captain give her a personal tour of the craft and explain its workings. While in London, she enjoyed the intellectual life, partaking of the city's culture and attending lectures on natural history, but she was frustrated that British women were not interested in politics, history, and intellectual pursuits.

Abigail was reunited in 1784 with her husband during his diplomatic appointment in France, where this daughter of Puritan New England was shocked by the social liberalism of Parisian society. In particular, she was offended by the ballet and theater and the attitudes, dress, and manners of Parisian women. A highlight of Abigail's European years was her daughter's marriage to the U.S. military attaché to England in 1786. The wedding ceremony was performed by none other than the archbishop of Canterbury.

Presidency

On April 30, 1789, John Adams became the nation's first vice president. Abigail was pleased with her husband's selection, although she grew to believe that the office offered little challenge or responsibility. She even chose to remain in Massachusetts to run the family farm during part of her husband's second term as vice president. The same difficulties the Washingtons faced in establishing parameters and precedents for the inaugural presidency also concerned the Adamses, and the role of the vice president was even less defined than the president's. They responded with ease and poise, however, generally enjoying their years in the vice presidency. Abigail befriended Martha Washington and assisted her with social functions, appearing beside her at many social and state affairs. Abigail drew on the valuable experiences she had gained as the wife of a diplomat and knew the social protocol of the courts of Europe, something Martha lacked. Later, however, during her husband's presidency, Abigail worried about measuring up to Martha Washington's great popularity and esteem.

When John Adams became president in 1797, Abigail excelled as a hostess as well as in her capacity as his political confidante. She brought her intelligence and gift for conversation to the office. She also enjoyed Philadelphia and distinguished herself from her predecessor through a more engaged, political style. Abigail was most atypical, as women of her time were not supposed to demonstrate an interest in politics. Only her sensitivity to criticism of Adams by his political enemies (especially if it came from supporters of Thomas Jefferson) appears to have occasionally clouded her otherwise keen political judgment. For instance, her hostility toward journalists who attacked him contributed to her support of the flawed Alien and Sedition Act. The subsequent move to restrict the press became highly unpopular. Albert Gallatin, one of John Adams's political enemies, even took to criticizing Abigail for her power and involvement, calling Abigail "her majesty." Perhaps in recognition of such criticism, Abigail denied and downplayed her influence. But she worked so hard during her husband's presidency that she became ill and was forced to return to Massachusetts at one point to rest and recuperate. Still, her political activism and advisory role with her husband had started long before her years as presidential spouse and went on long thereafter.

During the critical days leading up to the Revolution, Abigail expressed her view that its objective should be full independence from Great Britain, not simply an increase in freedoms or a negotiated reconciliation, as some had favored. Later she indicated that she was opposed to France's handling of its own revolution. Indeed, Abigail appears to have had opinions on all political issues of the day. She was a Hamiltonian, siding with Alexander Hamilton and George Washington in support of a strong role for the federal government during the founding days of the nation. She even debated Federalist policies with her husband, who was a Federalist but disagreed with the party's position supporting war with France. He opted for sending a peace mission to France; Abigail preferred the more hawkish position of most Federalists. She was disgusted by slavery, believing it was at odds with the ideals of America. Abigail is also credited with initiating the healing of one of the day's most celebrated political rifts, that between Adams and Thomas Jefferson. Abigail started the reconciliation by writing to Jefferson after his daughter's death; she continued exchanging letters with him, opening the door to the famous correspondence between the two founding fathers.

Legacy

In 1800, John Adams lost his bid for reelection to Jefferson. This upset Abigail, as she believed her husband deserved a second term. After the loss they retired to their home in Massachusetts, where they finally were able to have a private life together. Abigail enjoyed this period, spending time with her children and grandchildren at the large Adams home in Braintree. She also kept up her interest in politics and even came to support Jefferson's presidency.

Abigail Adams was one of the best-read and most politically powerful women of her time. John Adams felt that Abigail was a tribute to all women and referred to his wife as his "wisest friend." For her part,

Abigail continued to call her husband "the president" for the remainder of her life. She shared in her husband's political career and his strong sense of public duty. She made many sacrifices for her country and holds the distinction of being both wife and mother to a U.S. president, as her son John Quincy followed in his father's footsteps in 1825.

Abigail Adams became ill from typhoid fever in 1818 and spent her final days confined to her bedroom. Her cheerful, positive disposition had become somewhat eclipsed by a quiet resolve and growing religious conviction in her later years. She died at home on October 28, 1818.

Bibliography
Adams, Charles Francis. *Letters of Abigail Adams, the Wife of John Adams.* Boston: Charles C. Little and James Brown, 1848.

Levin, Phyllis Lee. *Abigail Adams.* New York: St. Martin's Press, 1987.

Mitchell, Stewart, ed. *New Letters of Abigail Adams.* Boston: Houghton Mifflin, 1947.

Smith, Page. *John Adams.* 2 volumes. Garden City, NY: Doubleday, 1962.

Withey, Lynne. *Dearest Friend.* New York: Free Press, 1981.

3

Martha "Patsy" Jefferson Mann and Mary "Polly" Jefferson Eppes

---

President: Thomas Jefferson (1743–1826), Third President
President's Term: 1801–1809 (Democrat-Republican)

Thomas Jefferson's wife, Martha, died almost two decades before his election to the presidency. Devastated by her death, Jefferson honored a pledge he apparently made to her on her deathbed that he would not remarry. He came to the office as a widower and asked his two surviving daughters to serve as hostess in the Executive Mansion. (See also Appendix 5.)

Hostess for Thomas Jefferson:
Martha "Patsy" Jefferson Mann (1772–1836)

Jefferson's eldest daughter, Martha ("Patsy"), served in place of her deceased mother, staying at the White House with her family and presiding over its social affairs during the winters of 1802–1803 and 1805–1806.

Patsy had married her cousin Thomas Randolph Mann (who was the governor of Virginia from 1819 to 1822) and would eventually have ten children, including a son who was the first child to be born in the Executive Mansion. The child was named after James Madison, Jefferson's secretary of state. When Patsy was not seeing to social affairs, Madison's popular wife, Dolley, often served as mistress of the

26

White House. Patsy's socials were simple gatherings, in line with her father's taste for the new spirit of democracy and the "common man," and a marked change from the more formal events of her predecessors, Martha Washington and Abigail Adams. For instance, Patsy abandoned the practice of hosting "levees," weekly receptions open to the ladies of the capital city. Jefferson himself often appeared at his daughter's socials, although dressed almost embarrassingly informally and wearing either dirty riding boots or slippers.

Martha "Patsy" Jefferson .

Patsy was well prepared for such hosting duties, as she had long ago traveled with her father to France, where she had been exposed to the courts of Europe. After his wife's death, Jefferson, in 1784, accepted a diplomatic post in Paris and took his firstborn daughter with him. He had always been meticulous about Patsy's education, sending her to the finest schools in Philadelphia and, during his service as U.S. minister to France, to Paris's Abbaye Royale de Panthemont. Patsy originally attended a convent school in the French capital, but when she expressed interest in joining the nunnery, her father quickly withdrew her and obtained the services of private, more secular tutors. Patsy's close relationship with her father continued after his presidency.

The 1820s were difficult times for Patsy. Both her father and husband experienced financial problems. Thomas Jefferson left severe debts when he died in 1826, and his grieving daughter was forced to sell his beloved estate to cover them. Two years later her husband passed away. She moved to Boston to live with her daughter, then lived briefly in Washington before joining her son at her Edgewood estate. She continued her interest in politics, closely following the debate over slavery. Although retaining some of the Jefferson family slaves, she taught her children that the institution was morally wrong. Her son, Thomas Jefferson Randolph, was elected to the Virginia legislature where he promoted gradual emancipation. Patsy was her father's lifelong confidante and the person closest to him during his long public career after his wife's death.

Hostess for Thomas Jefferson:
Mary "Polly" Jefferson Eppes (1778–1804)

The fourth child of Thomas and Martha Jefferson, Polly was just a child when her mother died. She was often placed in the care of Sally Hemings, the young slave girl with whom Jefferson apparently had a love affair. Polly was said to be like her mother: She was petite, attractive, and physically delicate. Although she neither shared her older sister's intellect nor extensive education, she did receive a formal education far superior to that of most girls of the period. When she was nine, Polly's father and sister traveled to France at the start of his ministership. Shortly thereafter, Polly sailed for Europe, too, staying for a brief time with John and Abigail Adams in London, then joining her father and sister in Paris, where she attended the same prestigious convent school as her sister.

While Jefferson was president, Polly assisted Patsy at the White House during the seasons the latter was unable to preside as hostess. Polly appears to have done an admirable job as presidential hostess. Although she had married her cousin, John Wayles Eppes, in 1797, because of the city's notorious marshes and the prevalence of disease there, Polly went alone to the Executive Mansion when she served. Patsy also refrained from moving her family to the capital city because of the health risks. Delicate like her mother, however, who had succumbed to the strain of childbirth, Polly also died (in 1804 at the age of twenty-five) not long after the birth of her second child.

4

Dolley Payne Todd Madison

Born: May 20, 1768; New Garden, North Carolina
Died: July 12, 1849; Washington, D.C.
President: James Madison (1751–1836), Fourth President
Husband's Presidential Term: 1809–1817 (Democrat-Republican)
Marriage: First: January 7, 1790, to John Todd; Philadelphia, Pennsylvania (widowed 1793). Second: September 15, 1794, to James Madison; Harewood, Virginia
Children: First marriage: John Payne (1792–1852); William Temple (1793). Second marriage: None

---

Early Years

Dolley Payne was born on May 20, 1768, near the town of Piedmont, North Carolina. Unlike the three presidential wives before her, Dolley came from a family of modest means and social standing. She was fairly well educated for a girl of her time, having been tutored at her family plantation, a home full of books where reading was stressed. She also attended a Quaker school.

Considering the vivaciousness and gala social events for which she was famous in the White House, it is surprising to learn that Dolley was raised in a strict Quaker family. Her parents, John and Mary Coles Payne, who had moved to North Carolina from Virginia, were members of the Society of Friends. In 1769, a year after Dolley's birth, John Payne took his family back to Virginia, and in 1783 resettled them in a Quaker community in Philadelphia, a region of the new nation in which the Quaker faith was well established. John Payne's faith appears to have grown with time; after the Revolutionary War he freed his slaves in accordance with Quaker beliefs.

Despite her disciplined and somber upbringing, Dolley developed a warm, engaging personality and a contagious sense of humor. She was an active woman who preferred a fast-paced life, with a taste for the latest fashions and a propensity for excess. It is even documented that later in life she enjoyed partaking of the snuffbox. As first lady she would certainly indulge these appetites. Yet throughout her life Dolley remained approachable, humble, and highly personable with everyone she met. Numerous accounts by those who met her remark on how much they liked her and were impressed by her warmth and attentiveness. Perhaps Dolley's most dominant personality trait, which became an asset later in life, was her genuine love of people.

In 1790 Dolley married John Todd Jr., a wealthy lawyer. Later that year she gave birth to a son, John Payne Todd. This happy occasion was, however, followed by tragedy. In 1792 Dolley's father died insolvent, and the following year her husband, his parents, and her second son, William Temple, only a year old, all died during a severe yellow fever epidemic. Like Martha Washington and Martha Jefferson before her, Dolley found herself a young widow with an infant child.

Marriage to James Madison

The twenty-five-year-old widow had many suitors, one of whom was U.S. Representative James Madison. The two had been introduced by the controversial politician Aaron Burr (who would soon become vice president), and were an unlikely match: Madison was seventeen years Dolley's senior, an Episcopalian, and as serious and staid as Dolley was cheerful and social. Irrespective of their differences in age and personality, he was instantly enamored. Although Dolley was hesitant in the initial stages of the courtship, they were married in September 1794, only four months after meeting.

Dolley converted to her husband's faith and was consequently disavowed by the Quakers. The Madisons enjoyed a happy though childless union, and James was a patient father to Dolley's notoriously troublesome son from her first marriage. The couple quickly became close friends, sharing a passion for politics, and Dolley threw herself into her husband's career. The two became lifelong partners in their very public lives.

Family Life

Dolley's life with her "little Jemmy" or "darling little husband" was defined by politics. She called him "the Great Little Madison," in reference to his slight stature, and made him and his political career the centerpieces of her life. Although she publicly stated she was not interested in politics and that it was a man's business, Dolley had both a fondness and a knack for all things political. She was a keen observer of the issues of the day and intimately familiar with her husband's policies, supporting all of his political positions. Dolley thoroughly enjoyed accompanying Madison to Washington and its social events. She also assisted him at home and in his career. In a time when furnishing the home was the purview of men, Dolley took it upon herself to redecorate Montpelier, the Madisons' home in Virginia. Even before her husband's presidency, Dolley established a reputation as Washington's most celebrated hostess.

Throughout her marriage to James Madison, Dolley's social and political activism and her magnetic personality benefited her husband, her charm and wit winning him many supporters. Not known for her physical beauty, Dolley was nevertheless considered a glamorous and fashionable woman. She enhanced her appearance with ample applications of makeup and shocking new styles guaranteed to create gossip. She soon became a fashion trendsetter, a role that later first ladies would also fulfill. Her taste in adornment favored low-cut, revealing dresses, peacock plumes in her hair, and elaborate turbans, which in combination became her signature look.

Presidency

Dolley Madison's rise to the nation's foremost social hostess began in Thomas Jefferson's presidency. As the wife of his secretary of state, Dolley occasionally presided over the widower's social affairs. She quickly gained fame and honed her social and political skills.

Madison assumed the presidency after Jefferson, and Dolley became the third first lady, ushering in a new social approach to the office and bringing even more visibility to the duties of the president's spouse. In 1809 she hosted the first large-scale presidential inaugural ball. From that moment, Dolley's social events became the toast of the capital city, and she became one of the most admired and well-known first ladies of all time. Dolley translated this gift for hostessing into political benefits for her husband, strategically manipulating the guest lists, timing, and seating arrangements of her events. Although she reduced the White House social calendar during the War of 1812, she threw socials to coincide with key events such as the capture of British ships or American military victories. The nation celebrated with Mrs. Madison.

It was not only her socials but Dolley herself who became the attraction and won over supporters for the president. Madison's enemies often left the White House less hostile than when they entered it, for almost everyone was affected by Dolley's personality and charm. Dolley apparently recognized her abilities and became quite conscious of her image and popularity, even seating herself at the head of table during state dinners.

Jefferson never fully furnished the White House during his eight-year tenure, and when he left office, the building was in a state of neglect. Thus Dolley undertook the first renovation of the Executive Mansion. To build political and financial support for her project, Dolley wisely invited members of the House and Senate to see firsthand the poor condition of White House furnishings. Her strategy produced the necessary funds, and she initiated another first for the office, establishing a role that many later presidential wives would exercise, that of overseeing the decoration and refurbishment of the White House. She also demonstrated foresight by enlisting the famous architect Benjamin H. Latrobe in the project. Dolley unveiled the new look to the nation by throwing a huge gala. Ever mindful of appearance and detail, she hired a leading chef and master of ceremonies to assist her in hosting the event. Dolley's renovation, like her socials, blended practicality with flair. She rearranged the rooms in the White House in pragmatic order to accommodate more guests and, ignoring her preference for French styles, opted for more symbolic and popular American designs to please the proud young nation. She achieved the sensitive balance between the standards of European elegance and the homegrown warmth and simplicity of the new nation.

Similarly, in her socials she often served American recipes solicited from or given to her by the women of the country. Dolley's expansive guest lists included the country's most famous artists and writers but also average citizens. So successful were her gatherings that she became one of the first women covered by the press and earned the nicknames "Lady Presidentress" and "Queen Dolley." Another first was that she appears to have eclipsed her husband in terms of popularity and as a public figure, becoming well known in her own right.

Another of Dolley Madison's contributions to her husband's presidency and the nation was her act of heroism during the War of 1812. When the hostilities broke out, the young country was ill prepared for war with England, but a group of outspoken hawks in Congress, mostly southerners, nevertheless pushed for a confrontation. Madison reluctantly acquiesced. During the ensuing conflict, the British enjoyed several decisive victories. This was a critical time for the republic, as some voices advocated surrender to England, and some British factions even clamored to recapture and reclaim the former colonies.

In spite of public criticism of Madison and rumors of assassination plots, Dolley maintained a public face, ignoring the threats. During the British invasion of Washington, she was advised to evacuate the White House but refused, even though her husband was away with the army. On August 24, 1814, as British troops overran and burned the capital city, Dolley watched with a spyglass from atop the White House, listening to the cannon blasts. With the British approaching the building, she finally vacated—but not before loading presidential papers and important, historic collectibles like china, silver, books, a copy of the Declaration of Independence, and the White House draperies onto a wagon with help only from a personal friend named Matilda and an army officer. They left in a carriage for Virginia just as the British started to sack and burn the White House. One priceless object Dolley Madison saved from inevitable destruction was the famous Gilbert Stuart portrait of George Washington. Thanks to her courage and quick thinking, the painting still graces a wall of the White House.

Only a timely rain shower saved the building from complete devastation. Dolley returned as soon as the British departed, ignoring advice to stay in Virginia for her own safety. She was met by cheering crowds when she proclaimed, "We shall rebuild Washington." The first lady held socials despite the damage to the White House, and in so doing, she helped inspire the populace and return the country to a degree of normalcy.

Legacy

Back at Montpelier after her husband's presidency, Dolley assisted Madison in his retirement by taking dictation and helping him organize his papers. She remained popular and continued to entertain the many visitors they received. After her husband's death in 1836, she experienced financial difficulties, partly from her son's considerable gambling debts, and consequently sold her home. She convinced Congress and President Andrew Jackson to purchase the Madison papers for the National Archives, receiving $30,000, a considerable sum at that time. She also was given a franking privilege by Congress, which covered her mailing costs for life.

Dolley Madison was the first presidential wife fully to embrace the office and truly enjoy the challenge of the presidency. She also helped frame the first ladyship office and created precedents for it by being the first to renovate the White House, preside at an inaugural ball, and make social hostessing and fashion prominent features within the office. To the present time, first ladies are expected to perform these same tasks, and many have also become public celebrities.

Dolley was easily the most popular woman in the country during her lifetime and the main public figure in the capital city for decades. At her eulogy President Zachary Taylor called her "our first lady for a half-century," an apt description given Dolley's long reign in the capital. After Madison's death and the sale of their home in 1836, Dolley moved back to Washington, D.C., where she continued to entertain and to enjoy great public admiration, even receiving an honorary seat in Congress by unanimous vote of that body, the only woman to have won this honor.

Although Dolley Madison was not considered an intellectual, she was an engaging conversationalist with natural political skills. Bold and nontraditional in her actions, she nevertheless managed to walk the narrow line regarding the "proper" role for women in public life. She did not seem to embrace women's equality and rarely voiced her opinions on issues of the day, yet she was a powerful political force in the White House and was her husband's biggest political asset. Charles Coteworthy Pinckney, an unsuccessful political opponent of Madison in 1808, best captured the influence of Dolley Madison when he bemoaned that he "might have had a better chance if I faced Mr. Madison alone."

Bibliography

Arnett, Ethel Stephens. *Mrs. James Madison: The Incomparable Dolley.* Greensboro, NC: Piedmont Press, 1972.

Cutts, Lucia Beverley. *Memoirs and Letters of Dolley Madison, Wife of James*

Madison, President of the United States. Boston: Houghton Mifflin, 1886.

Mayer, Jane R. *Dolley Madison.* New York: Random House, 1954.

Moore, Virginia. *The Madisons: A Biography.* New York: McGraw-Hill, 1979.

Wilson, Dorothy Clarke. *Queen Dolley: The Life and Times of Dolley Madison.* Garden City, NY: Doubleday, 1987.

5

Elizabeth Kortright Monroe

Born: July 30, 1768; New York City
Died: September 23, 1830; Oak Hill, Virginia
President: James Monroe (1758–1831), Fifth President
Husband's Presidential Term: 1817–1825 (Democrat-Republican)
Marriage: February 16, 1786; New York City
Children: Eliza Kortright (1786–1835); James Spence (1799–1800);
  Maria Hester (1803–1850)

Early Years
Elizabeth was the second of five children born to the Kortrights, a prominent family in New York City. Her father, Captain Lawrence Kortright, had been a British army officer and retained pro-British sympathies long after his service, although they lessened later in life. Ironically, the man that Captain Kortright's daughter would one day marry gained fame fighting the British and would go on to become president of the former colonies. Elizabeth's mother, Hannah Aspinwall, came from a prestigious New England family, but she did not live to see her daughter reach adulthood. Hannah died when Elizabeth was only nine years old, leaving her in the care of her grand-

mother, Hester Kortright. Grandmother Kortright was a strong, forceful woman, whose disciplined upbringing of her granddaughter appears to have contributed to Elizabeth's personal strength. Elizabeth would rely on this as an adult to face the challenges of public life and deal with the criticism she would experience as first lady.

Born in 1768, Elizabeth as a young woman was known for her beauty. Her blue eyes and contrasting dark hair earned her much attention from eligible bachelors. Raised in a monied, established family, she was refined and well mannered, but rather reserved and somewhat formal in demeanor and outlook. Her three sisters, also known for their beauty, had many suitors as well, and all married into powerful families; one sister married the son of Alexander Hamilton.

Marriage

James Monroe was a hero of the Revolution and a favorite of Thomas Jefferson. Like Jefferson, Monroe had attended the College of William and Mary, leaving to fight in the war. From 1780 to 1783 he studied law under Jefferson, and their friendship helped establish Monroe's political career. When James and Elizabeth met in 1785, he was a representative from Virginia to the Continental Congress under the Articles of Confederation. Even though his father was a judge, the Monroes were not members of the same class as the Kortrights. Nevertheless, after a brief courtship, James Monroe and Elizabeth were married in February 1786, when she was only seventeen, a decade younger than her new husband. That this teenage girl was courted by a well-known member of Congress speaks to the attractiveness, confidence, and poise she already displayed. Their first daughter, Eliza, was born the following year.

Family Life

Elizabeth and James Monroe spent most of their lives together in public service; only briefly did they enjoy a private family life during his political career. When Monroe received a diplomatic posting to France in 1794 during the Washington presidency, Elizabeth and their daughter joined him in Paris. Despite the political and social turmoil enveloping France, this was a very happy time for Elizabeth. She appears to have developed a taste for French food and culture, enjoying the life of a diplomat's wife and the social season and privilege that came with the position. While in France, Elizabeth befriended the mother of Napoleon III, even nicknaming her daughter "Hortensia," in honor of her friend.

The Monroes appear to have valued a solid education for their daughter; Eliza attended a fashionable school in Paris. Back home in 1799, a son was born, who died at sixteen months, and a second daughter arrived in 1803.

It was also in France that Elizabeth earned the nickname "La Belle Americaine." The story behind the name offers insight into her courage and charisma. In 1794 the Marquis de Lafayette, the flamboyant French military officer who had helped George Washington during the American Revolution, found himself and his family endangered by the forces fomenting the French Revolution. His wife, Adrienne Noailles de Lafayette, was imprisoned and facing death at the guillotine. In appreciation for Lafayette's role in its own revolution, the United States, through the efforts of statesman and founding father Gouverneur Morris, tried repeatedly but unsuccessfully to intervene on Madame Lafayette's behalf. Undeterred, Elizabeth Monroe rode to the prison housing Madame Lafayette and demanded to see her. Her conviction and her status as the wife of the American consul gained Mrs. Monroe entry, whereupon she comforted the prisoner and demanded her release. The authorities were duly impressed, and the request for a pardon was granted. This story of the pardon and Elizabeth Monroe's courage spread on both sides of the Atlantic, gaining for her not only a nickname but a reputation.

James Monroe enjoyed for the most part a charmed political career. First elected to the House of Burgesses in Virginia, he entered the U.S. Senate in 1790, then received a diplomatic appointment to France. Back in the States after being recalled, he served as governor of Virginia from 1799 to 1802 and again later in the decade. The election of his mentor Thomas Jefferson to the presidency brought Monroe an appointment as his special envoy to France, Spain, and later England. After Jefferson's presidency, James Madison assumed the office in 1809, and Monroe was his secretary of state from 1811 to 1817. In 1817 Monroe followed Madison into the presidency.

Elizabeth neither detested politics nor loved public office, but she followed her husband to each of his diplomatic posts and joined him in Richmond when he served as governor. Of their American homes, Elizabeth found Philadelphia most agreeable; she felt it had more culture than Virginia and it was also closer to her family in New York. She seems to have genuinely enjoyed their stays in France and England and was actively interested in her husband's career. Monroe respected her and relied on her support during the critical time that marked his service during mounting British-French tensions, with the United States divided in its loyalties.

Public life did not pay well, and many men who achieved distinction in it were wealthy before entering public service. Monroe was not as wealthy as the four previous presidents, and the family suffered financial difficulties in covering their travel expenses and the costs of the entertaining required of political leaders.

The Monroe home in Virginia was named Oak Hill, and Elizabeth's love of European culture was apparent in its decoration. During her adult life, public views on women were gradually changing, and the new image of the American "lady" was gaining popularity over the Federalist and Revolutionary notions of the practical, if plain homemaker. This is noticeable in the new image Dolley Madison projected compared to that of Martha Washington only a few years before. Since the founding of the office, first ladies have simultaneously reflected the nation's current attitudes toward women while being expected to fit traditional ideas about womanhood. Elizabeth matched the new image of a lady in her dress, attitude, and approach to the spousal duties of her husband's political offices.

Presidency

Elizabeth Monroe entered the White House well versed in the fine points of hosting, and being intimately familiar with the protocol of the courts of Europe, she seemed quite prepared to preside over the social affairs of the White House. But her practice of adopting elements of the European courts in her socials and French tastes in decor proved less an asset than it appeared to be. She was criticized for being too French and not being American enough. She was also attacked for her "excessive" taste in fashion. If the newly emerging image of a lady was appropriate for Dolley Madison, it was not publicly acceptable for Elizabeth Monroe. Indeed, she was criticized for many of the same practices that had earned Dolley Madison recognition and enduring fame as a hostess. Such fickle public perceptions of the first ladyship and the highly individualistic nature and treatment of the office continue to the present time. Furthermore, Elizabeth suffered from poor health while in the White House, thus limiting her activism and ultimately her success as a first lady. She had bouts with headaches and fevers, and a rumor circulated that she had had a miscarriage as well. She was assisted in her White House duties by her younger daughter Maria.

Early first ladies had endured the timely and burdensome custom of receiving endless streams of lady callers. They were also expected to return all calls, regardless of the number, impracticality, or time impositions involved. In part because of her poor health, Elizabeth chose to end the tiring tradition of returning all calls. She also limited calls on the wives of diplomats and members of Congress, minimized the full White House social calendar of her predecessor Dolley Madison, and started spending time away from the Executive Mansion. The custom of the day was that when the president's wife was not present or receiving, women generally did not join their spouses at White House functions. Thus, Elizabeth's absences were seen as a snub by women who felt they were not welcome at the Monroe White House. Political wives eager to attend presidential functions vented their wrath on Elizabeth. In 1819 several women boycotted her socials to show their displeasure with the first lady. James Monroe was even forced to call a cabinet meeting to deal with this "crisis." Not surprisingly, Elizabeth seems to have lost some of her enthusiasm for politics and public life. One of the few White House social occasions she threw herself into was the wedding of her daughter, which was held there. But she limited the guest list and was criticized for doing so.

Although she continued to agree with her husband's positions on political issues and took an interest in his presidency, she was not the active woman she had been earlier in his career. Fortunately, Monroe enjoyed widespread popularity, so whatever minor controversies Elizabeth occasioned did not negatively affect his presidency. Taking advantage of his popularity, the president and his wife embarked on a tour of the country, the first sitting president to do so.

Tired of the grind of politics and duties of public life, Elizabeth declined in health; indeed, she was so ill at the close of her husband's presidency, they had to delay their departure back home to Virginia.

Legacy

Elizabeth Monroe was a highly capable, sophisticated woman. If she is not remembered as a great first lady, in part it is because she had a difficult act to follow, that of Dolley Madison. Any presidential spouse would likely have struggled in the considerable shadow of Queen Dolley. Still, Elizabeth accomplished much and was an integral part of James Monroe's long political career. Moreover, her refinement, beauty, and regal White House socials were admired by many. In spite of her formal ways, she always preferred the simple title "Mrs. Monroe."

Elizabeth died on September 23, 1830. She was survived by her husband, who was so distraught at his wife's death that he burned many of their letters, depriving future generations of a better knowledge of Elizabeth Monroe.

Bibliography

Ammons, Harry. *James Monroe: The Quest for National Identity.* New York: McGraw-Hill, 1971.

Brown, Stuart Gerry, ed. *Autobiography of James Monroe.* Syracuse, NY: Syracuse University Press, 1959.

Cresson, W. P. *James Monroe.* Chapel Hill: University of North Carolina Press, 1946.

Morgan, George. *The Life of James Monroe.* New York: AMS Press, 1969.

Wootton, James E. *Elizabeth Kortright Monroe.* Charlottesville, VA: Ash Lawn–Highland, 1987.

6

Louisa
Catherine
Johnson
Adams

Born: February 12, 1775; London, England
Died: May 15, 1852; Washington, D.C.
President: John Quincy Adams (1767–1848), Sixth President
Husband's Presidential Term: 1825–1829 (Democrat-Republican)
Marriage: July 26, 1797; London, England
Children: George Washington (1801–1829); John Quincy II
(1803–1834); Charles Francis (1807–1886); Louisa (1811–1812)

Early Years
Louisa Johnson came from a powerful political family. Her paternal
uncle Thomas Johnson, one of the signers of the Declaration of
Independence, served as governor of Maryland and justice on the U.S.
Supreme Court. Louisa's American father, Joshua Johnson, was a
wealthy owner of a tobacco enterprise who moved from Maryland to
England in 1771 to pursue business ventures on the other side of the
Atlantic. Louisa was born in London in 1775; her mother, Catherine
Nuth, was British. Three years after Louisa's birth, the family moved
to France, where young Louisa spent part of her formative years, but
when her father was appointed U.S. consul to England by President

Washington, the family returned there, living near the Tower of London during Johnson's tenure as diplomat.

Louisa was the second child in a large household (records are unclear, but the Johnsons had eight or nine children). She enjoyed a privileged upbringing and a happy childhood. Indeed, in many ways her youth seemed idyllic, although one of the few ghosts in the family closet was a nagging rumor that she and her older sibling had been born out of wedlock.

Louisa's education was far better than that of most young women in the new United States. In France she attended a convent school and then an elite boarding school; her father also employed private tutors for her. As is clear from her letters, Louisa was a talented writer, and she learned both Latin and Greek as well as French. An avid reader, Louisa appears to have developed an inquisitive mind and an independence of thought rare for society women of the period. She took an interest in the status of women, believing they were as intelligent as men, yet balanced her bookish ways with social refinement and a deep passion for the fine arts, particularly music and the theater. Throughout her life she played instruments such as the harp and piano and demonstrated talent for sketching and poetry.

Marriage

Both Louisa and her future husband, John Quincy Adams, had previous love affairs with other persons that appear to have been serious but did not end in marriage. Adams fell in love with a girl named Mary Frazer, but his parents discouraged the relationship. Although he and Louisa eventually married after an on-and-off courtship, she apparently did not affect him as deeply as his earlier love. Their rocky courtship turned into a rocky marriage: They often argued and experienced both warm and difficult periods during their life together.

In fact, the marriage almost never occurred. The couple met in London in 1794, when he was twenty-seven and serving as U.S. minister to the Netherlands. Louisa was nineteen. After a formal courtship, they planned to marry, but Adams was hesitant, as he had been throughout the relationship. His formidable mother, Abigail, was cool toward Louisa, and he himself was concerned about his financial stability. A source of constant strife in their life together was Louisa's independence of thought, progressive views, and intelligence. Unlike his father, President John Adams, who appreciated his famous wife's intellectual partnership, John Quincy was more traditional and was even displeased with Louisa's love of literature and the type of books she read. He never fully respected or supported his wife's learned ways even though he himself was quite intellectual. It is unclear if he saw her as a threat or if he was simply very conservative in his personal life.

Nevertheless, they were wed on July 26, 1797. Even though Abigail disapproved of Louisa, finding her too weak and frail, the president felt that John Quincy's selection was the best decision his son had ever made. In many ways John and Louisa were opposites: She was as gentle as her husband was stern; she was impulsive and shy, and he was orderly and cold. Although he appears to have preferred a subservient wife, Louisa grew increasingly confident and independent as she matured. For these and other reasons, the marriage was difficult from the start. Around the time of the wedding, Louisa's father went bankrupt, and the newlyweds themselves had financial problems owing to the expenses of travel and the need to host social affairs associated with Adams's position. Soon after their marriage, Adams was posted to Berlin as U.S. minister to Prussia.

Family Life

Louisa had health problems in Berlin, and her first pregnancy ended in a miscarriage, one of several. Louisa eventually bore four children between 1801 and 1811, which drained her physically and mentally. She seems to have been naturally frail and suffered from poor health her entire life. The troubles in her married life—her husband's neglect, preoccupation with career, and long periods of absence—did not help matters. The long, difficult journeys were also hard on Louisa.

She did not set foot in the United States until 1801, when Thomas Jefferson was elected president and recalled the son of his political rival from his post. Stateside, John Quincy pursued a career in law but was soon elected to the Massachusetts State Senate. He next ran unsuccessfully for the U.S. House but was elected to the U.S. Senate in 1803. Louisa joined her husband part of the time during his political service in Boston and later in Washington. She was not fond of Boston or the Massachusetts farming community in which they lived first, but she did find the nation's capital agreeable.

Around this time her father died bankrupt, which she took hard, but the birth of John Quincy II in 1803 seems to have helped her recovery. In Washington Louisa lived with her widowed mother and her sister Nancy, which she found to be a pleasant respite from her husband and life in Massachusetts. Adams's Senate career went poorly, however, and he left for a teaching post at Harvard. The pregnant Louisa stayed behind in Washington but unfortunately suffered one of her several miscarriages.

When James Madison assumed the presidency in 1809, he appointed John Quincy Adams minister to Russia. He accepted without consulting Louisa and departed for Russia without her. He also failed to consult his wife when he arranged to have their sons George and John II remain in the United States with relatives. When Louisa sailed to join her husband, she went without her older sons and against her will, taking her two-month-old son Charles and only her niece and one maid. This and other diplomatic assignments would keep the Adams family away from the United States for eight years.

In Russia, Louisa distinguished herself in the social realm of the diplomatic world and was an asset to her husband. Her refinement, grace, and fluency in French made her popular at court. She apparently even made an impression on Czar Alexander and was his dancing partner. Louisa was not fond of Russia, however, and because the United States had almost no stipend available for its minister, Adams and Louisa were forced to live in rather spartan conditions and continually ran short of money. Frail Louisa somehow endured the brutal cold of the Russian winter and two additional miscarriages. A daughter was born in 1811, but she died in infancy, and Louisa and John grew even further apart.

In 1814 Adams was summoned to Paris to help negotiate the treaty ending the War of 1812, leaving his wife and young Charles behind in St. Petersburg. This was a long, lonely year for Louisa. Finally, in 1815, he sent word for her to join him in Paris. She departed in the dead of winter with her eight-year-old son, an elderly nurse, and two male servants. Crossing a continent by carriage in winter was a formidable challenge, one made worse by the unfortunate timing of Napoleon's escape from his prison at Elba. Napoleon was on a rampage, and Europe teetered again on the edge of war. Facing the threat of renewed hostilities and prospects of robbery, Louisa boldly held her small party together through the long trip. They became stuck in mud and snow, lost their way, and encountered mobs of Napoleonic loyalists hostile to a party traveling in a Russian carriage. Louisa quickly responded to the threat by crying, "*Vive Napoléon!*" After forty long days, the group arrived in Paris on March 23, 1815.

The trip was successful in another manner: Both her husband and mother-in-law were impressed by the strength Louisa demonstrated during the trip and treated her much better after the ordeal. She was also pleased when Adams received word that he was appointed minister to England. Later that year she returned to her childhood home in London and enjoyed a reunion there with her two older sons. This was one of the happiest times in her life, and even her health improved once she was back in England.

Presidency

John Quincy Adams was named secretary of state by President James Monroe in 1817, and the Adamses returned to the United States. With their relationship improving, Louisa took more interest in her husband's career and began fulfilling an advisory role, helping with his papers and supporting his growing bid for the presidency. She continued to mature intellectually and became more independent. Her interest in women's rights and the abolition of slavery defined her as her own woman and a progressive thinker. Louisa donated money to the abolition movement and freed her slave, who was the family cook. Her writing at this time reflects her belief that wives were at the "mercy" of their husbands and were "made to cook dinner, wash his clothes, gratify his sensual appetites." The letters also reveal that she saw a promising future for the status of women.

This period also reflects a change in Adams's view of his wife and his willingness to accept her help, which he was wise to do. Although his social stiffness and rudeness offended many, Louisa more than made up for her husband's shortcomings, charming both the public and important political leaders. This required effort on her part, as she was naturally shy.

There was not as much campaigning for office in the early 1800s as today, but candidates for the presidency still needed to court key supporters. Adams approached the office as an elite who felt he should not have to campaign, believing he simply deserved the presidency. His wife wanted him to become president but did not share his view of campaigning. Louisa made important contacts for him, opened their home to key political supporters each Tuesday evening when Congress was in session during the eight years of Monroe's presidency, and planned strategic political-social events to benefit her husband's campaign. She also helped him improve his rigid social demeanor.

As the wife of the secretary of state, Louisa substituted as White House hostess for Monroe's wife, Elizabeth, when the first lady was ill. On January 8, 1824, she hosted one of the grandest balls in the history of the country, inviting roughly one thousand to celebrate the anniversary of General Andrew Jackson's victory at the Battle of New Orleans.

This and other social events helped place John Quincy in a more favorable position to be elected. They also provided Louisa with valuable experience as a hostess.

Louisa's efforts on behalf of her husband's candidacy were successful, and she deserved partial credit for his election. In 1825 they moved into the White House. Ironically, she did not enjoy her time there. She grew tired of the social demands of the presidency and first ladyship and likened living in the White House to being in prison. The presidential years were difficult for both of them. Adams came under attack from a hostile Congress, and the marriage once again turned sour. In fact, his presidency seemed doomed from the beginning, when his electoral college victory was contested: Adams failed to garner a majority of electoral votes, and his opponent, Andrew Jackson, took the popular vote. Adams won only by a tie-breaking vote in the House of Representatives, thanks in part to his political deal making with the influential House leader Henry Clay to secure the necessary votes (Adams apparently promised to appoint Clay his secretary of state). Adams's motives were questioned, and the public voiced its disappointment with the election and the new president. While in office, Adams did push innovative and necessary programs such as publicly supported road and canal projects, and he expanded federal agriculture and education opportunities. But he was criticized for these initiatives and almost anything he did.

By 1826 the president and first lady were taking separate vacations and barely speaking to each other. Adams's already cranky personality and temper worsened as the press railed against him. He failed to take his wife's advice not to read the negative reporting and took his anger out on Louisa. Her health declined as she struggled with loneliness and depression. Nor did she escape criticism herself. When she hosted a dance at the White House, she was censured for allowing dancing. Consequently, the first lady curtailed much of her social entertaining.

As Louisa distanced herself from her husband and her official hostessing duties, she looked inward. She read prolifically and undertook new hobbies such as raising silkworms and writing plays and poetry. She also pursued her interest in art and preferred to be alone at the White House, often composing music and playing her harp in a private room on the second story of the building. Toward the end of the presidency, their oldest son, George, either fell overboard or committed suicide by jumping off the president's boat. Louisa believed her husband might have been to blame because of his harsh criticism of their son. Louisa looked forward to leaving the trials and political turmoil of the White House.

Legacy

Their marriage improved somewhat after leaving the White House. In "retirement" John was elected to the House of Representatives, the only man to become a congressman after his presidential term. He appears finally to have found contentment in his public service. Louisa continued to call him "the president," while he referred to her as "Mrs. Louisa C. Adams." Still, she was often depressed, as reflected in her memoir title: "Adventures of a Nobody," the first autobiography written by a first lady. She also wrote a play for her family called "The Metropolitan Kaleidoscope" that was something of a parody of her life; the lead character obviously was modeled after her husband—an ambitious statesman with a cold personality and poor parenting skills.

Louisa was the nation's first and only first lady born outside the United States, but there is more to her legacy. Although she did not directly impact her husband's policy decisions in the White House, she did much to secure his election. She was also one of the earliest public figures to embrace the causes of abolition and women's equality. She opposed the country's Indian removal policies, the annexation of Texas, and the war with Mexico, making her one of the first human rights supporters of either sex to reside in the White House. After their brief years of partnership in the White House, Louisa resumed this role by joining her husband and possibly even helping initiate his post–White House career as a vocal critic of slavery. Indeed, it is possible that Louisa was behind his newfound passion, for Louisa, after all, was a human rights crusader and social reformer long before John.

In 1847 the couple celebrated their fiftieth wedding anniversary together back home in Quincy, Massachusetts, in relative happiness. Only a year later, on February 1, 1848, John Quincy Adams collapsed on the floor of the House of Representatives after speaking out against the South's slave policies. He died two days later at age seventy-seven. Louisa died on May 15, 1852, also at the age of seventy-seven. On her death Congress adjourned for the day, the first time this had been done in honor of a woman.

Bibliography

Adams, Louisa Catherine. Diary. Available in the Adams Family Papers at the Massachusetts Historical Society.

———. "Narrative of a Journey from St. Petersburg to Paris in February 1815." *Scribner's Magazine,* October 1903. Adams Family Papers, Massachusetts Historical Society.

———. "Records of a Life: My Story" and "Adventures of a Nobody." Adams Family Papers, Massachusetts Historical Society.

Bobbe, Dorothie. *Mr. and Mrs. John Quincy Adams.* New York: Minton, Balch & Co., 1930.

Shepherd, Jack. *Cannibals of the Heart: A Personal Biography of Louisa Catherine and John Quincy Adams.* New York: McGraw-Hill, 1980.

7

Emily Tennessee Donelson
and Sarah Yorke Jackson

President: Andrew Jackson (1767–1845), Seventh President
President's Term: 1829–1837 (Democrat)

Rachel Donelson Jackson had once said about the White House, "I had rather be a doorkeeper in the house of God than live in that palace." She got her wish, dying several weeks before Andrew Jackson's inauguration. Even before his election, she and Jackson, anticipating the problems she might have as social hostess for the White House, had requested that Emily Tennessee Donelson and her husband, who was one of Rachel's nephews, live in the White House to keep Rachel company and help her. After Rachel's death, Emily took on the role of social hostess.

Hostess for Andrew Jackson:
Emily Tennessee Donelson (1809–1836)
Emily was the wife of Andrew Jackson Donelson, one of Rachel's nephews. Andrew and Rachel Jackson cared for the boy after the young boy's parents died in 1805. In 1824 Donelson married his sweetheart Emily Tennessee, a wealthy girl whose dowry included much land and many slaves. During Jackson's presidency, Donelson served as a presidential aide and his wife functioned as the White House hostess during the first two years of the Jackson presidency. Emily was only twenty-one but she served well and also took care of the president. Emily gave

birth to three of her four children while residing at the White House and hosted the many Jackson relatives who visited there.

Emily returned home to Tennessee when the Peggy Eaton scandal became too intense and was causing internal problems within the administration. Peggy Eaton was the wife of Jackson's secretary of war and the alleged mistress of several men whose affairs became public. After Secretary Eaton resigned and the scandal quieted, Emily returned to the White House in 1832. During the second term of the Jackson presidency, however, she became too ill to serve and ceased her hosting duties in 1834. Her husband also resigned to take care of her. Emily died of tuberculosis two years later.

Hostess for Andrew Jackson:
Sarah Yorke Jackson (1805–1887)

Sarah Yorke married one of Andrew and Rachel Jackson's foster sons. In 1834, when Emily Donelson became too ill to continue her service, Sarah assumed the role of hostess. Unfortunately, Sarah fared little better than Emily. The tone of the social affairs of Jackson's presidency was subdued from the beginning because of the untimely death of Rachel Jackson, and Emily's illness and subsequent death in 1836 weighed heavily on the president. Although Sarah hosted from 1834 to 1837, her White House functions are remembered as unremarkable.

8

Angelica Singleton Van Buren

President: Martin Van Buren (1772–1862), Eighth President
President's Term: 1837–1841 (Democrat)

Hannah Hoes Van Buren died on February 5, 1819, and Martin Van Buren never remarried. He assumed the presidency in 1837, almost two decades after his wife's death. He was a widower with four bachelor sons. Martin started his term without a first lady, and believing the White House did not need a social hostess, he undertook many of those duties himself. On taking office, he immediately began to refurbish the Executive Mansion, which had been sorely neglected during Jackson's two terms.

Hostess for Martin Van Buren:
Angelica Singleton Van Buren (1816–1878)
At the time of Van Buren's presidency, former first lady and recent widow Dolley Madison was once again living in the capital city and was still its leading socialite. One of Dolley's relatives by marriage, the beautiful and elegant Angelica Singleton, had come from South Carolina to visit Dolley in Washington. When Angelica accompanied Dolley to a White House function, she caught the guests' attention, including Van Buren's oldest son, Abraham. He immediately began courting Angelica, and they were married in late 1838, honeymooning

in Europe the following spring. Abraham had been serving as his father's private secretary, and after his marriage to Angelica, the couple resided in the White House, where she became social hostess. The capital city had not experienced much of a social season or entertaining in the White House during the eight years of Jackson's presidency; thus it was receptive to Angelica's full social calendar, and the events she hosted were quite successful. Angelica also won over the president, who was impressed with her and pleased to have her join his family. He clearly changed his position on not needing a hostess.

While living in the White House, Angelica gave birth but the infant lived only a few hours. This unfortunate event, however, did not limit her White House service. She thoroughly enjoyed her life there and her years of hostessing. After Van Buren's presidency ended, Angelica and Abraham lived in Europe and South Carolina before eventually settling in New York City, where she died in 1878.

9

Anna Tuthill Symmes Harrison

Born: July 25, 1775; Walpack township, New Jersey
Died: February 25, 1864; North Bend, Ohio
President: William Henry Harrison (1773–1841), Ninth President
Husband's Presidential Term: 1841 (Whig)
Marriage: November 25, 1795; North Bend, Ohio
Children: Elizabeth Bassett (1796–1846); John Cleves Symmes (1798–1830); Lucy Singleton (1800–1826); William Henry (1802–1838); John Scott (1806–1840); Mary Symmes (1809–1842); Carter Bassett (1811–1839); Anna Tuthill (1813–1865); James Findlay (1814–1817)

Early Years

Anna Symmes was born near Morristown, New Jersey, in 1775. Her father, John Cleves Symmes, was originally from Long Island, New York; he had married into a prominent family and enjoyed a prosperous career as a judge. He buried two wives while still a reasonably young man. Anna never knew her mother, Symmes's second wife, who died when Anna was only a year old.

Anna attended the prestigious Clinton Academy, a boarding school in East Hampton, New York, and studied Latin and Greek. It was unusual for girls of the late eighteenth century to receive a formal education, much less one with a classical curriculum, and to be away from their families for so long. Anna's grandmother saw to it that her granddaughter received a quality education; she raised her in the Presbyterian faith and most probably instilled in Anna the values of caution and discipline, strength, and courage that would become her trademarks in later years.

Anna's father was rarely present when she was growing up. He served in the Revolutionary War and was a member of the Continental Congress from 1785 to 1787 under the Articles of Confederation. When Anna was fourteen, her father led a group of early settlers west to what is now Cincinnati, Ohio, but she remained in New York to complete her education. Several years later, Symmes returned to the East Coast and married for the third time, this time to Susanna Livingston, the daughter of the governor of New Jersey. He then took his new wife and nineteen-year-old daughter to live in Ohio. As a young woman, Anna was bright and was described as attractive, short, and of a slight build. She was also said to have fine manners and an interest in the latest fashions. The trip and transition from New York to the frontier must have been difficult for her.

The family arrived in Ohio on January 1, 1795, but once there the judge again moved them, this time to a location on the north bend of the Ohio River. They prospered in the new territory, and Symmes became the first judge on Ohio's Supreme Court.

Marriage

It was on the long trip to the Ohio Territory that Anna met her future husband, William Henry Harrison, while visiting her sister in Kentucky. Anna and Harrison were immediately enamored with each other, but Symmes was opposed to his daughter's interest in the twenty-two-year-old lieutenant. Even though young Harrison was from an established Virginia family, was on his way to the rank of captain, and would in 1796 assume command of Fort Washington, a small outpost near the Symmes home, the judge did not want for his daughter the harsh life of a military wife, living in forts along the rugged frontier. This seems odd, given that he himself had uprooted her and moved to the frontier, but possibly he had other reasons for opposing the marriage. The headstrong Anna defied him, marrying Harrison secretly on November 25,

1795, when her father was out of town. Upon learning of the marriage, Symmes at first refused to talk to his new son-in-law, but after seeing that his daughter was happy, he relented.

Family Life

The couple apparently shared deep feelings for each other. Anna called William "Pah," and he referred to her as "Nancy." On September 29, 1796, Anna gave birth to the first of ten children, Elizabeth Bassett. The next year Harrison was promoted to the rank of captain, but only a year later he resigned his commission and bought land for his new family. In 1799 he was elected as a delegate to Congress from the Northwest Territory. This position not only offered Harrison important exposure for his political and military career, but it afforded Anna the opportunity to travel with him to Philadelphia and Richmond, Virginia; they also visited the Harrison family home on the James River. During a visit to Richmond in 1800, she gave birth to their third child. Later that year Harrison was appointed the first governor of the Indiana Territory, a position he would hold for the next twelve years, and he was the first representative to Congress from the new territory as well.

Accepting the governorship meant moving the family even farther into the uncharted West. Life was exceedingly tough along the frontier, and Anna's home lacked many of the basic amenities of life back east. There was, for instance, no well-trained physician available in the western outpost to assist Anna when she gave birth to a son in 1802. Nevertheless, she was happy there and enjoyed raising her growing family. She took responsibility for educating the children, as the small outposts often lacked sufficient schools or teachers. She also endured a lack of female companionship because so few women lived at the military posts in the territory.

Except on Sundays—being religious, she always kept the Sabbath—Anna hosted the few families and military officers visiting the outposts in the simple, informal manner expected on the frontier. The Harrison home at Vincennes was a mixture of plantation, fort, and house. Powder kegs and military supplies were part of her furnishings, and the home even had locations for sharpshooters to defend the occupants against Indian attacks.

Relations between the white settlers and the new territory's native people were strained at best, and Harrison was often called from his post to lead the military against Indian "uprisings" in the new territory.

Harrison negotiated numerous treaties with the Indians and also pushed for a greater military presence in the area to protect the settlers. Although Anna missed him a great deal when he was away, she dealt courageously with his absences and the threats against the small settlements. At times Anna was one of the few adults left at the outpost. During an 1811 campaign against the Indian leader Tecumseh, which would become one of Harrison's most famous victories, Anna gave birth to another son, named Carter Bassett. Although Harrison worried about her safety, Anna found the countryside beautiful and withstood its hardships with stoic discipline. She bore five more children during their time in Indiana. For a short while around the outbreak of the War of 1812, however, Anna returned to the safety of Cincinnati to live with her family at their North Bend home. She had her ninth child there, a daughter born in 1813, also named Anna.

William Henry Harrison reentered military service during the War of 1812, rising to the rank of general in charge of the Indiana troops, and built on the fame he had gained earlier as an Indian fighter. Although he was regarded as a war hero and would later—as a presidential candidate running under the slogan "Tippecanoe and Tyler too"—become known for his victory at the battle of Tippecanoe in 1811, Harrison's postwar military career did not progress as he had hoped. Disenchanted, he returned to civilian life. But neither he nor Anna was adept at managing money, and private life appears not to have been tenable for Harrison; they never enjoyed a peaceful or prosperous life. In 1817 a newborn son died, and Anna's ever-present strength momentarily wavered under the pain of the loss.

In the years following the War of 1812, Harrison concluded several important Indian treaties, which brought peace and increased settlement to the territory. Indiana became a state in 1816, and Harrison served first as a congressman, then as senator (1825–1828). In 1828 Harrison was appointed U.S. minister to Colombia. Anna stayed in the United States while her husband was gone, for a year only, as Harrison was recalled when Andrew Jackson took office. He again tried private life, living at their home, the Berkeley, in North Bend, Ohio. When Harrison returned to military life, he enjoyed further success as an officer but did not achieve the promotion or command he desired. Thus he again retired from active duty. Remarkably, his career was resurrected from relative obscurity in the mid 1830s by Whig Anti-Masons interested in promoting him as a presidential candidate. This probably had less to do with Harrison's suitability for the office than with a weak field of candidates and the need for a compromise candidate between different factions of the Whig Party. Although "Old Tippecanoe's" image as a war hero would sit well with the public, he was one of the most unlikely presidential candidates in the nation's history.

Presidency

When Anna heard from her home in North Bend that Harrison had won a landslide victory in the 1840 presidential election, she said simply, "I wish that my husband's friends had left him where he is, happy and contented in retirement." After a long, difficult life and career on the frontier, Anna was not ready to go back to public life; she had opposed her husband's bid for the office. At sixty-eight, William was the oldest man elected to the office, and Anna, at sixty-five, was the oldest first lady. Neither enjoyed robust health.

Anna chose not to accompany her husband when he departed for his inauguration in 1841. It appears she made this decision not only because of her coolness toward politics, but because the long journey by steamboat, rail, and carriage from Ohio to the capital in the cold of winter understandably held no appeal. Moreover, Anna was not well at the time, and her doctor discouraged her from traveling.

The new president-elect asked his daughter-in-law Jane Irwin to serve as White House hostess; she was the widow of the Harrisons' son William. Anna planned to make the trip in the spring, as soon as the weather improved and her health returned. She also intended to assume the White House hosting responsibilities, probably with her daughter-in-law's assistance.

Anna never made it to the White House, however, because her husband died only one month into his term. President Harrison had given a lengthy, outdoor inaugural address on a bitterly cold day and caught pneumonia. He died on April 4, 1841. The news of her husband's death reached Anna as she was packing and making plans to join him.

Legacy

Anna's frontier life had been arduous but generally happy. Her later years, though, were filled with tragedy. The Harrisons experienced financial troubles throughout much of their married life, and money problems continued to threaten Anna after her husband's death until she received a pension from Congress. In addition to William Henry

Harrison's tragic death, Anna buried nine of ten children, including an alcoholic son, William Jr., who died in debt; Lucy, who died at a young age in 1826; and John Cleves, who passed away four years later.

Anna accepted the loss of her husband and the tragedy that surrounded her final years much as she had lived her whole life: with dignity and courage. She stayed in her home in North Bend for over a decade after Harrison's death, until it was destroyed in a fire. She then moved in with her sole surviving child, John Scott Harrison, who lived nearby, remaining there until her death at eighty-eight in February 1868.

Some have claimed that Anna Harrison held much influence over her husband, that she even "ruled" him. Because not much information exists on her, it is difficult to substantiate this claim. It is known, however, that she did not permit her husband to campaign on Sundays and that she kept abreast of the political issues of the day. We know she opposed slavery and that she ran the household during her husband's many absences. She was certainly a strong, courageous woman and endured years in rugged military outposts. She also established important political contacts and used them for the benefit of her husband and to obtain attractive military appointments for her sons.

President William Henry Harrison remained popular after his death, partly because Anna worked to keep his memory alive, organizing his memorabilia and dispensing her late husband's autographs. Her legacy is noteworthy, given that she never formally served in the White House. Anna was the first first lady to have the benefit of a quality, formal education and the first to receive a pension.

She was married forty-six years and lived to be almost ninety. Anna Harrison was one of the earliest and among the most prominent settlers of the new Ohio and Indiana territories. She also holds the distinction of being wife to one president and grandmother to another: Her only surviving son, John Scott Harrison, was the father of Benjamin Harrison, who became president at the end of the century.

Bibliography

Bond, Beverly W., Jr., ed. *The Correspondence of John Cleves.* New York: Macmillan, 1926.
————. *The Intimate Letters of John Cleves Symmes and His Family.* Cincinnati: Historical and Philosophical Society of Ohio, 1956.

Cleaves, Freeman. *Old Tippecanoe: William Henry Harrison and His Times.* New York: Scribner's, 1939.

Goebel, Dorothy Burne. *William Henry Harrison: A Political Biography.* Indianapolis: Historical Bureau of the Indiana Library, 1926.

Holloway, Laura C. *The Ladies of the White House.* Philadelphia: A. Gorton, 1881.

10
Letitia
Christian
Tyler

Born: November 12, 1790; New Kent County, Virginia
Died: September 10, 1842; Washington, D.C.
President: John Tyler (1790–1862), Tenth President
Husband's Presidential Term: 1841–1845 (Democrat; Whig)
Marriage: March 29, 1813; New Kent County, Virginia
Children: Mary (1815–1848); Robert (1816–1877); John (1819–1896);
   Letitia (1821–1907); Elizabeth (1823–1850); Anne Contesse (1825);
   Alice (1827–1854); Taxwell (1830–1874)

Early Years
Letitia Christian was born not far from Richmond, Virginia, on
November 12, 1790, one of six girls born to Mary Browne and Robert
Christian. Her father was a wealthy plantation owner with an interest in
politics, who counted many influential political leaders among his circle
of friends; he was an acquaintance and ardent supporter of George
Washington. As a young girl Letitia was widely praised for her beauty.
She was shy, gentle, quiet, and also very religious, which appears to
have influenced her simple tastes and preference for a simple lifestyle.
Although she did not have a formal education, her experiences growing

up in a prominent family provided the skills necessary to run a large plantation home, as well as the art of social entertaining.

Letitia's daughter-in-law, Priscilla Cooper Tyler, remembered her as "the most entirely unselfish person you can imagine. . . . Notwithstanding her very delicate health, mother attends to and regulates all the household affairs and all so quietly that you can't tell when she does it." Unfortunately, none of Letitia's personal letters survive, and little is known about her early years; however, her husband, John Tyler, does refer to her in his writings. This, along with other old letters, makes it is possible to piece together some information about her life.

Marriage

John Tyler followed in the footsteps of his father, an early political leader in Virginia who served as governor of the Old Dominion state. John's career started early, just after his graduation from the College of William and Mary, when he was elected to the Virginia statehouse in 1811. The Tylers knew the Christian family, and John met Letitia on a visit in 1808. Later, on his travels to the capital in Richmond, Tyler often stopped at the Christian household. After a five-year courtship, the couple were married on March 19, 1813, his twenty-third birthday. Their marriage joined two of the most prominent families in the Richmond area. Letitia's conservative father, however, disagreed with his son-in-law's political views and his allegiance to Thomas Jefferson and the Jeffersonians.

Less than four months after their wedding, Tyler was commissioned as a captain in the War of 1812. Not long thereafter, Letitia's parents died, leaving her a sizable inheritance. In addition, John inherited a home, and the young couple prospered in all facets of their lives. From the love letters and sonnets he composed for Letitia, it is quite clear that Tyler was deeply in love with his wife.

Family Life

John Tyler's political career advanced at an impressive rate. He was elected to the U.S. House of Representatives in 1816, while still in his twenties, and at thirty-five became governor of Virginia. After a term as governor, he was elected to the U.S. Senate in 1827. Preferring the comforts of her home, Letitia did not join her husband in Washington when he served in Congress, even though he requested that she do so. She participated in the capital's winter social season only once, but during his governorship she did preside as first lady of Virginia, where she was an effective hostess.

Tyler's successful political life kept him busy, and his public duties often required him to be away from home. Letitia does not appear to have been interested in politics, nor did she influence her husband's political decisions. Her contribution seems largely within the Tyler household. She raised the children and managed the plantation during her husband's absences—no easy undertaking, for the Tyler plantation was a large enterprise. Letitia hosted guests, cooked, sewed, oversaw the business, and supervised slaves. She worked to provide a tranquil refuge for her husband at home, a respite from his turbulent political life. Letitia saw herself simply as a wife and mother and believed women should be subservient. John's letters reveal that he held his wife in high regard.

Despite their inheritances, the Tylers encountered financial trouble later in life. The costs of their large family and the burden of entertaining during his long political career drained their finances. With their plantation, they were land rich but cash poor, and after Tyler's Senate tenure ended in 1836, they retired to Williamsburg.

Letitia's hobbies included music and reading; she was also an avid knitter. She gave birth to nine children, seven of whom lived. Her sixth child, Anne, lived only three months, and a ninth, unnamed child died at birth. She was a devout Episcopalian who read her Bible and prayer book daily. By the late 1830s her health was declining, and she suffered a serious stroke in 1839 that confined her to bed. She became even more religious, reading little else but the Bible from that time on.

Presidency

John Tyler was selected as vice president on the 1840 presidential ticket with William Henry Harrison. After Harrison's death only one month into his term, Tyler became the first vice president to ascend to the presidency. He had been fulfilling most of his vice presidential duties from his home in Williamsburg; when he learned of his succession, he wanted his wife to join him in the White House. Letitia chose not to accompany her husband, however, because of her stroke and weak physical condition. Priscilla Cooper Tyler, the wife of their son Robert, presided as White House hostess for her mother-in-law. Priscilla had been an actress, and with her poise and famous beauty she fulfilled the duties ably. She also received tips from none other than the capital city's foremost hostess, Dolley Madison, whom the younger woman befriended.

Priscilla offered a full social calendar at the Executive Mansion, which included two formal dinners for around thirty guests per week when Congress was in session. She also hosted biweekly evening receptions open to the public and large, monthly parties for as many as one thousand guests. She entertained many luminaries at her functions, including writer Charles Dickens. In the nineteenth century all White House hostesses held huge, public socials on New Year's Day and Independence Day, and during the summer months Priscilla added concerts on the south lawn by the Marine band. Priscilla was glad to serve, and unlike her mother-in-law, who had little interest in politics or the social functions associated with public office, she found hostessing fun. Tyler's daughter Elizabeth also assisted as hostess. While living in the White House, Letitia remained nearly invisible, secluded on the second floor because of her disability. She did, however, continue to fulfill her family responsibilities. When Elizabeth married on January 31, 1842, Letitia made her only public appearance downstairs for the occasion.

Tyler's term as president was not easy, owing to bitter infighting among his fellow Jeffersonian Democrats. So bad was Tyler's rift with his party that in his first year the entire cabinet resigned, except for Daniel Webster, his secretary of state. These challenges may also have contributed to Letitia's withdrawal from public life, although even if she had been healthy, it is doubtful she would have engaged in any political affairs.

The White House needed repairs, but Letitia was not up to the task nor did the Tylers have the funds to undertake an extensive restoration. At the time, presidents were required to cover the expenses of office themselves. The mansion's heating and lighting costs and the financial demands of entertaining used up much of the Tylers' remaining money.

Legacy

Letitia suffered a second stroke and died in the White House shortly thereafter, on September 10, 1842, the first first lady to die while her husband was in office. She also appears to have been the first presidential spouse who was not a significant factor in her husband's life or success. Indeed, even though Elizabeth Monroe had been limited by poor health and thus occasionally asked her daughters to hostess on her behalf, Letitia was the first spouse to live in but not preside over the White House. Official Washington and the public seem to have grown accustomed to surrogate hostesses and were fairly understanding of

Letitia's limitations, for the Tylers received minimal public criticism when she did not uphold her social duties.

Had Letitia not suffered the debilitating stroke in 1839, she would likely have presided over at least some of the White House's social events. She had served as an official hostess earlier, when her husband was governor of Virginia, albeit reluctantly. Because she was somewhat reclusive by nature, however, she probably would have maintained a minimal social calendar and would have enlisted the assistance of her daughter and daughter-in-law regardless.

Bibliography

Chitwood, Oliver Perry. *John Tyler: Champion of the Old South*. New York: D. Appleton-Century, 1939.

Coleman, Elizabeth Tyler. *Priscilla Cooper Tyler and the American Scene*. Birmingham: University of Alabama Press, 1955.

Seager, Robert. *And Tyler Too*. New York: McGraw-Hill, 1963.

Tyler, Lyon Gardiner. *Letters and Times of the Tylers*. 3 volumes. Richmond, VA: Whittet & Shepperson, 1884–1886.

Willets, Gilson. *Inside History of the White House*. New York: Christian Herald, 1908.

11

Julia
Gardiner
Tyler

Born: May 4, 1820; Gardiners Island, New York
Died: July 10, 1889; Richmond, Virginia
President: John Tyler (1790–1862), Tenth President
Husband's Presidential Term: 1841–1845 (Democrat; Whig)
Marriage: June 26, 1844; New York City
Children: David Gardiner (1846–1927); John Alexander (1848–1883);
    Lachan (1851); Julia Gardiner (1853–1935); Robert Fitzwalter
    (1856–1927); Pearl Taylor (1860–1947)

Early Years

Julia Gardiner was born on Gardiners Island near Long Island, New York, on May 4, 1820. Her mother and father, Catherine and David, were very wealthy, prominent members of the East Hampton community and were well known in the state. Gardiner was elected to the state senate, serving from 1824 to 1828. Julia was educated at home until 1835, when at age sixteen she was sent to New York City to attend Madame Chagaray's, a prestigious finishing school. Her parents wanted a high-quality education for their daughter, along with the requisite refinements expected of a society girl of the period. While boarding at

Madame Chagaray's, Julia studied French literature and music as well as math and history.

Julia was the third of four Gardiner children. She led a charmed life and was known for her beauty and outgoing manner; she was described as both elegant and flirtatious. She possibly gained much of her confidence and boldness from her highly opinionated and domineering mother, who raised her daughters to be aware of their privileged position in life and to believe in their social superiority and the importance of marrying into a family of similar status. Apparently this lesson was not lost on Julia, despite her somewhat rebellious personality.

At age fifteen Julia had her official society debut, and her coming out was capped off later by a tour of Europe. She enjoyed not only England and France but the many suitors she attracted on her travels as well. The family also visited Virginia and Washington, in part to expose Julia to the world and, in turn, the world and its eligible bachelors to Julia. Washington was especially pleasing to Julia, and once back in East Hampton, she complained of being bored and wanted to return to the capital city. Apparently, she developed early on an affinity for politics, the Washington social scene, and the considerable romantic attention she received from the city's politicians, who were drawn not only to her beauty but her intelligence, energy, and charm as well. This early trip to Washington seems to have kindled what would become a lifelong fascination with all things political.

At age nineteen Julia appeared on a handbill for a clothing store in New York wearing a fancy fur coat, with feathers adorning her hair. Julia's likeness was used to sell the company's merchandise with the caption, "I'll purchase at Bogert and Mecamly's, No. 86 Ninth Ave. Their goods are beautiful and astonishingly cheap." At the time it was deemed improper for a girl to appear in such an advertisement, especially one from Julia's background. The ad created a minor scandal and embarrassed her parents. The *Brooklyn Daily News* found the ad and story newsworthy and on the newspaper's front page referred to the young model as "The Rose of Long Island." An admirer was even moved to write a poem titled "Julia—The Rose of Long Island," which was published in the same paper. This nickname stuck and, when she became first lady, would be recognized by many.

Marriage

In 1842, the same year that Julia Gardiner and her family once again visited Washington, Letitia Tyler, the wife of the president, died after a prolonged illness. Julia attended many social events in the capital and enjoyed the company of its most prominent families and their eligible sons. She received numerous offers of courtship, and such was her appeal that even married men and several leading political figures were quite enamored of the Rose of Long Island. At her request, the family returned for the city's winter social season in 1843.

During their second visit, the Gardiners were invited to a White House dinner and party. Julia's father and President Tyler became friends while playing cards together. The president also noticed David Gardiner's daughter. In fact, only two weeks after meeting her, the widower president proposed to Julia. She turned him down, but they began a courtship that produced a stream of poetic, deeply romantic love letters from the president. In February 1844 Tyler again proposed to Julia at a White House ball, but she again rejected him. A month later, however, she accepted his proposal.

In the interim between Tyler's marriage proposals, the Gardiners accepted the president's invitation to join him and a group of dignitaries aboard the U.S.S. *Princeton,* which set sail down the Potomac on February 22, 1844, for Mount Vernon, George Washington's former home. While on board, Captain R. P. Stockton treated the passengers to a demonstration of the steam frigate's new cannon, named "the Peacemaker." The big gun misfired and the ensuing explosion killed five on board, including two members of the cabinet and Julia's father. So distraught was Julia that she reportedly fainted, and President Tyler carried the young woman off the ship. During Julia's recovery in Washington, Tyler seems to have assumed something of a fatherly role in her life, even as the courtship continued. A secret engagement soon followed.

Julia was twenty-four and the president thirty years her senior when they married on June 2, 1844. Not surprisingly, when the story of their wedding became public, it generated much public interest—and criticism. But it was more than the age difference that contributed to the gossip prompted by the wedding. Tyler was the first president to marry in office, and the country was both curious and uncertain about the event. Some thought it was improper for the president to remarry in the White House; others saw the marriage as coming too quickly after Letitia Tyler's death less than two years before. Tyler rebutted the criticism, stating that he was in his "prime" and not too old to marry Julia. Mrs. Gardiner attempted to slow down the courtship and wedding, apparently in an effort to allow her daughter time to be sure of her love for Tyler. John Tyler had had seven children by his first wife, and the older ones were surprised and upset by their father's marriage to Julia. It took them some time to come to terms with their young stepmother.

Family Life

In spite of the tragedy and controversy that surrounded the wedding, the couple quickly became close friends and political allies, and John grew to admire and rely on Julia. She both enjoyed and excelled at hostessing in the White House. Theirs was a loving marriage, and the first child was born in 1846, a son, David Gardiner, named after his maternal grandfather. She and Tyler would have five more children (a sixth died in infancy), the last one when the former president was seventy, making him the president who sired the most children. Julia's life was devoted to her family and her husband's political career, but rather than simply supporting him, she shared his political views and challenges, closely following the political events of the day. Tyler's political projects and positions became her own.

One event she felt passionately about was the 1846 war with Mexico. Julia was hawkish, embracing her husband's argument in favor of armed conflict to the extent that she even criticized her brothers in New York for their opposition to it. The U.S. soldiers engaged in the conflict received her full backing, and she regularly shared stories of their heroism and courage with her audiences at the White House. On the matter of annexing Texas, Julia was so proud of her husband's initiative that she wanted to wear around her neck the gold pen he used to sign the annexation treaty. She read all John's speeches and found them to be "inspirational" and "poetic," and she was often vocal and aggressive in attacking her husband's critics and political enemies. Although Julia was from the North, she adopted her husband's secessionist stance, rallying behind the South, state's rights, and even the practice of slavery.

The Tylers' home life both during and after their presidential years was happy, and the two appear to have genuinely enjoyed each other's company. They shared an interest in more than just politics and frequently played music together, with Julia playing the guitar and singing and Tyler accompanying her on the violin.

Presidency

Perhaps more than any other of her predecessors, Julia Tyler loved being first lady. She was ambitious and wanted to host the best and largest socials ever held in the White House. Although her tenure as first lady was short, it was highly successful. Julia benefited from the public and press fascination with the new, young, beautiful first lady. Both as a socialite before her marriage and once in the White House, she seems to have used her popularity, appearance, and charm to great advantage. Even the notoriously difficult congressional leader and secretary of state, John C. Calhoun, was under her spell. Powerful New York congressman Richard D. Davis, also old enough to be her father, sought Julia's audience and attention as well.

Julia took command of the White House, enlivening it with some of the grandest events the capital city had yet seen. She inherited a White House in disrepair and was only too happy to renovate the neglected building immediately. French furniture and the best French wines were procured for the Executive Mansion, often at the Tylers' own expense. She also used her fortune to buy an elaborate wardrobe. Just as Dolley Madison before her had become a fashion symbol, Julia's peacock plumes, elegant dresses, and latest styles became the talk of Washington social circles. Her tastes were regal, as were her socials. She even seated herself on a raised platform to receive guests. Julia's 1845 New Year's Day reception attracted over two thousand people; her final social event hosted over three thousand guests. Joining the first lady at these affairs was an entourage of maids of honor, consisting of her sister Margaret and her cousins, along with Julia's pet Italian greyhound.

Before marrying Julia, the president had opposed including the waltz at White House functions on grounds that the music and dance were immoral. His new wife quickly changed his mind and featured the waltz at her socials; she also introduced the polka to the White House. Much like Dolley Madison before her, Julia's socials blended politics and social hostessing. But Julia was much more openly political than Dolley or other early first ladies in building support for her husband's programs through her social events and using these events to herald his accomplishments. Her considerable influence did not end there, however, for she gave her husband political advice as well.

After Letitia Tyler's illness and minimal social calendar, the capital city was ready for Julia Tyler and opened its arms to her. She served for only eight months, but her first ladyship was appropriately described as her "reign." Although she was widely admired and her first ladyship was very successful, criticism of her self-centeredness seems to have been on the mark.

Julia hated to leave the White House after Tyler's single term in office. Reluctantly, she "retired" to Sherwood Forest, his home near the James River in Virginia. Here Julia continued to stay busy, helping her husband manage the plantation with its sixty to seventy slaves. Julia also renovated her husband's home, redecorated his boat, and had his carriage refurbished. She continued to host impressive parties at Sherwood Forest and in the Hamptons in New York during summers. She called her husband "the President" for the remainder of her life and continued her interest and activism in politics. As hostilities grew between the North and South, Julia became a leading spokesperson for the Confederacy and the practice of slavery.

In 1853, concerned women in England, led by the duchess of Sutherland, began a letter-writing campaign appealing to southerners, and southern women in particular, to end slavery. The initiative drew Julia's ire. She drafted an open letter to newspapers rebuking the British abolitionists, which was published in the *New York Herald* and *Richmond Inquirer*. In her letter Julia argued that southern slaveowners were kind to their slaves and that the British women had no business meddling in U.S. affairs. This prompted criticism from some northern abolitionists, who called Julia a "dough face," a common term describing someone from the North who held southern views. But this failed to silence the former first lady. She attacked the North as "fiendish" and defended the southern cause as "holy."

In 1861 Julia accompanied her husband, who was a delegate, to what proved to be an unsuccessful peace conference attempting to prevent war. At the outbreak of the Civil War, she also joined him in Richmond when he was asked to serve in the provisional congress of the Confederacy. Julia flew the rebel flag at her home and was proud when two of her sons joined the Confederate Army. During the war Union forces seized the Tyler home but held it in safekeeping until after the close of hostilities. Julia was forced to move back with her New York relatives during part of the war. Although she refused to sign the Union's oath of allegiance, she managed to obtain a special federal pass to travel to New York, sailing by way of Bermuda. While in the North, Julia joined a pro-Confederacy group known as the Copperheads and proceeded to distribute anti-Lincoln pamphlets and peace literature, purchase Confederate bonds, raise funds for the Confederacy, and send money to Confederate soldiers in northern prisons while simultaneously working to obtain their pardon. Her family, former neighbors, and the northern public tolerated Julia's campaign against the Union but were obviously upset by her aggressive support of the South.

Legacy

Shortly after the outbreak of the Civil War, John Tyler's health began to fail. In January 1862 he suffered a stroke and died at the age of seventy-two. Julia took her husband's death hard, suffering from depression and writing poetry to him. This was a difficult time for a still-young widow trying to raise her children under the strain of war. She also experienced money problems, for it was not until much later that presidential widows were provided with pensions. In 1870 Mary Todd Lincoln was voted a pension, so Julia successfully lobbied for her own; her prompting led to pensions for others. In 1880 she received a $1,200 pension from Congress and a year later, following the assassination of President James Garfield, presidential widows Mary Lincoln, Sarah Polk, Julia Tyler, and Lucretia Garfield were all given $5,000 annually.

Julia moved back to Richmond after the war and lived there until her death in 1889. She suffered from malaria in her final years but ultimately succumbed to a stroke, dying in the same hotel where her husband had died.

Julia Tyler's legacy is vast. From the moment she wed John Tyler, making her the first woman to marry a sitting president, she made history. Heralded as "the most beautiful woman of the age," she initiated the practice of having the Marine band play "Hail to the Chief" when the president entered a room or appeared in public. Guests to her social functions were honored by having their names announced as they entered, and so grand were her parties that she was given the nickname "Lady Presidentress." Julia thoroughly enjoyed serving as first lady, and the president was proud of her and her many accomplishments. She was one of the most charming and successful hostesses in the history of the White House, despite some criticism of her excessive tastes and the blemish of her post–White House advocacy of slavery. Yet even her defense of the Confederacy and the many wartime activities in which she was involved marked the first time that a first lady or former first lady was so publicly active in politics.

She was most likely one of the best-known people in the country. A song titled "The Julia Waltz" was composed in her honor and became a popular hit. She takes her place alongside Dolley Madison as one of the most famous and admired first ladies.

Bibliography

Durbin, Louise, and Marie Smith. *White House Brides*. Washington, D.C.: Acropolis Books, 1966.

Gardiner, John Lion. *The Gardiners of Gardiner's Island.* East Hampton, NY: Star Press, 1927.
Gardiner, Sarah D. *Early Memories of Gardiner's Island.* East Hampton, NY: East Hampton Star, 1947.
Seager, Robert. *And Tyler Too.* New York: McGraw-Hill, 1963.

12

Sarah Childress Polk

Born: September 4, 1803; Murfreesboro, Tennessee
Died: August 14, 1891; Nashville, Tennessee
President: James K. Polk (1795–1849), Eleventh President
Husband's Presidential Term: 1845–1849 (Democrat)
Marriage: January 1, 1824; Murfreesboro, Tennessee
Children: None

Early Years

The Childress family relocated from Virginia to the frontier of Tennessee, where Captain Joel Childress prospered as a planter, tavern owner, and merchant. Sarah was born into this thriving frontier family in the town of Murfreesboro in 1803. Both parents placed great importance on education and wanted to give their children the best possible, mixing the traditional refinements of a finishing school with a classical education. Sarah and her sister were tutored at home, then sent to the Ambercrombie School in Nashville, where they attended balls and a party at the home of Andrew Jackson. Sarah later went to the Moravian Female Academy in Salem, North Carolina, one of the few schools devoted to higher education for women at the time. She studied art, geography, grammar, history, music, and the Bible. It was an impressive education, especially compared to that afforded to most frontier girls.

One of the major influences on Sarah was her mother, Elizabeth. Sarah's father died at age forty-two, but Elizabeth was a strong woman who encouraged Sarah's healthy appetite for reading, which she would enjoy throughout her life. The eldest daughter, Sarah had nine siblings and grew up in a household with many privileges courtesy of her parents' wealth. This included a home life that exposed young Sarah to politics and social hosting when the Childress family entertained guests.

Marriage

James Polk, a graduate of the University of North Carolina, was practicing law and working as a clerk in the Tennessee legislature in 1821 when he met Sarah Childress, who was roughly eight years younger than he. She reportedly made her acceptance of his marriage proposal conditional on his agreement to pursue a political career and run for the legislature, although it is hard to verify the story. It is clear that both of them were ambitious and loved politics. He did run, and one year after their marriage on New Year's Day 1824, James Polk was elected to the U.S. House of Representatives.

Polk was an eligible bachelor for several years and courted many women, but Sarah was an attractive possible spouse for him. None other than Andrew Jackson, Polk's mentor, encouraged his political protégé to marry Sarah because Jackson was so impressed with the bright young woman from his home state.

Family Life

The Polks did not have children. Because the lives of most women of the early and mid-nineteenth century revolved around their children and the role of motherhood, childlessness must have been difficult for Sarah. But it did permit her to devote herself to her husband's career and to become his full-time political partner. She often joined Polk in the capital city in a time when few wives traveled such distances for such purposes, especially those from frontier regions. On the rare occasions she did not accompany him to congressional sessions, the two exchanged letters, revealing the warmth of their relationship and Sarah's strong interest in politics and her role as his adviser.

Polk's political star rose rapidly, aided by his wife's valuable assistance and his friendship with Andrew Jackson, who appears to have continued to be impressed with the young Mrs. Polk. Within a decade James Polk was positioning himself for the speakership of the House. When his initial bid for the office failed, Sarah increased their visibility in capital social circles, hosting events aimed at building political support for her husband. It was said she held some of Washington's best socials, and Polk did ascend to the position of Speaker in December 1835. After his long tenure in Congress, Polk returned to Tennessee, where his wife's support and social contacts helped elect him to the governorship in 1839.

Samuel Laughlin, the editor of Nashville's newspaper, referred to Sarah as the "membress of Congress," and Supreme Court Justice Joseph Story honored Mrs. Polk by penning a poem for her. Franklin Pierce, later president, stated that while serving in Congress he preferred to discuss politics with Sarah rather than most men. She was a regular in the congressional gallery, where she kept up with the latest legislative developments.

In the capital city Sarah Polk was known for being outspoken. Her opinions were bold and her participation in politics exceeded what was considered appropriate for a woman. In many ways her disposition complemented her political pursuits: She disliked the traditional home life that governed most women's lives and even proclaimed that she would not cook or clean when she was in the White House. The couple had much in common. Both were ambitious, loved politics, and worked hard, and James's public life was their joint undertaking. They agreed on almost all political issues, including one of the most pressing matters of the day: westward expansion. Both advocated expansion, including the war with Mexico and the push westward and north, even into Canada. One of the few areas in which they disagreed was the basis for the country's currency. Polk supported a standard founded on gold and silver, whereas Sarah favored paper money and a strong role for banks. She appears to have been thoughtful and cautious, especially on sensitive issues such as slavery, the Civil War, and women's rights, but she could be bold, as in her rejection of the prevailing views against a gold or silver standard.

Throughout his political career Sarah served as her husband's personal secretary, copying his correspondence and editing his speeches.

James Polk had so much confidence in his wife's judgment that he regularly solicited her opinion on political issues; he even requested her to read newspapers for him and then provide reports of newsworthy events. Polk frequently commented on his wife's intelligence and appears to have appreciated her activism. Sarah also helped with his campaigns for public office. Recognizing her husband's tendency to work himself to exhaustion, she frequently tried to get him to slow his pace.

Another of Sarah's passions was religion. While in Washington, she regularly attended the First Presbyterian Church and succeeded in getting her husband to attend with her. She always kept the Sabbath, refusing even to entertain visitors on Sundays. Sarah also would not attend the theater or horse races because of her beliefs, but she was more lenient for political activities and the social events of the Washington winter social season.

Their family life was not all politics. Only a few years after their marriage, Polk's father died, and James and Sarah assumed care of the family. Sarah's father and older brother died as well, leaving the couple to run the Childress family estate.

Presidency

Sarah was thrilled by her husband's election to the presidency and assumed her role as first lady with confidence and ease. She did attend the inaugural ball but, bowing to her strong religious views, declined to dance. This act somewhat set the tone for Sarah Polk's first ladyship. Her tenure was more subdued than the extravagant and glamorous eras of Dolley Madison (to whom she paid a courtesy call) and Julia Tyler. But with practiced efficiency and good manners, Sarah succeeded in her social responsibilities. Although it was said she did not allow wine at White House dinners, some accounts of her events reveal that wine was in fact served on occasion. These records also document rather impressive social affairs in the Polk White House. If her manner was understated and her socials were not lively, they were nevertheless up to the standards of the office.

Sarah's social calendar consisted of two evening receptions each week, which appear to have been well attended and somewhat informal. In the summer months she held concerts on the White House lawn each Wednesday evening featuring the Marine band. And of course she hosted the gala socials every first lady was expected to offer, the July Fourth celebration and the New Year's Day open house.

One of Sarah's assets was her skill as a conversationalist. She talked openly with reporters, and her personality and intelligence appear to have won her many supporters. She also preferred joining the men after dinner to discuss politics, finding the small talk over tea with the ladies of Washington boring. When Sarah dismissed herself from the dinner table to join the men, many of the female guests responded with criticism, feeling snubbed by the first lady's unwillingness to keep their company.

Although she is said to have attempted to hide her political bent from the public, Sarah did attend cabinet meetings and discussed politics with White House guests, though she was careful to preface her comments with, "Mr. Polk believes . . . ." Yet the first lady weighed in on the war with Mexico, a divisive issue that was generally backed by the South and opposed by the North. Sarah supported her husband's position in favor of the war and was at his side when he signed the peace treaty ending the conflict. As she had done during his congressional career, Sarah served as her husband's private secretary and close political confidante in the White House as well, and even attempted to build support for him by circulating favorable newspaper clippings to key backers and political figures. So serious was she about Polk's political positions that she never invited his critics and rivals to White House events.

Not everyone greeted Sarah's involvement in politics with admiration. Rumors circulated that she "ruled" her husband. Vice President George Dallas even quipped, "She is certainly mistress of herself and I suspect of somebody else also." Whether the charges were true remains unanswered, but it is clear that James Polk did at times defer to his wife on political matters.

James K. Polk stepped down after a single term in office. Sarah left Washington with a fair amount of praise, including the admiration of the formidable Henry Clay and a fond farewell from the city's newspaper. They retired to their new home in Nashville, Polk Place.

Legacy

Both James and Sarah were workaholics, but he was often sick and lacked his wife's strength and robust physical health. As a child he had experienced many bouts of illness and had had bladder stones surgically removed at a young age, which some historians speculate might have left Polk sterile. Although he left office reasonably young at fifty-five, he died only three months later. Sarah, still in her forties, did not handle his death well. She became depressed and essentially stopped socializing except to attend church. She did recover, however, whereupon she dedicated the remainder of her life to preserving her husband's legacy. She organized his papers, maintained his study as it was when he died, and somewhat reluctantly opened their home in Nashville to visitors.

During the Civil War Sarah Polk was careful to remain neutral and welcomed both Union and Confederate officers into her home, offering them her hospitality and the memories of her husband. Despite her somewhat enlightened views on slavery and her husband's suggestion in his will to free their slaves, Sarah failed to do so. One might have expected otherwise of Sarah, given her self-professed belief that she was an emancipator who did not abuse those who worked for her. She continued to run the family-owned cotton plantation in Mississippi, managing its affairs from her home in Tennessee.

Sarah Polk loved politics and made her husband's career the centerpiece of her life. She is remembered as the first first lady to serve as the president's closest political confidante since Abigail Adams some four decades earlier. In many ways Sarah was also the prototype of modern partners who are intimately involved in all aspects of their spouse's political career. She spent the remaining forty-two years of her life in Polk Place as a widow always dressed in black and was nearly ninety when she died in 1891.

Bibliography

Claxton, Jimmie Lou Sparkman. *88 Years with Sarah Polk*. New York: Vantage Press, 1972.

Nelson, Anson, and Fanny Nelson. *Memorials of Sarah Childress Polk*. New York: Anson D. F. Randolph, 1892.

Nevins, Allan, ed. *Polk: The Diary of a President, 1845–1849*. New York: Longmans, Green, 1952.

Sellars, Charles. *James K. Polk: Jacksonian Democrat*. Princeton, NJ: Princeton University Press, 1957.

———. *James K. Polk: Constitutionalist*. Princeton, NJ: Princeton University Press, 1963.

13

Margaret Mackall Smith Taylor

Born: September 21, 1788; Calvert County, Maryland
Died: August 18, 1852; Pascagoula, Mississippi
President: Zachary Taylor (1784–1850), Twelfth President
Husband's Presidential Term: 1849–1850 (Whig)
Marriage: June 21, 1810; Jefferson County, Kentucky
Children: Ann Mackall (1811–1875); Sarah Knox (1814–1835); Octavia Pannel (1816–1820); Margaret Smith (1819–1820); Mary Elizabeth "Betty" (1824–1909); Richard (1826–1879)

Early Years

As was the case with so many of the women who eventually became first ladies, Margaret Smith came from a wealthy family. Her mother was Ann Mackall, and her father, Major Walter Smith, was a plantation owner who had served as an officer in the Revolutionary War. They lived in Calvert County, Maryland, where Margaret was born in 1788.

Even though her family was rather well-to-do, Margaret, like most eighteenth-century girls, did not receive a formal education but apparently was tutored at home. Young "Peggy" was described as thin, with brown hair, and is said to have displayed a southern demeanor throughout her life. Very little is known about her, and most scholars believe that no verifiable portrait of her exists.

Marriage

In the eighteenth century it was uncommon for most women, much less young girls, to venture far from their place of birth. This was certainly not true of Margaret Taylor, however, whose birth, marriage, and death all occurred in different states. Indeed, travel defined much of her life. When she was twenty-one, while visiting her sister and family in Kentucky in 1809, Margaret met a twenty-five-year-old army lieutenant named Zachary Taylor, who was on leave visiting his parents near Louisville, Kentucky. Apparently, they fell in love immediately. After a courtship of almost six months, they

Betty Taylor Bliss

were married in June 1810. Margaret called her new husband "Old Zach."

Family Life

Zachary Taylor was not a West Point graduate and thus lacked the political connections to ensure a smooth, rapid advancement through the military ranks. Although he enjoyed some success as an officer, Taylor spent most of his career commanding small military posts in the western territories of Michigan and Missouri and in remote regions of the South such as Louisiana and Florida. Most of the Taylors' approximately four decades together were spent in rugged, rural locations. Margaret loyally followed her husband from one outpost to another, raising a family with few of the basic amenities she had been accustomed to as a child; she spent much of her life housed in log cabins or old military barracks. It was not until Taylor was given command of Fort Crawford in the Michigan Territory that she finally moved into a decent home with a kitchen. Religion helped her through the ordeals of frontier living; she was an Episcopalian who maintained her faith and read Scripture throughout her life.

Between 1811 and 1826 Margaret gave birth to six children. During these years, her husband was often away on duty, leaving Margaret alone at the garrison with the children, five daughters and a son. She had the assistance of two slaves who traveled with the Taylors, but she was often lonely. She showed impressive courage and strength in the face of constant challenges and the threat of confrontation with natives.

Margaret was often one of the few white women living in the vicinity of the military posts. Believing in the merits of a solid education, she tutored the children herself; then they were sent back to Kentucky and the East Coast for formal schooling. Her daughter Ann attended an academy for girls in Lexington, Kentucky; Sarah went to schools nearby in Louisville and in Cincinnati, Ohio; and her youngest daughter, Betty, was enrolled in a boarding school in Philadelphia. The Taylors' youngest child and only son, Richard, born in 1826, graduated from Yale. "Dick" went on to become a general in the Confederate Army.

The year 1820 was especially difficult for Margaret. Her three-year-old daughter, Octavia, died while they were living in the Louisiana bayous, and that same year she lost an infant child named after herself. Both children appear to have died from "bilious fever," a malady that plagued Margaret off and on throughout her life. She suffered from periodic bouts of poor health at the forts, and the deaths of two daughters devastated her. As she would do repeatedly during her life, however, Margaret rebounded from the challenges and recovered. She did not complain of the lack of adequate medical treatment, supplies, housing, and other necessities others took for granted. She was a simple, kind woman who lived a demanding, often spartan life.

Perhaps because of their own hardships and, possibly, frustration with Taylor's slow advancement—promoted to major in 1812, he served twenty years before becoming a colonel in 1832—both Margaret and Zachary Taylor opposed having their daughters marry career military men. Sarah Knox fell in love at age eighteen with a lieutenant in his twenties. Over her parents' objections, Sarah went forward with the marriage plans, but apparently neither even attended the ceremony, as Sarah's uncle gave her away on the wedding day. She died from malaria only three months later; her husband, Jefferson Davis, went on to become president of the Confederacy during the Civil War. Davis eventually remarried, and the Taylors appear to have reconciled their differences with their son-in-law, retaining their acquaintance with him and becoming close friends with his second wife, Varina. At age eighteen, another daughter, Ann, married Robert

Crooke Wood, an assistant military surgeon working at Fort Crawford under Zachary Taylor's command. The parents grudgingly accepted this marriage, too.

Taylor often was called into sudden service. When hostilities between the Seminole Indians of Florida and white settlers reached a crisis point, Taylor was sent to Fort Brooke in Tampa. During the Second Seminole War, he achieved a degree of fame for his military victories, one of them on Christmas Day 1837 at the battle at Okeechobee against the Seminole and Mikasuki tribes. It was then that Taylor earned the nickname he would carry into the presidency: "Old Rough and Ready." He was also promoted to brigadier general. After the conflict, Margaret joined her husband in Florida, where she helped nurse wounded soldiers.

In need of rest, Taylor requested leave for himself and his family, which was finally granted in 1840. The Taylors were accustomed to traveling and spent their leave doing anything but relaxing. They embarked on a multistate tour, first to Pensacola and other locations in Florida, then to New Orleans and Baton Rouge in Louisiana, New York state, and Washington, D.C. En route they visited relatives in Kentucky and stopped in Philadelphia to see their daughter Betty, who was attending school there.

After his leave, Taylor assumed command of a fort in Baton Rouge. In spite of the hardships she had faced for so many years, or perhaps because of them, Margaret declined the opportunity to live in a large home, choosing a small cottage instead. With the help of her slaves and some of the fort's soldiers, she renovated the little house. This was possibly the happiest time in her life. Her husband finally enjoyed a more prestigious command, and she felt contented in her modest home while enjoying her children's company. Upset that there was no Episcopalian church near the fort, Margaret designated a room at the post for church services and later helped establish an Episcopal church in Baton Rouge.

Margaret Taylor's tranquillity did not last. She was once again deprived of her husband's company when war with Mexico broke out. In 1845 General Taylor was ordered to Texas; she stayed at their beloved cottage in Baton Rouge. Her children continued to visit and comfort her, but she worried continuously about Zachary's safety and seems to have taken this separation harder than earlier ones. During this period Margaret supposedly vowed that should her husband return safely from the war, she would never again participate in society life. He did return, and she seems to have honored her vow and avoided social life—although she had never spent much time in society circles and did very little formal entertaining as mistress of the military garrisons where they were stationed. Regardless of whether or why she made such a vow, we do know that this final separation of his long career was difficult for Margaret.

After the war ended in 1847, Margaret traveled by ship with her daughters to visit Taylor in December. She arrived in the port of New Orleans to share in the city's celebration honoring the general; he had returned as a hero with victories at Palo Alto, Resaca de la Palma, and the decisive one at Buena Vista. After the celebration the Taylors retired to their cottage in Baton Rouge. Margaret was pleased to have her husband safe at home and enjoyed visits from their children and grandchildren, but unfortunately, her health had begun to deteriorate by this time.

Presidency

As a popular hero, Taylor was nominated and elected to the presidency on the Whig ticket in November 1848. Margaret did not want him to be president and even prayed he would lose the election. Recognizing the demands of the office, she worried about his declining health and feared the presidential duties would shorten his life. She was also a very private individual who longed for a quiet retirement. By this time her health was so poor she was probably a semi-invalid, but she supported her husband nonetheless.

As first lady, she joined her husband in the White House but did not attempt to fulfill any duties associated with the office. She remained largely out of the public eye during her time there, confining herself to the private living quarters on the second floor, with the exception of her church attendance. Despite her claims of poor health, Margaret went to services daily at St. John's Episcopal Church. A more likely reason for her lack of involvement is that she simply was not interested in being first lady. She declined an invitation from outgoing President James Polk to dine with him before Taylor's inauguration, then failed to attend the three inaugural ceremonies. And although she had spent decades enduring the harsh conditions of frontier military life with barely a protest, in the White House Margaret complained frequently about Washington's heat and humidity. She still enjoyed the company of her children and grandchildren, however, and was pleased with their frequent visits.

Although Taylor's enemies criticized him because of his wife's lack of enthusiasm, the attacks were tempered because of his popularity as a war hero. But his opponents and the press did not let up in their allegations that Margaret was a bumpkin. Caricatures in newspapers even showed her smoking a corncob pipe. Historians have disagreed about whether she did in fact smoke a pipe, but most cite her poor health as the reason she did not.

The Taylors asked their daughter Betty Taylor Bliss to serve as White House hostess; she also attended the inaugural festivities in place of her mother. Betty had married Lieutenant Colonel William S. Bliss, the president's personal secretary, and she is generally credited with being a successful hostess.

After an Independence Day party in 1850, Zachary Taylor became ill with cholera morbus. He steadily worsened, dying on July 9. Margaret did not attend her husband's funeral and moved out of the White House that very day.

Legacy

A few days after the funeral, Margaret Taylor left the capital and visited her daughter Ann in nearby Baltimore. After a brief stay, they traveled to New Orleans to visit the Taylors' son, Richard. With his assistance the family divided the inheritance and attended to Taylor's will. Margaret took the death of her husband hard and never again mentioned the White House.

She retired to Pascagoula, Mississippi, to live with her daughter Betty's family. There she remained very private, assisted only by a few family members and five slaves. Margaret Taylor died a largely forgotten woman, and she remains just as obscure today, for none of her letters survived. Margaret herself possibly destroyed them after Zachary's death, or they may have been lost in a fire that destroyed her family home during the Civil War. Although it is difficult to assess her legacy, she appears to have been one of the few nineteenth-century first ladies who played virtually no role in their husbands' presidencies.

Bibliography

Brainerd, Dyer. *Zachary Taylor.* New York: Barnes & Noble, 1967.
Holman, Hamilton. *Zachary Taylor: Soldier in the White House.* Hamden, CT: Archon Books, 1966.
———. *Zachary Taylor: Soldier of the Republic.* Hamden, CT: Archon Books, 1966.

Klapthor, Margaret Brown. *Maryland's Presidential First Ladies: Mrs. Zachary Taylor and Mrs. John Quincy Adams.* Calvert County, MD: Calvert County Historical Society, 1966.

Whitton, Mary Ormsbee. *First First Ladies, 1789–1865: A Study of the Wives of the Early Presidents.* New York: Hastings House, 1948.

14

Abigail Powers Fillmore

Born: May 13, 1798; Stillwater, New York
Died: March 30, 1853; Washington, D.C.
President: Millard B. Fillmore (1800–1874), Thirteenth President
Husband's Presidential Term: 1850–1853 (Whig)
Marriage: February 5, 1826; Moravia, New York
Children: Millard Powers (1828–1889); Mary Abigail (1832–1854)

Early Years

New York's Saratoga County was still a rather remote wilderness at the end of the eighteenth century. Abigail Powers was born into the small community of Stillwater there in the spring of 1798. Her father, Lemuel, was a Baptist preacher who died only about two years after his daughter's birth. Abigail's mother, Abigail Newland Powers, was a strong, resourceful woman who, after her husband's death, took her family farther west in New York State to live with relatives in the town of Sempronius. Like Stillwater, Sempronius was a rural place only sparsely settled.

The widow raised her family in the Baptist faith and used her deceased husband's library to educate her children. This home tutoring was supplemented with some formal schooling in the nearby town of

New Hope. A schoolteacher, Mrs. Powers imparted to her daughter an appreciation for learning. Abigail developed a love of reading that continued into adulthood, and she grew up to be much like her mother: strong and intelligent.

Marriage

Like her mother, Abigail also became a schoolteacher. She began teaching at the New Hope Academy near the town of Sempronius at age sixteen. It was while working at this country school that she met Millard Fillmore, who enrolled as a student in 1818. Although Abigail was approximately two years older than her new student, they were both ambitious individuals who shared a love of learning. A romance soon developed, and they were engaged a year after meeting, when Abigail was twenty.

Fillmore's education was irregular, but he read law and credited Abigail with enabling him to achieve his dream of becoming a lawyer. She supported him in his pursuit, even though his studies caused them to be apart for several years and put their courtship on hold. It was important to Fillmore to establish himself in his career and achieve some financial stability before marrying. Abigail's formidable mother and family appear not to have been supportive, initially opposing the union on grounds that Fillmore had little to offer Abigail. The struggling lawyer came from a family of poor farmers and was a Unitarian, whereas the Powers family were strict Baptists.

Abigail continued teaching and founded a library in Sempronius while Fillmore was completing his education. Because the couple lacked the money for travel to see each other, they corresponded. Eventually his career picked up, and the couple married in February 1826.

After the wedding the Fillmores moved to East Aurora, New York. Abigail continued to teach, making her the first future first lady to be employed after marriage. Most women of the period ceased working after they wed, many after becoming engaged. But Abigail was by nature a teacher; she loved reading and learning, was naturally inquisitive, and wanted to help others. She was a major influence on the education of her husband and their two children.

Family Life

In 1828 Abigail gave birth to her first child, a son named for his father. In 1832 her second child, Mary Abigail, was born. Just as her mother had instilled the value of learning in her, so did Abigail stress a sound education in raising her children. She challenged and pushed them in their educational pursuits and corrected the grammar in their letters. But even though she could be very demanding, she also praised her children.

As Fillmore's legal practice improved, he became better known—to the extent that in 1829 he entered public life with his election to the state legislature. Abigail stopped teaching only temporarily when she had children, but even while she was raising her infants, she studied French. The Fillmores had a close marriage and were intellectual partners; the two spent time reading and studying together and he gave books to his wife as presents.

Abigail developed an interest in politics corresponding to her husband's growing political career. They discussed political affairs together, and Millard often sought his wife's opinion on pressing issues. Abigail did not, however, accompany Millard to Albany when he attended legislative sessions. This was difficult for her because of the long separation during their engagement. Moreover, she worried that her husband would find the women in the capital "fairer" and "more accomplished" than herself. She often repeated this concern when Fillmore traveled without her, a curious insecurity because she seemed otherwise to be a strong woman.

The following year, 1830, Fillmore relocated his law practice to Buffalo, where he finally found the success he had sought. The couple enjoyed their financial prosperity. Abigail joined her husband's Unitarian church and remained active in educational issues, helping to start a library and book-lending program and working to improve the quality of education in the community. She continued to study French and also horticulture, developing an interest in gardening. At the heart of their union was their shared love of learning, and together they built a family library that contained over four thousand books.

Fillmore was elected to the U.S. House of Representatives in 1832, as a member of the Anti-Mason Party. Abigail remained in New York when he traveled to Washington for the congressional session. He served one term, then returned to his law practice in 1835, but he was reelected the following year after joining the Whig Party. This time Abigail joined him in Washington. Their children stayed in New York in the care of relatives. They repeated this arrangement each session from 1836 through 1842, although their daughter, Abby, visited them in Washington occasionally.

In 1840 Abigail was asked to deliver a speech at the dedication of a building in the capital city. She declined the offer, perhaps out of convention; it was unusual for a woman to be asked to give a public address. Or possibly she was uncomfortable speaking in such a forum. Although as a teacher she often spoke before others, at times Abigail seems to have lacked self-confidence. Regardless of the reason, that she was asked to dedicate the building demonstrates the high regard in which others held her. Although some historians have implied that Abigail was not interested in women's rights, she clearly placed a high priority on education for both sexes. Moreover, even though she was often conventional, she did continue to work after marriage and publically advocated educational improvements, which suggests at least a marginal interest in the status of women and that she practiced what she preached.

In 1842 Millard Fillmore decided not to run for reelection to Congress and once again resumed his law practice. But he returned to politics only two years later, in an unsuccessful attempt to run for vice president on the Whig ticket. He also lost a bid for governor of New York, but in 1847 he was elected state comptroller. The Fillmores moved to Albany when he assumed his new office. Their children went to Massachusetts to continue their education in college.

Two events limited Abigail's enthusiasm and activism during Fillmore's career. In 1838 her mother died, and the loss deeply affected her. Then, after Fillmore's stint in the U.S. House of Representatives and they returned to Buffalo, she fell and badly injured her foot and ankle. Abigail never fully recovered from this nagging injury, and it apparently not only limited her mobility but also often caused her to be depressed. She used crutches for several years and later cited the injury as the reason she could not attend certain social affairs. Although she complained about it, however, she may have used it as an excuse to avoid events she was reluctant to attend. It is clear that Abigail disliked ceremonies and found elaborate social functions unnecessary, and she was ill at ease in the company of those who attended them. Around this same period, her general health began to deteriorate; she suffered from headaches, a bad back, and a chronic cough.

In 1848 Abigail met a professor of theology with whom she became very close friends. Their lively, intellectual conversations appear to have reinvigorated her moods and passion for learning. That same year the Whigs selected Fillmore as Zachary Taylor's running mate for the 1848 presidential election. Although she was pleased with the results, Abigail did not accompany her husband to Washington after the election because of her poor health. It appears she genuinely wanted to go with him because she complained of being lonely and wrote that she missed him terribly, as he did her. While they were apart, she followed political events and exchanged letters with Millard offering him political advice.

Presidency

Fillmore was in Washington and Abigail was vacationing in New Jersey with the children when President Taylor died in 1850. She had always been supportive of her husband's career and shared his ambitions; moreover, she enjoyed politics herself. But she received the news of his ascension to the presidency with mixed emotions. Even as the Fillmores and the nation mourned the loss of its war hero and president, Abigail was happy and proud of her husband's achievement. But she also worried about her ability to fulfill the duties of the first lady and was concerned that her poor health and foot injury would limit her. She also feared she would be considered an inadequate and boring hostess. After Margaret Taylor, public expectations were possibly not so high for the first ladyship as they would have been after Dolley Madison, but despite this and despite her intellectual abilities and skills as a conversationalist, Abigail suffered from doubts.

Nevertheless, she followed the issues closely, attended congressional sessions and debates, and combed the newspapers for political news. In letters to friends and relatives, she discussed politics and showed herself to be well informed. Indeed, Abigail Fillmore was a valuable political adviser to her husband, and he often solicited her counsel. They remained close partners during his presidency.

But in her capacity as White House hostess she struggled. She did attend political and social events and hosted her obligatory functions, but she avoided the limelight and at times felt uncomfortable in her role. Her style was very informal and simple, and her intensely private persona was apparent in her approach to the office. Abigail's old injury prevented her from dancing or standing in long receiving lines, and the death of her sister in 1851 also dampened her enthusiasm for entertaining. As it happened, her subdued social events and hosting manner matched the general consensus that, owing to President Taylor's death and the growing tensions between North and South, White House social affairs should be more reserved. The Fillmores' daughter, Abby, assisted her mother and seems to have been a highly capable hostess, earning praise for the gatherings she held and also her beauty. Toward the end of Fillmore's term, Abigail relinquished most of the social duties to her daughter for health reasons.

While still able, however, Abigail appears to have performed the first lady functions adequately. The Fillmore social calendar included Friday evening receptions, Tuesday morning receptions, and evening dinner parties on Thursdays and Saturdays. Ever the intellectual, Abigail invited famous thinkers and writers to the White House; among her guests were Charles Dickens, Washington Irving, and William Thackeray. Beyond guest lists, Abigail initiated a practice subsequent first ladies would follow, that of making the White House a center for the nation's culture, arts, and learning. Abigail also oversaw the refurbishment of parts of the White House, adding new wallpaper where needed, installing the first iron range in the kitchen, and improving the building's heating systems.

Even though she was uncomfortable in some social settings, Abigail did cherish her time in the White House. She celebrated her husband's political triumphs and made the most of her days in the capital, frequently attending concerts, lectures, art exhibitions (and even horse races) while in Washington. In earlier times it was uncommon for women to travel about in a city without their husbands, and this was especially true for presidential wives. But Abigail attended concerts and other events unaccompanied by the president. It is clear that the intellectual life of the capital and its variety of social and intellectual amenities agreed with her.

In private, she devoted herself to running the household, sewing and cooking, and pursuing her personal studies. Abigail preferred quiet family time and passed many hours alone in the upstairs living quarters reading. Abigail played the piano and harp, and her daughter was an accomplished musician who sang and played the piano, guitar, and harp. The two of them often played music together and occasionally gave small concerts for friends and invited guests.

Given Abigail's love of books and her vocation as a teacher, it seems natural that she found the lack of a library in the White House distressing. Having previously founded at least two libraries, Abigail once again acted and pushed her husband to secure funding from Congress to create a White House library. With the subsequent $2,000 appropriation, she personally undertook the task of obtaining books for it, which she located in the second floor Oval Room. She took the job very seriously and invested considerable time and energy in the matter, personally reading many of the numerous books she selected. She acquired both new and old books, classic texts, personal favorites like Shakespeare and Dickens, biographies, books on history and religion, maps, and musical instruments. She was proud of the library and spent many hours reading there.

Another issue Abigail took up with her husband was the practice of flogging; it appears she is to be credited for ending this form of punishment in the U.S. Navy. Her political instincts and advice seem to have been at least equal to those of her husband and perhaps even better at times. She advised him not to sign the Fugitive Slave Act, legislation that allowed the government to participate in capturing and returning runaway slaves to the South. Abigail opposed slavery on moral grounds but also predicted that this controversial piece of legislation would hurt her husband politically. He rejected her advice and signed the bill into law, and it indeed became one of the factors that prevented his reelection. Fillmore's position alienated him from key northern supporters in the Whig Party, and in the next campaign he was not even renominated as its candidate.

During her years in the White House, Abigail spent her summers visiting friends and relatives in New York, partly to escape the capital city's heat and humidity and partly because she missed New York. At the conclusion of her husband's term, she looked forward to returning there. While attending the inauguration of Fillmore's successor on a windy, snowy day, however, she caught cold. Abigail died of bronchial pneumonia on March 30, 1853, as the couple were preparing to return to their home state. Congress adjourned upon learning of her death, public offices closed, and President Franklin Pierce canceled his scheduled cabinet meeting. Many turned out to pay their respects, and the city's newspaper spoke highly of the "dignified" first lady.

Legacy

Millard Fillmore found it difficult to carry on after his wife's death; and his daughter died only a year later. Fillmore is remembered only as a marginal president in the pages of history. Because of her husband's lack of distinction, Abigail Fillmore is not well known either. Although her health did limit her effectiveness in the White House, she was nevertheless a partner in her husband's long political career and presidency. She should be remembered as an early leader in educational access for women and an advocate for educational quality, as well as the founder of the White House library.

Bibliography

Grayson, Benson Lee. *The Unknown President: The Administration of Millard Fillmore*. Washington, D.C.: University Press of America, 1981.

Rayback, Robert J. *Millard Fillmore*. Norwalk, CT: Easton Press, 1959.

Severance, Frank H., ed. *Millard Fillmore Papers*. Buffalo, NY: Buffalo Historical Society, 1970.

Snyder, Charles M. *The Lady and the President: The Letters of Dorothea Dix and Millard Fillmore*. Louisville: University Press of Kentucky, 1975.

15

Jane Means Appleton Pierce

Born: March 12, 1806; Hampton, New Hampshire
Died: December 2, 1863; Andover, New Hampshire
President: Franklin Pierce (1804–1869), Fourteenth President
Husband's Presidential Term: 1853–1857 (Democrat)
Marriage: November 19, 1834; Amherst, Massachusetts
Children: Franklin (1836); Frank Robert (1839–1843); Benjamin (1841–1853)

Early Years

Jane Appleton was born to Elizabeth Means and Jesse Appleton on March 12, 1806, in Hampton, New Hampshire. Jane's father was a well-known Congregationalist minister and the president of Bowdoin College in Maine. The Appleton family prospered, but the reverend tended to overwork, and he died when Jane was only thirteen. Jane's mother was left a comfortable inheritance, and she then moved her daughters to Amherst, New Hampshire.

Jane enjoyed a life of privilege, but she was always physically weak and described as "frail, nervous, and sensitive." Although not many details of her education are known, it is clear that she was bright, loved literature, and had a classical education, most probably taught at home by private tutors employed by her father. Jane was close to her sisters, and the strict, religious upbringing they received seems to have greatly affected Jane, whose piousness tended toward the extreme. Even though her mother instilled in her a sense of self-worth, a consciousness of image, and a capacity for discipline, Jane seems also at times to have been judgmental, elitist, and proper to a fault.

Marriage

One story suggests that Jane met Franklin Pierce at Bowdoin College, where he was a student and Jane's father had been president. Reportedly, she had taken refuge under a tree on campus during a thunderstorm; Franklin noticed the attractive young woman and, recognizing the danger in hiding under a tree during lightning strikes, rushed to escort her to a safer place. More likely, however, Jane was introduced to Franklin after his graduation from the college in 1824, through her sister Elizabeth's husband, Alpheus S. Pachard, a professor at Bowdoin who knew Franklin from his law studies.

Either way, Pierce began courting Jane shortly after they met, even though Jane's domineering mother opposed the prospective marriage. It was an unlikely attraction, as the two were complete opposites. While they were courting, Franklin was beginning his political career, having been elected to the House in New Hampshire's General Court in 1829. But Jane, and apparently her mother as well, considered politics to be an undesirable and demeaning vocation, one not suited to a well-bred person like herself. This appears to have been a major reason for Elizabeth's opposition to her daughter's suitor; in all other respects he would have been a worthy husband and son-in-law. He was a graduate of the college of which Jane's father had been president, his own father was the sitting governor of New Hampshire, and his law practice was progressing well. But Pierce was an Episcopalian, not a Congregationalist, and the two had different personalities and outlooks. Jane was introverted and Franklin gregarious. He was outgoing and fun loving, and had a passion for debating and drinking with his friends. Jane felt alcohol was sinful, would rather stay home than socialize, and was shy and reclusive. Moreover, he was a Jacksonian Democrat committed to social progress and political reform, while Jane and her family were elitist, traditional, and stubbornly closed-minded.

Nevertheless, the young couple got along better than one might imagine given these differences, perhaps because Pierce took great pains to adjust his lifestyle to suit that of his fiancée. Their courtship was a long one; they did not wed until 1834, when Jane was twenty-eight, considered quite old in the nineteenth century for a woman's first marriage.

Family Life

As Pierce's career in politics progressed, Jane would have nothing to do with it. She was unhappy when his popularity and success took him from the U.S. House of Representatives (1833–1837) to a more prestigious seat in the Senate (1837–1842). In fact, she frequently asked him to end his political career and tried to persuade him to pursue other occupations. Although she was impressed with President Andrew Jackson, Jane thought little of other politicians. She had especially harsh words for Davy Crockett, describing the self-promoting politician as "conceited, stupid, silly." She rarely accompanied her husband to Washington when he traveled there for each legislative session, preferring to remain in New Hampshire. She did not like the capital and did not like politics; indeed, she equated politics with sin.

When they were apart, which was often during their marriage, they exchanged warm letters and appear to have been on reasonably good terms even though they did argue over his political career.

Because of her frail health, Jane did little housework. Her husband hired a married couple to take care of the household and assist Jane with other matters. Jane devoted herself to little beyond her children and religion. In Concord, New Hampshire, she was an active member of the South Congregational Church. The first of three sons, named for his father, was born in 1836 but died after a few days. In 1839 a second son, Frank Robert, was born, and the last one, Benjamin, was born two years later. Frank Robert died of typhus at age four, and thereafter Jane appears to have become mildly obsessed with her surviving child, Bennie. She spent all of her time with him and raised him in a strict religious manner. The two prayed throughout the day and went to church regularly, and she sang hymns to him. Mother and son were inseparable.

During the 1840s Pierce's political career went very well. But at Jane's urging, at the height of his popularity in the Senate he retired from politics; she argued it would be better for their two sons living at the time. Pierce returned to New Hampshire to practice law, and despite tragedy in her own life—little Frank died in 1843—Jane was pleased he was out of politics. The decision was difficult for Pierce, and he reluctantly declined an offer from President James Polk to join his cabinet as attorney general in 1846. He also declined offers to run for governor of New Hampshire and his old seat in the Senate. He served as a brigadier general of volunteers during the war with Mexico and, as was the case with most officers with war experience, enjoyed the hero status that came with service.

Pierce's friends continued to press him to reenter politics, and although he failed to inform his wife, he appears to have worked quietly with them on a possible return to public life. He kept his foot in the door by chairing the state Democratic Party and working briefly as a federal district attorney for New Hampshire. When supporters tried to get him to run for president in 1852 as a "dark horse," he rejected the opportunity—but only initially.

Presidency

Reversing his earlier decision to stay out of politics, Pierce accepted the Democratic Party's nomination for the presidency. When Jane found out, she denounced the news, saying, "I hope he won't be elected." When she learned he had worked behind the scenes (and her back) to return to politics, she was disgusted and angry with her husband. Franklin Pierce was elected in the fall of 1852; Jane reportedly fainted at the news. During the campaign Jane refused to help or support Franklin, even though he tried to convince her that his presidency would one day help Bennie's life and career.

Just two months before the inauguration, Pierce, Jane, and their thirteen-year-old son were traveling from Boston back to their home in Concord, New Hampshire, on the Boston and Maine Railway. On January 6, 1853, the train's axle broke, causing the train to derail. The resulting wreck killed Bennie, crushing his head in a gruesome scene witnessed by his mother. After the death of her beloved last son, Jane Pierce was never again the same. She directed her anger and grief toward her husband and politics, believing God had taken Bennie so that the child would not interfere with Pierce's ambition and presidency. His son's death profoundly affected Franklin as well; he accepted responsibility for the tragedy.

A cloud hung over Pierce's election, as the nation mourned the loss of the new president's son. Jane Pierce did not accompany her husband to his March 4 inauguration, but she did join him at the White House later that month. Because of the tragedy, Pierce was sworn in with a simplified ceremony. Also in March Abigail Fillmore, wife of the outgoing president, died, followed by Vice President Rufus King in April. This chain of death was too much for the sensitive, grieving wife of the president. At the beginning of Pierce's term, Jane rarely appeared in public and remained in mourning for some time thereafter. She did not entertain guests during the first year of her husband's presidency. To deal with her grief, Jane turned even more deeply to religion; she remained in seclusion in their second-floor quarters of the White House, praying and writing letters to Bennie in heaven.

As first lady, Jane was not often seen with the president and did not attend concerts or public events in the capital city. She did little entertaining, and when she did serve as hostess, she was lethargic and uninspired. She occasionally forced herself to make appearances at social affairs and went to church with her husband. Jane also kept the Sabbath in the White House, effectively shutting down the Executive Mansion on Sundays. She also attempted to get the White House staff to hold religious services.

To carry out the first lady's duties, the president hired the couple who had tended their household in New Hampshire to join them in the White House. Varina Davis, the wife of Jefferson Davis, Pierce's secretary of war, also hosted for him, as did Abigail Kent Means, one of Jane's closest friends and an aunt by marriage. Abigail also stayed with and helped comfort Jane. Obviously, the Pierce White House was somber and had a limited social calendar. Jane even became known as "the Shadow of the White House."

Legacy

Jane Pierce lost much of her will to live after the death of her third son. Her legacy reflects her grieving and lack of enthusiasm as White House hostess. She detested politics and not only failed to support her husband's political career in any manner, but openly opposed his lifelong commitment to public service. Jane was not without her supporters, however. She befriended the writer Nathaniel Hawthorne, who attended her funeral, and Mrs. Robert E. Lee also spoke highly of her as having served admirably as first lady.

After the White House, the Pierces returned to New Hampshire. In waning health, Jane traveled to Europe and the West Indies to seek a cure for her weakness and melancholy, but her search was unsuccessful. Jane remained in mourning for Bennie, keeping locks of his hair and those of her other sons with her. She also carried Bennie's Bible with her at all times. At fifty-seven Jane's suffering came to an end, on

December 2, 1863. In her will she left money to the American Bible Society, the American Society for Foreign Missions, and the American Colonization Society. Her husband survived her by six years.

Bibliography

Boas, Norman F. *Jane M. Pierce.* Stonington, CT: Seaport Autographs and the Pierce-Aiken Papers, 1983.

————. *Jane M. Pierce, Supplement.* Stonington, CT: Seaport Autographs and the Pierce-Aiken Papers, 1989.

Holloway, Laura C. *The Ladies of the White House.* Philadelphia: A. Gorton, 1881.

Nichols, Roy. *Franklin Pierce: Young Hickory of the Granite Hills.* Philadelphia: University of Pennsylvania, 1958.

Whitton, Mary Ormsbee. *First First Ladies, 1789–1865: A Study of the Wives of the Early Presidents.* New York: Hastings House, 1948.

16

Harriet Rebecca Lane Johnston

Born: May 9, 1830; Mercersburg, Pennsylvania
Died: July 3, 1903; Narragansett Pier, Rhode Island
President: James Buchanan (1791–1868), Fifteenth President
Uncle's Presidential Term: 1857–1861 (Democrat)
Marriage: January 11, 1866, to Henry Elliot Johnston; Lancaster, Pennsylvania
Children: James Buchanan (1866–1881); Henry Elliot (1869–1882)

Because James Buchanan never married, his niece Harriet Lane served as surrogate first lady during his presidency.

Early Years
She was born in Mercersburg, Pennsylvania, on May 9, 1830. Her parents were the president's sister Jane and Elliot Tole Lane, a merchant. When her mother died in 1839, Harriet went to live with her uncle, Reverend Edward Buchanan. Two years later tragedy struck again when her father died. Her three siblings were sent to other relatives, but Harriet, the youngest, was taken in by her favorite uncle, James Buchanan, who became the girl's legal guardian. "Nunc," as she called him, had been very close to Harriet's mother.

Buchanan, a wealthy lawyer and U.S. senator, took a keen interest in Harriet's education and sent her to prestigious schools. She did well

Harriet Rebecca Lane Johnston

in school and developed a love for learning, especially literature, history, and astronomy. But in addition to being intelligent, Harriet was somewhat "undisciplined," by all accounts, an independent-minded, spontaneous child who was occasionally a bit too much for her teachers. Buchanan even sent her to the Visitation Convent, a Catholic school in Georgetown, because of concern for her "mischievous" nature. Harriet also attended finishing school in Charleston, Virginia (now West Virginia).

Harriet grew into an impressive young woman, with an interest in horseback riding, a talent for the piano, and compassion for human suffering and need. Nicknamed "Hal," she was of average height with blond hair and was known for her beauty. Apparently outgrowing her youthful lack of discipline, Harriet was elegant and poised, although she retained her confidence and independence and had a fun-loving, outgoing personality.

Marriage

With such attributes, she attracted many suitors. Surprisingly, Harriet postponed marriage until she was thirty-six, marrying Henry Elliot Johnston, a well-to-do banker from Baltimore, Maryland, in 1866. Some historians have speculated that she may have waited so long to marry because of loyalty to her uncle and his political career. For his part, Buchanan seems to have been overly protective of his niece, at times discouraging her amorous interests. Her eighteen-year marriage to Johnston, however, was a happy one, although both their children died young.

Family Life

After Buchanan became her guardian, Harriet lived at his estate in Franklin County, Pennsylvania, known as Wheatland. Buchanan encouraged his niece to participate in his political career and took her to London when President Pierce appointed him U.S. minister to Great Britain in 1853. Harriet loved London and developed a passion for politics during their three-year tenure there. She met Queen Victoria and so impressed the royal family that she was granted the title of "ambassador's wife." Harriet also met Napoleon III and Empress Eugenie, the archbishop of Canterbury, and other members of the diplomatic corps, while enjoying the social events of the diplomatic seasons. Although young, she handled herself gracefully and worked hard to learn about diplomatic protocol and English history, thus becoming very popular with her British hosts. While living in London, Harriet fell in love with a wealthy British aristocrat and jurist, Sir Fitzroy Kelly. But he was forty years her senior, and Buchanan discouraged the affair.

When Buchanan returned home in 1856, the Democrats nominated him for the presidency. Harriet again accompanied her uncle in his political pursuits, this time to Washington. She continued her involvement in his career, and Buchanan, a well-educated and stubbornly demanding man, solicited his niece's opinions. She always spoke her mind. Buchanan's career defined Harriet's family life, as she made it her primary focus. When he was elected to the presidency that November, she was well prepared to become White House hostess.

Presidency

At twenty-six, Harriet's youthful attractiveness and charm served her well in her new role. Even though the Buchanan years were troubled times for the country, with the rise of sectionalism and the threat of southern secession, after the limited social agenda of the grieving Mrs. Pierce, the country was ready for Harriet's lively events; like Julia Tyler in the 1840s, she featured dances like the waltz and polka. Indeed, the Buchanan years came to be known as the "gayest administration," largely because of Harriet.

It did not take Harriet long to make her presence known in the capital. She hosted many events during Buchanan's campaign, which helped his bid for office. After the election, the elegant gown she wore to the inaugural ball established her as a fashion trendsetter and popular figure in the city. Her lifestyle contributed to her romantic image. Harriet often wore white, had a fondness for carrying bouquets of roses, and traveled widely, pampering herself at exclusive spas. A government steamship was named in her honor, and she attended the christening of the battleship *Lancaster.* Returning the hospitality she received while living in Great Britain a few years earlier, Harriet entertained the prince of Wales, Edward Albert, in 1860. The prince's visit was followed closely by the U.S. public, as was their tour together of George Washington's home. They spent time in each other's company and even danced together. For his part, the prince seems to have been rather enamored of his gracious hostess; his appreciation of lovely ladies was well known.

Some believe the term "first lady" was initially used to describe Harriet, when *Frank Leslie's Illustrated Newspaper* of March 31, 1860, featured her photograph with the caption, "First Lady of the Land." While in the White House, she invited artists to her social affairs and began an art collection, becoming a well-known collector in later years. Harriet also closely followed the political issues of the day but remained neutral on the most pressing one, slavery. She recognized the sensitivity surrounding it and was careful not to voice her opinions too strongly in either direction. She also insisted that White House guests avoid the topic and arranged the seating at her functions with sectional tensions in mind. Harriet hoped for compromise. She appears to have opposed both slavery and southern secession personally but felt that neither freed slaves nor the country would fare well if slavery were abolished, because of the poverty and general social unrest that would result.

Although Harriet's concerns about these problems seem callous by today's standards, she was seen as a humanitarian in her time. One issue she embraced while in the White House was the welfare of Native Americans. She promoted education and health care for American Indians and interceded to stop the sale of liquor on reservations. For her work, the Chippewa Nation called her the "Great Mother of the Indians."

Harriet's tenure in the White House was not without negativity, however. She lost her brother Eskridge and sister Mary just before Buchanan's election. Then allegations arose that she spent congressional funds too lavishly to redecorate the Executive Mansion and that she used the naval ship named for her as if it were her own personal ship. Nevertheless, Harriet was immensely popular. That her uncle was the only bachelor president and that she served as a surrogate first lady did not seem to limit her in any way. On the contrary, official Washington was captivated by the enchanting, single woman presiding over White House social affairs. Harriet Lane would most likely be better remembered today if Buchanan had not been so criticized by both North and

South and if history regarded his tenure more favorably. She was a most capable hostess and earned her nickname, "the Democratic Queen."

Legacy

After Buchanan's term ended just before the Civil War, he and Harriet retired to his Wheatland estate in Pennsylvania. There she continued to support the former president, taking care of him as his health declined. In 1866, however, she married Johnston and moved to Baltimore. Two years later Buchanan died. As heir to her uncle's estate, she worked to save and organize his presidential papers and defended his tarnished reputation.

Harriet and Henry Johnston had two sons, both of whom died young. Their firstborn died in 1881 of rheumatic fever, as did the remaining son the following year, despite her efforts to find a cure for him in France. As would be expected, Harriet was devastated by the losses. She responded by championing children's causes, including the establishment of a pediatrics department in 1883 at Johns Hopkins Hospital in Baltimore. In 1884 Harriet's husband died; the widow sold the estate she had inherited and her home in Baltimore. Because she still had many friends in Washington, she returned to the capital city, where the social and cultural amenities she so loved there helped ease her losses.

Harriet had long enjoyed material plenty and luxury, and the deaths of those closest to her left her even wealthier. She put the money to good use, promoting social causes, establishing churches, setting up memorials to James Buchanan, and endowing scholarships as well as one of the first homes for invalid children. Her life was devoted to philanthropy, but she is best remembered for her art collection. By the time of her death, she had amassed one of the country's foremost collections, which she bequeathed to the Corcoran Gallery. It would later form the basis of the Smithsonian's National Gallery.

Harriet Lane Johnston died in Rhode Island in 1903. She holds the distinction of being the only woman to serve as hostess for the nation's only lifelong bachelor president.

Bibliography

Hoyt, Edwin P. *James Buchanan*. Chicago: Reilly & Lee, 1966.
Klein, Philip Shriver. *President James Buchanan*. University Park: Pennsylvania State University, 1963.

Shelley, Mary Virginia, and Sandra Harrison Munro. *Harriet Lane: First Lady of the White House*. Lilitz, PA: Sutter House, 1980.

Smith, Elbert B. *The Presidency of James Buchanan*. Lawrence: University Press of Kansas, 1981.

17

Mary Ann Todd Lincoln

Born: December 13, 1818; Lexington, Kentucky
Died: July 16, 1882; Springfield, Illinois
President: Abraham Lincoln (1809–1865), Sixteenth President
Husband's Presidential Term: 1861–1865 (Republican)
Marriage: November 4, 1842; Springfield, Illinois
Children: Robert Todd (1843–1926); Edward Baker (1846–1850);
    William Wallace (1850–1862); Thomas "Tad" (1853–1871)

Early Years

The Todds were among the first settlers in Lexington, Kentucky, and are considered the city's founders. A descendant of this pioneer family, Robert Smith Todd was a well-known banker and political figure there in the early nineteenth century. Mary Ann Todd was born to Robert and Eliza Parker Todd on December 13, 1818, in Lexington, the third of three girls; she also had two brothers. When Mary was only six years old, her mother died and her father remarried; however, she and her siblings did not care for their stepmother, Elizabeth Humphries Todd. For this reason and others, Mary began spending more time with her maternal grandmother, who helped raise the young girl.

Mary received a sound education, attending the Shelby Female Academy (also known as the Wards Academy) and later boarding at Madame Charlotte Mentelle's finishing school. In total she received roughly twelve years of formal schooling, which was considerable for either a boy or girl living in Lexington at that time. Mary learned French, history, reading, mathematics, needlework, and etiquette. A popular girl and leading debutante, she attracted numerous suitors with her blue-eyed beauty and outgoing personality. Mary was, however, unlike the class of well-bred southern ladies she aspired to join. Even as a young girl she was outspoken and opinionated, and had a fondness for politics. She even dreamed of becoming president. The Todd family was active in politics, affiliated with the Whig Party, and hosted many politicians at their estate. Thus, Mary grew up around politics. One individual she admired greatly was her fellow Kentuckian and a leading politician of the age, Henry Clay.

Mary was close to her sisters and seems to have become even closer to them after their mother's death and father's remarriage. In 1832 Mary's sister Elizabeth married a politician named Ninian Edwards Jr. and moved to Springfield, Illinois. Mary went to live with her sister and immediately became a popular participant in Springfield's social season.

Marriage

Abraham Lincoln had won a seat in the Illinois state legislature in 1834, serving four successive terms. He got his attorney's license in 1836 and moved to Springfield, the capital, the next year. In 1839 Abe and Mary met, although they did not begin a courtship immediately. Mary was not overly impressed with Lincoln; she had been courted by many well-known figures, such as Judge Stephen Douglas, a powerful politician and Lincoln's eventual rival in the famous 1858 debates. Lincoln was also interested in other relationships.

But in 1841 Abe began to court Mary, who was twenty-three at the time. It was an unlikely relationship. The thirty-one-year-old lawyer was tall (six feet, four inches), rail-thin, prone to depression, homespun, and described by Mary's sister Frances as "the ugliest man in Springfield." Mary, in contrast, was five feet two, plump, aristocratic, and described by many as quite flirtatious. Their courtship was stormy, and their engagement was on-again, off-again for three years. Both were to blame: Mary's extreme jealousy disrupted their relationship, and Lincoln got cold feet when it came to committing to marriage. Mary herself was somewhat hesitant about their prospects; her family opposed the wedding, feeling that the self-taught lawyer from the heartland was socially beneath the Todds.

The couple eventually did marry on November 4, 1842, in Springfield. Despite their many differences, they got along surprisingly well and shared many qualities. For instance, both (but especially Mary) could be materialistic, they shared a passion for poetry, and perhaps most important, they loved politics and were ambitious. They also complemented each other. Lincoln helped calm some of Mary's nervousness and insecurities, and although her phobias would eventually become a problem for both, he did succeed in tempering Mary's impulsiveness and recklessness when shopping, spending money she did not have. In fact, Abe good-naturedly teased his wife about her knack for getting into trouble, even nicknaming her his "child-wife." In turn, Mary's high-spirited personality and prominence as a socialite helped enhance Abe's visibility and popularity in social settings, and she improved his notoriously rugged manners and disheveled style of dressing.

Family Life
Abe called his wife "Mother"; Mary called him "Mr. Lincoln." Their first years together were busy with raising a growing family and working on his legal and political career. Their first son, Robert Smith Todd, was born in 1843; the second, Edward Baker, was born in 1846 but died in 1850 from tuberculosis. The death of their second child was especially difficult for Mary, perhaps more so because a third child, William Wallace, arrived later the same year and her father had died only the year before. Thomas, or "Tad," was born in 1853.

After Lincoln's election to the U.S. Congress in 1846, Mary joined him in the capital, even though most spouses from the frontier declined to make the long trip. While there, she frequently observed congressional sessions from the public gallery. Together they compiled notes on every member of Congress to help in legislative battles and making political contacts. Mary continually encouraged her husband's political career and in 1855 helped him with his unsuccessful campaign for the U.S. Senate. She followed political events closely and often traveled with him, attending the well-known debates with Stephen Douglas that were held throughout Illinois in 1858. Mary loved being involved in politics. She regularly discussed politics with Abe and wanted to be a helpful part of his career. She grew to adore her husband and was very proud of his accomplishments.

In the 1856 election, Lincoln had received a few votes for president. The debates with Douglas two years later gained him a national audience and a reputation as a reformer and critic of slavery; even though he was not an abolitionist, he saw it as evil and opposed its spread. By the end of the decade, with utmost confidence in him, Mary had started to focus on the presidency. Lincoln's star was rising.

Presidency

Abraham Lincoln was the underdog at the 1860 Republican Party convention in Chicago. Mary assisted him in the campaign, building his confidence and working as a gracious hostess with key elements of the public, press, and political establishment. Lincoln's long-shot bid proved successful, greatly helped by the three-way split among the Democrats. When he learned of his election to the presidency, Lincoln reportedly shouted, "Mary, Mary, *we* are elected!"—a comment that underscored their long-standing political partnership.

Mary continued her political activism in the White House. In spite of the huge obstacles Lincoln faced in fighting the Confederacy and reuniting the nation, she was confident he would succeed. Her support must have been critical to her husband, because he suffered from episodes of depression and self-doubt about his efforts.

Mary's belief in her husband did not necessarily extend to herself. She was somewhat insecure, hypersensitive to criticism, and self-conscious to an extent that ultimately led to her undoing. Although apparently highly capable and charming, she worried continually about what to wear, how she looked, and what others would think of her social events. She loved hosting social functions but expended considerable energy fretting about their outcome. After the election she worried that the public and the press would see her as unrefined and "country." To impress would-be critics, Mary traveled to New York City for a lavish shopping spree that set the Lincolns back financially and sent the wrong message to a country more concerned with war than the first lady's wardrobe. This was not her only social faux pas.

When the Lincolns arrived at the White House, Mary found it in disrepair and, realizing its symbolic value to the nation, endeavored to make the country proud of its Executive Mansion. She was right to be concerned: Furniture was broken, rugs were soiled, and the china didn't match. Brushing aside concerns for her safety at the outbreak of the

Civil War, she went to New York and Philadelphia to shop for furnishings. But the first lady's renovation of the White House was seen as excessive and unnecessary, and her choices extravagant. In one instance, she sent an assistant to Paris to purchase wallpaper and china for the White House and ordered an extra set for her personal use. In addition, Mary failed to use channels to pay for the improvements. Apparently a White House gardener named John Watt helped her find ways to finance her renovations by padding his expenses, practices that were possibly illegal and at least gave the appearance of impropriety. She further damaged her case by dismissing the commissioner in charge of the White House budget and replacing him with a friend, Benjamin French. He too found ways to accommodate Mary's spending habits, making matters worse.

Earlier presidents had traditionally covered the expenses of running the White House and entertaining from their own pockets; some even paid for renovations to the mansion themselves. Several endured financial difficulties as a result of the burden of public service. Mary was determined that the Lincolns' finances would not be drained by presidential expenses, and she insisted on using public funds to cover them. At least some of the criticism she received for spending "on behalf of the White House" was a result of the change in convention regarding White House expenditures.

Lincoln understandably was upset with what he deemed his wife's "flub-a-dub" bills. And the press launched an unprecedented attack on Mary, calling her "the American Queen" in a derogative manner. Another attack came when one of Mary's frequent guests to the White House, Henry Witkoff, stole the president's state of the union speech and sold it to a New York newspaper, which printed it in advance of the president's address. Indeed, her every move seemed to invite criticism, including her family life and her fondness for low-cut gowns. That the Lincolns' oldest son, Robert, was attending Harvard and not fighting in the war was also criticized. Although he wanted to join the Union army, Mary opposed it because she had already lost family members in the fighting and her young son Edward eleven years earlier. The president eventually secured a position for Robert on General Ulysses Grant's staff.

The Lincolns were criticized by some members of the Washington establishment who felt they were too common and "country." In fact, some people boycotted the first lady's inaugural balls and socials apparently for no other reason than their origins. Mary's connections with the South created controversy. Northerners never seemed to trust her, and southern relatives who visited the White House and condemned the North were accused of treason. When Mary's half-sister, the widow Emilie Todd Helm, refused to take the Union's oath of allegiance while visiting, Lincoln overlooked the matter, thinking family visits might be helpful to his wife. But instead of consoling Mary, Emilie blamed her for their relatives' deaths. Mary's family did indeed support the Confederacy, and she was greatly distressed when her brothers died in combat. Rumors circulated that Mary herself was not loyal to the Union. This could not have been less true, as she was wholeheartedly behind her husband's policies and was even an emancipationist. The South saw her as a traitor, and she received hate mail and even death threats from southerners. These constant attacks had their effect on Mary, who publicly ignored the threats and disapproval but in private allowed them to erode her confidence and happiness.

As first lady, Mary worked hard to offer a full, well-planned social calendar. Even though it was customary to rely on the secretary of state and other government officials to assist with the preparation and protocol for state affairs and formal events, Mary organized them without help from anyone else in the administration, and the results were impressive. Caterers from New York City and Philadelphia provided her menus (which alienated her from local businesses and caterers), and her guest lists included intellectuals, writers, and many well-known public figures. Mary even hosted Napoleon's nephew in 1861 and impressed him with her command of French. But because of other blunders and the wartime hardships, what could have earned praise for her was viewed as inappropriate and excessive.

Throughout her husband's presidency, and in spite of attacks on her character, Mary continued to be politically active. Like First Lady Sarah Polk, she preferred to discuss politics with gentlemen guests at the White House rather than adjourn with the ladies for tea. She offered advice on her husband's cabinet appointments and seems to have had better instincts than Lincoln for spotting potentially troublesome appointments. She was, however, prone to criticize, in particular, cabinet members including Edwin Stanton, the secretary of war, Salmon P. Chase, the secretary of the treasury, and Secretary of State William Seward, as well as Generals George McClellan and Ulysses Grant. She followed the war closely and appears to have been knowledgeable about its details. She demonstrated courage when she refused to leave Washington as the war approached the capital and rumors were circulating that the Confederates planned to take her and her children hostage.

Mary was already under enormous stress and somewhat unstable emotionally when their third son, Willie, died of typhoid fever in February 1862. He was her favorite and his death devastated her; she never seems to have recovered fully. She became more emotional, less rational, and began having visions, seeking the help of spiritualists and holding seances in the White House. When this became public, it provided even more fodder for the press and her political enemies.

Mary had always been extremely jealous, but her jealousy began to seriously embarrass her husband. She demanded that he avoid the company of other women, and her public outbursts were yet another source of trouble for the embattled president. One of her worst displays was in March 1865, when the commander in chief was visiting troops. She found out that one of the officer's wives had been permitted to attend the event with the president and, in a jealous rage, interrupted the entire inspection. On this occasion and others, Mary became uncontrollable. She suffered from severe migraine headaches that seemed to coincide with her fits of jealousy.

In many ways, because of the criticism she invited and her personal problems, Mary drained the president's already waning energy. It is surprising their marriage endured. Although Mary did help him, the problems she caused outweighed the support she offered. She became a liability in his bid for reelection in 1864, possibly the first time a first lady was actually a campaign issue.

In response to the criticism and the challenges of office, Lincoln began taking his family to their summer residence, "Soldier's Home," and resorts in New Hampshire and New York, to provide some relief for Mary and because their youngest child, Tad, was in poor health.

Legacy

On Good Friday in April 1865, the Lincolns, enjoying the president's reelection, the start of his second term, and the successful conclusion of the Civil War, attended the play *Our American Cousin* at the Ford Theater. They were in the company of Major Henry R. Rathbone and his fiancée, Clara Harris, who had replaced General and Mrs. Grant when they backed out at the last moment. During the third act John Wilkes Booth, a disgruntled actor and southern sympathizer, stole into the Lincolns' box and fatally shot the president in the head.

Mary was sitting next to the president and witnessed the horror. She collapsed after the shooting and was too devastated even to attend her husband's funeral. As her distress continued and she sank deeper into grief, she moved to Chicago with her two remaining sons, Robert and Tad. Poverty threatened because of the bills she owed, and in an attempt to avoid bankruptcy, she sold her jewelry and dresses in New York. The proceeds did not cover her debts. In 1868, perhaps to escape her creditors and critics as well as to seek a healthier situation for Tad, the two went to Europe for three years. Sadly, Tad died shortly after their return in 1871; he was only eighteen.

Faced with still another personal disaster, Mary became very depressed and was unable to eat or sleep; her behavior became quite eccentric. Questions arose about Mrs. Lincoln's sanity, and her critics seized upon an opportunity to destroy her. Among them was her remaining son, Robert, who was motivated largely by financial greed. In May 1875 Robert Lincoln initiated a sanity trial against his mother; the former first lady was declared insane by a Chicago jury and admitted to a sanitarium for the mentally ill in Batavia, Illinois. The trial was suspect, however, and the decision was reversed a year later. She escaped once more to Europe, spending approximately four years overseas. She found France to her liking, and it offered her some happiness in her otherwise tragic life.

On her return to the United States in 1880, Mary moved to Springfield, Illinois, to live with her sister. She found some relief from her debts when Lincoln family friend Charles Sumner obtained a pension for her from Congress in the amount of $3,000 per year. Just before her death, it was raised to $5,000 annually. Her final years, however, were no better. She was often sick and bedridden, had begun to lose her eyesight, and remained deeply depressed. Mary slipped into a coma and died of a stroke in July 1882.

Mary Todd Lincoln is remembered as one of the most highly controversial and most criticized of all first ladies. The range of criticism is nearly without equal in the office; she was accused of being ignorant, corrupt, vulgar, wasteful, vain, and both an inadequate and an extravagant hostess. Mary's actions invited attack, but under different circumstances they might well have earned her acclaim. For instance, because of the methods she employed to renovate the White House, she was reproached for her efforts whereas most other first ladies have been applauded for the same.

Mary remains a polarizing figure, but most historians agree that she was an able political partner. She loved politics and was an active hostess and adviser to Lincoln throughout his career, even though she often was also a personal and political liability for him.

Bibliography

Baker, Jean. *Mary Todd Lincoln.* New York: Norton, 1986.

Helm, Katherine. *The True Story of Mary, Wife of Lincoln.* New York: Harper, 1928.

Randall, Ruth Painter. *Mary Lincoln: Biography of a Marriage.* Boston: Little, Brown, 1953.

Ross, Ishbel. *The President's Wife. Mary Todd Lincoln: A Biography.* New York: Putnam's, 1973.

Turner, Justin G., and Linda Levitt Turner. *Mary Todd Lincoln: Her Life and Letters.* New York: Knopf, 1972.

18

Eliza
McCardle
Johnson

Born: October 4, 1810; Leesburg, Tennessee
Died: January 15, 1876; Greeneville, Tennessee
President: Andrew Johnson (1808–1875), Seventeenth President
Husband's Presidential Term: 1865–1869 (Union)
Marriage: May 17, 1827; Greeneville, Tennessee
Children: Martha (1828–1901); Charles (1830–1863); Mary (1832–1883); Robert (1834–1869); Andrew (1852–1879)

Early Years

Eliza McCardle was born into a family of very modest means. Her father, a shoemaker and part-time innkeeper, struggled financially his whole life. Eliza was born in Leesburg, Tennessee, on October 4, 1810, and was the McCardles' only child. When she was a young girl, the family moved to Warrensburg, then Greeneville, Tennessee, in search of better employment.

These were small, rural towns and most likely lacked adequate—if any—schools. Eliza's mother, Sarah Phillips, seems to have been a literate, intelligent woman who taught her daughter to read and write and was a tutor for several other children. Eliza also attended a school in her

116

community possibly named the Rhea Academy; historical records are unclear. As a girl, she helped her family by making quilts and sandals, and being a bright young woman, she acquired enough education to later work as a teacher.

Marriage

In 1826, when Eliza was a teenager, her father died. These must have been difficult years for Eliza's mother; the family was already poor and now she faced the prospect of caring for the two of them without a husband. The widow married a man named Moses L. Whitesides in 1833.

Andrew Johnson's family also had moved to Greeneville in search of work. Like the McCardles, the Johnsons were poor. Eliza met Andrew around 1826, and he immediately began courting her. Apparently, Andrew attended the small school where Eliza was teaching. In fact, some scholars have said she taught him to write and improved his reading. The accounts are mixed, however, and others suggest he was already literate when they met. Either way, records show that Eliza did provide Andrew with much of his formal education—and he credited her with this schooling. Just as the romance was blossoming, however, his family moved to the town of Rutledge, Tennessee, again in search of decent jobs. In 1827, after being away for a few months, Andrew returned to Greeneville to open his own business as a tailor. During the separation the two exchanged letters, and their courtship continued.

Eliza was only sixteen when she wed seventeen-year-old Andrew Johnson on May 17, 1827, less than a year after meeting. They hold the distinction of having married at a younger age than any other presidential couple. They enjoyed a close and warm marriage.

Family Life

Andrew Johnson's tailor shop prospered, permitting them to buy a home. Their first child, Martha, was born in 1828. During the next several years, Eliza was occupied with raising her family. Charles was born in 1830, followed by Mary two years later, and another son, Robert, in 1834. Their last child, named for his father but nicknamed Frank, came much later, in 1852. All the children survived childhood, but the boys died in their twenties or thirties. Moreover, the boys were unsuccessful and apparently were alcoholics by the time of their deaths.

Andrew Johnson's political career began very early. Less than a year after marriage, he was elected alderman in the town of Greeneville and became mayor at twenty-two. His political career progressed at an impressive rate, following the usual path, with service in the Tennessee state legislature from 1835 to 1843, then in the U.S. House of Representatives (1843–1853). He was elected governor of Tennessee in 1853 and reached the U.S. Senate in 1857. During her husband's terms in the Tennessee legislature and his trips to Washington for the legislative sessions, Eliza stayed home, opting to raise their children and tend to the household. She successfully ran the Johnson estate during her husband's long, frequent absences, and she may also have managed the family and business finances. They also owned a few slaves and a farm. Even though Eliza did not join her husband in Washington until 1860, she does appear to have been somewhat interested in politics.

Eliza deserves partial credit for her husband's success, as indeed Johnson himself acknowledged. He had little formal education and could be stubbornly difficult and argumentative; his demeanor suggests he had a chip on his shoulder and a need to prove himself. Still, it says something about the man that he rose from poverty and a tailor's apprenticeship to succeed in so many public offices. The education and advice he received from his wife assisted him in his endeavors; her counsel was always to follow his heart and conscience. Although she did not offer advice on politics and policy issues per se, she continually provided practical advice and moral support. She also helped him with speeches and urged him to practice public speaking, even encouraging him to join a debate society.

The tensions between the North and South and the outbreak of the Civil War were difficult for the Johnsons. By the mid-1850s Eliza's health had begun to deteriorate, and by the outset of war she was weak and often ill. Although the state of Tennessee joined the Confederacy, the eastern region of the state, where Andrew and Eliza lived, supported the Union. It was an uncomfortable relationship for the inhabitants of East Tennessee, especially the Johnsons. In March 1862 President Lincoln appointed Johnson military governor of the pro-Union section of the state. When the president of the Confederacy, Jefferson Davis, declared martial law in eastern Tennessee the next month and ordered Union loyalists to evacuate, Eliza was caught at home with ten-year-old Frank. Given only three days to leave, she fled to relatives elsewhere in the state, but the Johnson home was sacked by Confederate troops and their furnishings stolen or destroyed. Eliza then worked to promote federal interest in protecting loyal U.S. citizens living in the South during the war.

Eliza was given permission to travel north and courageously under-took the trip through Confederate lines without her husband and while ill. In September 1862 she traveled first to Nashville and then to Cincinnati, where she visited her son Robert and tried unsuccessfully to help him with his many personal problems. She next went to Indiana to visit daughter Mary, then returned to Ohio. In 1864 she went to New England with Frank. Eliza and Andrew lost their son Charles and a son-in-law during the war. As the conflict began to wind down, Johnson was selected to be Lincoln's running mate on the Union ticket in 1864, and the former tailor's apprentice from a poor family in rural Tennessee was elected vice president that fall. Eliza, however, remained in Tennessee.

Presidency

Andrew Johnson was in Washington and Eliza at the family home in Tennessee when President Lincoln was assassinated in April 1865. Johnson assumed the presidency, and Eliza left for the White House, accompanied by her two sons; her daughter Martha, her husband, and three children; and her widowed daughter Mary and her two children.

The capital was a difficult place to be. Tensions between the North and South remained high, and the specter of Lincoln's death hung over the country. His widow remained in the White House for a short period after her husband's assassination. Eliza, in particular, was alarmed by Lincoln's murder and worried about her own husband's safety and the challenges facing his presidency. Johnson would be responsible for implementing Lincoln's Reconstruction policies, and the country was divided over the controversial plan for rebuilding the South.

The physical condition of the White House needed attention. Fortunately for Eliza, her daughters assisted her in overseeing the mansion's cleaning, repairing dirty and broken items, and renovating parts of the building. Martha assumed most of the responsibility for hostess-ing because her mother was neither interested in the duty nor up to it physically. Martha appears to have risen to the task despite her simple, unsophisticated upbringing, and she invested a great deal of energy in acting as hostess, more from duty to her parents than from real interest. To provide fresh milk and butter for the family, she even grazed cows on the White House lawn. Her husband, David T. Patterson, was in the U.S. Senate during the Johnson presidency, so Martha and her children often visited and comforted Eliza, as did her other children and grand-children.

Eliza spent her time in the White House sewing, knitting, and reading. Although her overall health problems, especially a bout with tuberculosis, limited the first lady's effectiveness, Eliza never wanted to participate in public life or preside over social affairs. She was ill but perhaps not so much as she let on; however, some accounts suggest she was unable to walk and was confined to a chair. She secluded herself largely on the second floor of the residence and saw very few people, appearing only twice at public events during her first ladyship: once at an 1866 celebration for Hawaii's Queen Emma and the other at a children's ball in 1868 given by Martha in honor of the president's sixtieth birthday.

She did continue to assist Johnson in preparing his speeches and offered him advice on a regular basis, calmed his temper and frequent outbursts, and even selected his wardrobe. In a way Eliza had always mothered her husband, and the pattern persisted in the White House.

The defining event of Andrew Johnson's presidency was his impeachment trial in 1868. Johnson was certainly not a great president, and some believe that neither he nor Eliza was up to the challenges of the White House. But the impeachment proceedings were purely political, the result of post–Civil War tensions and dissatisfaction with the controversial policies of Reconstruction. The president's relations with Congress were terrible, and he managed to alienate both the advocates of an aggressive Reconstruction policy and its critics. For her part, Eliza followed the impeachment hearings closely in the newspaper and was a major source of moral support for her husband during these trying times, remaining confident in his abilities. Johnson escaped removal from office by the thinnest of margins; Eliza felt vindicated by the outcome and proclaimed she had known all along the president would be acquitted.

Legacy

Eliza and Andrew Johnson returned to Tennessee at the conclusion of his term in office. Shortly after, in 1869, their son Robert committed suicide. Despite the trials and tragedy they had faced, however, the former president did not retire. He was motivated to salvage his tarnished reputation and prove himself a capable public figure. This was the stubborn side of Andrew Johnson. He twice ran for Congress and was twice defeated, but on his third attempt he was elected to the U.S. Senate in 1874. When he took his seat early in 1875, Eliza felt that their political healing and public vindication had been completed. After their days in Washington, Eliza spent a great deal of time away from her husband, even traveling without him, for unknown reasons. Shortly after taking office in the Senate, Johnson died. Eliza was too distraught and weak to attend the funeral. She outlived him by only a few months, dying on January 15, 1876, and is best remembered as his constant adviser and supporter, even though she was rarely involved in politics or public life. She was one of the least active first ladies, and her most significant contribution was possibly the major part she played in the future president's education.

Bibliography

Beale, Howard Kennedy. *The Critical Years: A Study of Andrew Johnson and Reconstruction.* New York: Unger, 1958.

Graf, Leroy P., and Ralph W. Haskins, eds. *The Papers of Andrew Johnson.* 9 volumes. Knoxville: University of Tennessee Press, 1967–1983.

Jones, James Sawyer. *Life of Andrew Johnson.* Greeneville: East Tennessee Publishing, 1901.

Lately, Thomas. *The First President Johnson: The Three Lives of the Seventeenth President of the United States.* New York: Morrow, 1968.

McKitrick, Eric L., ed. *Andrew Johnson: A Profile.* New York: Hill and Wang, 1969.

19

Julia
Dent
Grant

Born: January 26, 1826; St. Louis, Missouri
Died: December 14, 1902; Washington, D.C.
President: Ulysses S. Grant (1822–1885), Eighteenth President
Husband's Presidential Term: 1869–1877 (Republican)
Marriage: August 22, 1848; St. Louis, Missouri
Children: Frederick Dent (1850–1912); Ulysses "Buck" Simpson (1852–1929); Ellen "Nellie" Wrenshall (1855–1922); Jesse Root (1858–1934)

Early Years
Julia's mother, Ellen Wrenshall, was born in England; her father, Frederick Dent, was from St. Louis, Missouri, where Julia was born on January 26, 1826. "Colonel" Dent, as her father was called, owned a plantation near St. Louis and was fairly well-off financially. Julia, the oldest daughter in her family, had a happy and privileged upbringing and was a very popular and friendly young girl. She attended the Mauro boarding school in St. Louis, then was sent to a boarding school in Philadelphia. Although she was a marginal student, she did develop a love of reading.

Marriage

Ulysses Grant was a good friend of Julia's brother, Frederick; they attended the U.S. military academy at West Point together. Grant was a welcome guest in the Dent home and visited them in 1848, when Julia had recently returned home after finishing her studies at boarding school in the East. Ulysses immediately fell for Julia, then eighteen. She was only somewhat interested, although she did want to marry a military officer and seemed at least somewhat attracted to this aspect of her suitor. Mr. and Mrs. Dent were not overly impressed with Grant and discouraged even her minor interest in the twenty-two-year-old officer. Julia's father appears to have opposed the marriage because he felt Grant was too poor and had little potential. His observations were not far off the mark: Ulysses Grant lacked polish, and his social skills were marginal. He was shy, awkward, and prone to bluntness in his speech and manner; later in life, he would experience a string of failures and bankruptcies. But Grant was stationed near the Dent home, which allowed him to continue the courtship. Julia soon became engaged to the young lieutenant.

The marriage was delayed by the onset of the Mexican War, in which Grant participated, serving in Louisiana. Nevertheless, the courtship was brief, and Julia and Ulysses were married at the Dent home on August 22, 1848. Julia's parents coolly offered their blessing. Regardless of the unpromising start, Julia's feelings for her husband grew to be quite strong, and they enjoyed a happy marriage. A charming story suggests the tone of the Grant marriage: Julia always chose to show her profile in portraits and photos, because she had a crossed eye. She longed to have corrective surgery, but her husband would not hear of it, insisting she did not need it and that he loved her as she was.

Family Life

During their first four years of marriage, from 1848 to 1852, the Grants lived in Detroit and Sacket's Harbor, New York, moving with Ulysses's military postings. In 1850 Julia gave birth to her first child, Frederick, named for her father and brother. Grant's career proceeded slowly, and he contemplated using his talent for mathematics to start a new career teaching at his alma mater, West Point. But in 1852 his commission took him to the West Coast; Julia was pregnant at the time and went to live with relatives in Ohio, where she had her second child, Ulysses Jr.

Things did not go well for Grant at Fort Humboldt in northern

California; loneliness and unhappiness marked his experience there. He suffered from severe toothaches, he contracted malaria, and to make matters worse, his commanding officers did not regard him well. As would be the case throughout his life, Grant had problems with finances and appears to have started drinking habitually. In 1854 he resigned from the military and returned to be with his wife and two infants. To help out his daughter and son-in-law, Frederick Dent offered them land and four slaves; Captain Grant thus became a farmer. The year after his return, Julia had another child, a daughter named Ellen, or "Nellie." The next two years were difficult: In 1857 their farm failed and Julia's mother died. To comfort and assist Mr. Dent, the Grants moved in with the widower. A year later their fourth child, Jesse, was born.

While Julia tended to her father and her four young children, Grant went to St. Louis in search of work. Unable to find a decent job, he went to Galena, Illinois, to assist his father with the family farm and his leather goods store. This string of failures depressed both Ulysses and Julia, who joined her husband at his father's farm. With business and financial prospects looking slim, the outbreak of the Civil War offered the former military officer a new opportunity. Grant was upset with the actions of the Confederacy and eagerly reenlisted. The North, lacking trained officers, was only too pleased to accept the West Point graduate, and in August 1861 he became a brigadier general of volunteers. Julia's family had owned slaves, and her father, born and raised in the South, sided with the Confederacy. Grant's alliance with the Union caused Dent to disown his son-in-law. Although this must have been difficult for Julia, she completely supported her husband and the Union.

Not only was she loyal but she made every effort to join Grant in camp. Her presence was reassuring, and she was proud of his successes, especially his famous victory at Vicksburg. After the battle Julia boasted she would rather be the wife of the hero of Vicksburg than of the president, and she took to calling him "Victor." Near the end of the war, Julia was with her husband during the important siege at Petersburg, where they opted to reside in a small cabin rather than a mansion nearby, as had been proposed. She even joined him when he met with the Confederate peace delegation in April 1865.

Even though Grant valued his wife's company and assistance and they regularly discussed the war, he did not solicit her opinion on matters. For her part, Julia, though keen on the details of the conflict, was not one to offer political advice. Even when she tried to get him to secure the release of her captured brother, Grant would not budge. He was known for his stubbornness. In an effort to broker peace, General

Longstreet, one of the South's foremost officers and an old friend who had been a member of the Grant wedding party, suggested once that the officers permit their wives to participate in the discussions to boost the stalled talks, but Grant refused to entertain the idea.

By the end of the war, Ulysses Grant was a hero throughout the Union. The Grants went back to Galena, but his celebrity took them to the nation's capital shortly after. Grant disliked Washington and politics; Julia loved both, especially the excitement of social events. Although the Grants were received by an appreciative president, Mary Lincoln was jealous of the fame of her husband's top general and his wife. When they were invited to join the Lincolns at Ford's Theater the night the president was assassinated, Mary's envy was the reason they declined.

Inevitably, Grant's renown propelled him—reluctantly—into the political spotlight. The former general was not entirely apolitical, however, as he had strong feelings about President Andrew Johnson's handling of the postwar Reconstruction. Grant felt Johnson was too soft and appeased southern interests, especially regarding the rights of newly freed blacks. Although uncomfortable with the role, Grant emerged as the leading candidate for the presidency after Johnson.

Presidency

Not surprisingly, Julia threw her full support behind her husband's bid for office. She expressed interest in the specifics of the campaign and after the election discussed cabinet appointments with the president, although she probably had little role in its selection. It is unfortunate that Grant did not seek his wife's counsel on the matter, as his administration would go down as one of the most corrupt in the history of the office and, according to Adam Badeau, Grant's own secretary, Julia's political skills and judgment exceeded the president's. Despite rumors that she was behind many of the president's decisions, Julia Grant was not her husband's partner in politics. Grant's stubbornness and independence make such a claim doubtful. Although she discussed politics with him and took an active interest in all facets of his presidency, Julia herself claimed to be uninterested in politics, but she opposed anyone not fully supportive of her husband.

Julia's contribution to her husband's presidency came in the social realm. At the beginning of Grant's administration, she befriended the wife of Hamilton Fisk, Grant's secretary of state and a wealthy New York aristocrat. Mrs. Fisk offered her services and taught Julia much about the art of social hosting. She was an apt pupil, even though she had little experience with entertaining on the scale of the White House. She became one of its most celebrated hostesses, offering a full social calendar of events. After the traumas of the Civil War and the dour administration of Johnson, the nation and capital city seem to have been in the mood for celebrating. Julia gave them what they wanted. She was always more ambitious than her husband, and the majesty of the presidency agreed with her. She especially fancied entertaining visiting dignitaries at the White House and emerged as a celebrity herself.

When Julia moved into the White House, she was disturbed by the physical state of the building and arranged for minor renovations to make the building more presentable. She also required servants to wear white gloves, hired prominent chefs and new attendants, and procured new china. She herself bought new jewelry and clothing for her first ladyship and instructed female visitors to her socials to wear hats, while the men had to leave their weapons behind. Julia did not permit smoking in the White House and even made her husband take his pipe outside. She could not, however, persuade him to give up cigars. The alcohol flowed at her socials, and her state dinners were immensely popular. The press covered Julia's reign, and she obliged them not only with gala events but by talking with them.

In addition to her elegant socials, Julia brought a warm, personal touch to the first ladyship. She loved her position and enjoyed the company of people; approachable and down-to-earth, she even attempted to personally greet each guest to the White House. Each Tuesday afternoon she held informal afternoon teas open to the public. Julia spent the happiest moments of her life in the White House. Her widower father, apparently having resolved his objections to Grant's support of the Union, came to live with them, and the Grant children also liked their years there, although the youngest son, Jesse, spent part of this time in school in Philadelphia. The child of their oldest son, Frederick, was born at the White House, and daughter Nellie married Algernon Sartoris, a wealthy Briton, there. Another son, Ulysses or "Buck," worked in the Executive Mansion. Julia closed the building's back lawn to the public to create a private area for her children and grandchildren.

In spite of the numerous scandals and charges of corruption in his administrations, Ulysses Grant was a popular president and could possibly have been elected to a third term, something Julia urged him to consider. But he declined to seek reelection, making his decision without first informing his wife, perhaps because he knew she would be upset.

Nevertheless, their marriage remained solid during their eight years in the White House, and the notoriously disagreeable Grant even appears to have lightened his mood while living there.

Legacy

Grant left office a relatively young man at age fifty-five, the youngest president to complete his terms in the nineteenth century. The couple then embarked on an extensive world tour, visiting numerous countries in Europe, the Middle East, and Asia. The two years they spent traveling were also among the happiest times of Julia's life and helped her get past missing the White House. The Grants were well received everywhere they went and were presented with many fine gifts. Julia, a devout Methodist, especially enjoyed visiting the Holy Land.

After their return in 1879, Julia continued to encourage her husband to run again for the presidency. Known as the "hero of Appomattox," Grant received some support at the 1880 Republican Party convention, for his political stock remained high in spite of the previous scandals. Julia was disappointed in her husband's hesitancy and the eventual nomination of James Garfield at the convention, but she did come around to support Garfield's presidency.

After their international travels, the Grants retired to New York City, where their son Buck held an investment position on Wall Street. This was a challenging time because Grant once again faced financial ruin. In yet another poor move, he invested his money in his son's firm, only to have the business and the investment go under in 1884, leaving the Grants bankrupt. Fatally ill with throat cancer, Grant raced to write his memoirs so that his wife might have financial security after his death. None other than Mark Twain helped him secure a publisher for the memoirs, which were completed only a few days before he died. As he had hoped, they sold well, providing Julia with comfortable financial support.

The hero of Appomattox died in Mount McGregor, New York, on July 23, 1885. Julia was too emotional to attend the funeral. In her final years she lived with her daughter in Washington, D.C., the city she loved so much and whose residents still loved her. She became the first first lady to compile her memoirs, dictating them because of her poor writing skills; she finished them before her death on December 14, 1902. She was buried in Grant's Tomb in New York City, which had been completed in 1897.

Julia Grant is remembered not only as a lifelong supporter of her husband's career throughout its many extremes but also as one of the most successful and admired hostesses in the history of the presidency.

Bibliography

Grant, Jesse R. *In the Days of My Father, General Grant.* New York: Harper, 1925.

Grant, Ulysses S. *Personal Memoirs of U. S. Grant.* 2 volumes. New York: Charles Webster, 1885.

Meredith, Roy. *Mr. Lincoln's General U. S. Grant.* New York: E. P. Dutton, 1959.

Ross, Ishbel. *The General's Wife.* New York: Dodd, Mead, 1959.

Simon, John Y., ed. *The Personal Memoirs of Julia Dent Grant.* New York: Putnam's, 1975.

20

Lucy
Ware
Webb
Hayes

Born: August 28, 1831; Chillicothe, Ohio
Died: June 25, 1889; Fremont, Ohio
President: Rutherford B. Hayes (1822–1893), Nineteenth President
Husband's Presidential Term: 1877–1881 (Republican)
Marriage: December 30, 1852; Cincinnati, Ohio
Children: Birchard Austin (1853–1926); James Webb Cook (1856–1934); Rutherford Platt (1858–1927); Joseph Thompson (1861–1863); George Crook (1864–1866); Fanny (1867–1950); Scott Russell (1871–1923); Manning Force (1873–1874)

Early Years

Lucy Webb was born on August 28, 1831, in Chillicothe, Ohio. Her family line—the Webbs and Cooks—included many strong individuals involved in politics. Her mother was Maria Cook, whose father, Isaac, had been a politician. Her father, James Webb, came from Lexington, Kentucky, and was a medical doctor. Even though the Webbs had roots in Kentucky and owned prosperous plantations, James Webb opposed slavery. In fact, he freed the approximately twenty slaves he inherited. Lucy's family also embraced the temperance movement and supported education. Among those relatives who played a role in shaping young Lucy was her grandmother, who made her pledge to avoid alcohol throughout her life.

In the 1830s a tragic cholera epidemic broke out in Ohio, claiming the lives of Lucy's paternal grandparents and many others. Lucy's father was tending to the victims of the epidemic when he contracted the disease himself, and he died when Lucy was only two years old.

The Webb family was well off financially, and Lucy's mother and maternal grandmother appear to have been intelligent, highly capable women who raised a successful brood of children. The Webb sons all followed in their father's footsteps as physicians. Lucy was also very bright and extremely well educated. She had initially joined her brothers at Ohio Wesleyan University, an almost exclusively male school, and was something of an educational pioneer, as very few women of the time enrolled in universities alongside men. But Lucy's mother, concerned that her daughter would marry too young without finishing her studies, eventually sent her instead to the Cincinnati Wesleyan Female College, one of the first colleges to grant degrees to women. Lucy did well there and earned a degree in 1850 at age eighteen, making her the first future first lady to have a college diploma. While at Cincinnati Wesleyan, Lucy was inducted into one of the school's prestigious societies, the Young Ladies Lyceum.

In addition to being intelligent, Lucy was described as kind and friendly as well as very disciplined and religious. She was also praised for her beauty.

Marriage

Rutherford B. Hayes was a young lawyer practicing in Cincinnati when he met Lucy Webb in the summer of 1847 while visiting her family. She was only sixteen at the time. Hayes appears to have been impressed with the girl but believed she was too young to court. He visited her again at the college when she graduated. Hayes was taken with her educational accomplishments and physical attractiveness, commenting on her intelligence, soft voice, and beautiful eyes. The summer after her graduation they were secretly engaged. Just over a year later, on December 30, 1852, they were married at her family's home in Cincinnati. He was twenty-seven; Lucy was twenty-one. "Rud," as she called him, had also established a successful law practice by the time of their marriage.

Family Life

The newlyweds lived in Cincinnati. Their life together was happy and prosperous. They shared a strong religious faith and were both opposed to slavery. Lucy had a total of eight children, three of whom were born before the outbreak of the Civil War and five living to adulthood. Her first child, Birchard Austin, was born in 1853, followed by another son, James Webb Cook, in 1856, and Rutherford Platt two years later. During this third childbirth, Lucy developed rheumatism and was quite sick; the illness would bother her periodically for the rest of her life. In 1861 she had a fourth child, Joseph Thompson, who lived only two years.

Although Rutherford Hayes opposed slavery, he was not an ardent supporter of the abolitionists, believing they were too radical. Lucy's support of abolition changed her husband's mind, and she eventually persuaded him to represent runaway slaves who had fled to Ohio. Lucy and Rutherford Hayes became well-known opponents of slavery and were so identified with the issue that an abandoned black baby was once delivered to their doorstep. Lucy kept in touch with former slaves owned by the Hayes and Webb families and their descendants. She also offered employment to several former slaves, including Winnie Monroe, the daughter of a slave freed by Lucy's family, who worked as a cook and nurse in the Hayes household. The future first lady, clearly influenced by her mother's strong belief in education, taught other former slaves, such as Eliza Jane Burell, to read and write. Lucy instructed her own children as well and later sent her daughter, Fanny, to Oberlin College.

The birth of four children and her bout with rheumatism weakened Lucy. Although her mother assisted her in raising her family, Lucy often commented on the work involved in motherhood and frequently felt the strain of managing a large family. She also began suffering from migraine headaches. The Civil War and her husband's participation as a major of volunteers probably contributed to her malady. Moreover, Hayes was wounded several times during the war: In 1861 he was shot in the arm at Antietam, and he was seriously injured during the Battle of Cedar Creek in Virginia in October 1864. The trials of the war were compounded by the death of her youngest child in 1863 and the birth of another son in 1864, who was named for Union general George Crook. After the Civil War Lucy gave birth to their only daughter, Fanny, in 1867. Another son, Scott Russell, was born in 1871, and their last child, Manning Force, was born two years later but died when only a year old.

Lucy did not allow the war events to stop her. She was proud when Rutherford volunteered at the outbreak of the war and proud of his successes and rise to the rank of colonel. She followed the war closely and even remarked after the Union surrender at Fort Sumter when the war began that had she and other women been at the fort, they never would have surrendered. When Hayes was recovering from the wounds he suffered at Antietam, she visited him at the hospital in Maryland, nursing other soldiers as well while there.

Lucy seems to have had a gift for bringing comfort and joy to the wounded troops, which she often did and for which she became well known. She became known as "Mother Lucy" to the men of the Twenty-third Ohio Volunteer Infantry, the unit under her husband's command that included future president William McKinley as one of its young officers. The troops and McKinley admired Lucy. Her presence at camp lifted their spirits as she offered the soldiers pep talks before battle. Lucy also asked her husband and the other officers not to return runaway slaves to the South and to be charitable to all wounded, Union and Confederate soldiers alike. Her brothers, who also fought in the war, received the same instructions from their sister. Joe was a surgeon for the Union, and Lucy frequently visited and assisted him in his hospital.

Lucy was critical of the Confederacy for the atrocities of the war, feeling that the high cost of human life was unnecessary and laying much of the blame on the South. The assassination of President Abraham Lincoln deeply disturbed her. She and Rutherford had met and accompanied Lincoln on his presidential train when it passed through Ohio. After the war she joined her husband on a visit to the White House to meet President Andrew Johnson and General Ulysses Grant. Hayes returned home to Ohio at the close of the war as a hero and was elected to the U.S. Congress in 1865 and the Ohio governorship in 1867 and 1869.

Lucy actively participated in her husband's political career even when she had young children. She traveled with him to the capital for each legislative session and accompanied him when he toured the sites of race riots in Memphis, Tennessee, and New Orleans. Lucy took an interest in politics and the events of the day, especially the end of slavery and the Reconstruction program. After his election to governor, the family rented a home in Columbus, the capital, and Lucy became possibly the best-known woman in the state, admired for her intelligence, refinement, and outstanding skills as a hostess. Hayes proved to be a reformer, and the politically astute Lucy visited public facilities such as hospitals, schools, and prisons around the state to generate support for his programs. She took the lead in pushing him to obtain state monies to support orphanages for child victims of the war.

She also was somewhat intrigued by women's suffrage. As a student she had written papers expressing strong views in favor of women's rights. Hayes's sister, Fanny Platt, was a suffrage supporter and appears to have encouraged Lucy's enthusiasm, but he himself, always more cautious than his wife, did not believe in women's suffrage, and this tempered her interest in the issue.

Hayes's terms as governor were highly successful, and he was encouraged to seek a third term. Being so well known, he was also positioned to make a run at the presidency. Both he and Lucy were concerned by the federal government's failure in the South to enforce the Fourteenth and Fifteenth Amendments to the Constitution, providing for the rights of former slaves.

Presidency

Even though Hayes and his wife were early advocates of civil rights, the Hayes presidency would mark the end of the controversial Reconstruction program. This was in part the result of the close, contested presidential race of 1876 in which he tied Samuel L. Tilden. Right up to the inauguration, Hayes was uncertain of his victory, which was decided by an electoral commission that gave him a majority of one in the electoral college. This weakened Hayes. Also, by the time he was elected, Congress, especially those politicians living in the South, had lost enthusiasm for Reconstruction.

After the election, however, he and Lucy were generally well received by the country. In the White House Lucy picked up where she had left off in Ohio, serving as a skilled hostess and active partner in her husband's career. The press was especially interested in Lucy Hayes, and the White House staff loved the new first lady, who invited them to join her for Thanksgiving dinner parties. Lucy was glad to have several young female relatives from Ohio to assist her with her duties, and she also called upon the wives of her husband's cabinet secretaries to help her entertain. Lucy's social style was refined but informal, as she found formal state dinners to be somewhat intimidating and uncomfortable. Lucy had many guests and friends visit her home full of children and pets, including two dogs, a bird, a goat, and the first Siamese cat in the United States. A musician who played the guitar and sang, Lucy featured musical performances at the Executive Mansion. It was a fun and active White House. The couple celebrated their silver wedding anniversary there, with Lucy wearing her wedding dress to renew her vows.

Even though she was generally a successful first lady, Lucy was perhaps best known for her advocacy of temperance. As a rule, she did not serve alcohol at the White House and was criticized for this, earning the nickname "Lemonade Lucy," but she was supported by the Women's Christian Temperance Union and others. And records suggest she did allow wine at a formal event for a visiting Russian diplomat and on a few more occasions. A devout Methodist, Lucy spent much time in prayer, reading the Bible, attending church, and singing hymns.

Lucy celebrated the country's natural assets by having the American artist Theodore R. Davis design new White House china featuring patterns of flora and fauna found in the United States. She joined her husband on extensive travels around the country, during which the press referred to her as the "first lady of the land"—according to some, one of the first uses of the title.

Legacy

Lucy Hayes received rave reviews from many politicians and the press; some considered her the best first lady yet to serve. She was active in her husband's legal and political career and appears to have had some influence over his decisions, especially in her bold stance in support of temperance and the abolition of slavery. She was the first presidential spouse to visit California and the first to have a college education.

More so than any previous spouse or White House hostess, Lucy was interested in the history of her office and in those who had preceded her. She slept at the home of George and Martha Washington, Mount Vernon, on her visit to the famous landmark and visited Montpelier, the home of James and Dolley Madison. Lucy also visited several first ladies still living, including Sarah Polk, Julia Tyler, and Julia Grant, as well as Lucretia Garfield and Ida McKinley, who followed her.

After the White House Lucy remained active in religious matters, serving as the president of the Woman's Home Missionary Society of her denomination. She spoke out for improving the condition of women's lives, perhaps recapturing the views on women's rights she had held as a young woman. Always an animal lover, Lucy had a pet greyhound that brought her much happiness and was always in her company.

After the presidency, the Hayeses enjoyed eight years together at their home, Spiegel Grove, in Fremont, Ohio, where she died on June 25, 1889. She was survived by her husband, who lived until 1893, and five of their children.

Bibliography

Davis, Mrs. John D. *Lucy Webb Hayes, a Memorial Sketch*. Cincinnati: Cranston & Curts, 1892.

Davison, Kenneth E. *The Presidency of Rutherford B. Hayes*. Westport, CT: Greenwood Press, 1972.

Geer, Emily Apt. *First Lady: The Life of Lucy Webb Hayes*. Kent, OH: Kent State University Press, 1984.

Williams, Charles R., ed. *Diary and Letters of Rutherford B. Hayes*. 5 volumes. Columbus, OH: Archaeological and Historical Society, 1922–1926.

Woman's Home Missionary Society. *In Memoriam: Lucy Webb Hayes*. Cincinnati: Women's Home Missionary Society, 1890.

21

Lucretia
Rudolph
Garfield

Born: April 19, 1832; Hiram, Ohio
Died: March 14, 1918; South Pasadena, California
President: James A. Garfield (1831–1881), Twentieth President
Husband's Presidential Term: 1881 (Republican)
Marriage: November 11, 1858; Hiram, Ohio
Children: Eliza Arabella (1860–1863); Harry Augustus (1863–1942);
James Rudolph (1865–1950); Mary "Molly" (1867–1947); Irvin
McDowell (1870–1951); Abram (1872–1958); Edward (1874–1876)

Early Years
Lucretia Rudolph was born in the town of Hiram, near Garrettville, Ohio, in April 1832. Her mother, Arabella Mason, was from Vermont. Zeb Rudolph, her father, was from Virginia and was of German heritage. Lucretia grew up in a strict, pious family who were active members of the Disciples of Christ Church.

The oldest of four children, Lucretia was often sick as a child, suffering from respiratory problems, and was a somewhat insecure, shy, and emotional young woman. She developed a love of learning and was an avid reader, traits that would stay with her throughout her life.

Perhaps surprising considering her upbringing, Lucretia was an independent, progressive thinker. In an essay titled "Women's Station" in her school's student literary magazine, she questioned the strict tradition of domesticity for women. She also addressed the low pay women received for work, asking, "Is it reasonable that the same number of stitches equally good should be worth less because [they were sewn] by women's weaker hand? Is it equitable that the woman who teaches school equally well should receive a smaller compensation than the man?" Lucretia advocated equal educational opportunities for women and felt that women had made many contributions to society for which they had not received due credit.

Lucretia was fortunate to have grown up in a community with rather progressive views on the role of women. Her family and community were supportive of her education, and she received excellent schooling for a girl of the times. Lucretia attended the Geauga Seminary, a Baptist school in the town of Chester, Ohio, and later studied at the Western Reserve Eclectic Institute in Hiram, an experimental school affiliated with the Disciples of Christ; her father was one of the school's founders. It was at Geauga in 1849 that she met James Garfield. The young man who would capture her heart also attended Western Reserve Eclectic, and they renewed their friendship there around 1851, although they did not become romantically involved until later. By 1853, Garfield had developed a deeper interest in his former classmate, and when he left the institute to continue his education at Williams College, in Williamstown, Massachusetts, they became pre-engaged. The relationship between "Jim," as she called Garfield, and "Crete," as he called her, was slow to build.

Marriage

James Garfield's family was one of modest financial means and considerably lower on the social ladder than the Rudolphs. Garfield was a troubled youth, but he overcame his past and grew to be an ambitious and popular young man. A religious conversion and the college experience appear to have provided the necessary focus to transform the wayward boy. In college he became a campus leader and in 1856 returned to his alma mater in Hiram to teach ancient languages; he went on to become the school's president at the age of twenty-five. The courtship between James and Lucretia was not as smooth as his career, however, and at times it appeared their romance would end. At Williams College Garfield fell for a woman named Rebecca Selleck, for whom he had much more passion than for Lucretia. This nearly ended their relationship and was apparently only the first of several affairs James had during his life with Lucretia.

They were eventually married on November 11, 1858, but had no honeymoon. Garfield was hesitant, almost reluctant, to marry. Things were no better after marriage. Immediately after the wedding Garfield lost interest in his wife and turned his attention and energy to his post at the college and a budding political career. Their initial years as husband and wife were as rocky as their courtship, and they often disagreed. In many ways they were opposites: She was shy and introverted, while he was outgoing. When he was elected to the state senate, he spent much time away from her, traveling alone to the state capital in Columbus. This pattern set the course for the early years of the Garfield marriage.

Family Life

James Garfield at first regretted marrying his wife and viewed their union as a "great mistake." He pursued other women, including the daughter of Salmon P. Chase, secretary of the treasury for Abraham Lincoln, and his affair with Rebecca Selleck did not end after Garfield completed his studies at Williams. Lucretia suffered through these affairs but appeared willing to forgive her husband for his infidelity. In addition to their marital difficulties, the Garfields' family life was defined by their many children, to whom both were devoted. Otherwise, their family life was dull and without warmth. They were both rather stodgy in their lifestyles and attitudes.

Their marriage eventually improved, however, and the couple would later refer to the first part of their life together as the "years of darkness." Several incidents seem to have strengthened the Garfield marriage. The birth of their daughter Eliza, or "Trot," in 1860 brought them a little closer, and although the mending of their relationship was interrupted by the Civil War, James's experience in it actually helped the marriage. During his tour of duty as a Union colonel, he contracted jaundice and dysentery and nearly died. When he returned home, Lucretia nursed him back to health, which momentarily moved him to appreciate her more. When he returned to the war, however, he met Lucia Calhoun, a writer from New York with whom he had an affair. Crete confronted her husband about the affair, and their marriage endured more strain.

Around this time Lucretia decided to share her diary with her husband. Garfield apparently was affected by the passionate, caring words his wife wrote about him. The incident started a real healing process in their marriage. Likewise, Lucretia's feelings toward her husband began to warm. The Garfields' second child, Harry, was born in 1863, the same year little Eliza died. Her death devastated Garfield, and he appears to have stopped seeing other women at this point in his life. The tragedy brought the couple closer together, and they had several more children: a son James, born in 1865, Mary (called "Molly") in 1867, Irvin in 1870, Abram two years later, and another son, Edward or "Neddie," in 1874.

All the while, Garfield's career was progressing. In 1863 he resigned from the military as a major general of volunteers and minor war hero and was elected to the U.S. House of Representatives. Garfield distinguished himself and was reelected several times, his career in the House spanning sixteen years and eventually bringing him to the speakership.

Lucretia began traveling with her husband and attended social functions with him in the nation's capital. She realized she was interested in and had a knack for politics and gradually became his most trusted adviser. The distance between them continued to diminish, and they found they even shared many of the same political views, as well as deep religious convictions and an interest in reading. Together they participated in literary clubs. Lucretia's progressive ideas moderated the thinking of her more traditional husband, and by the time of his presidential bid, the two had become close intellectual partners.

Presidency

Lucretia believed in her husband's abilities and felt he was a great leader. She was also proud of his accomplishments. His long, successful congressional career and growing national exposure had positioned him to seek the presidency in the 1880 election. Although Lucretia supported her husband's ambition, she was somewhat hesitant about assuming the role of White House hostess. A very private person, she was intimidated by the prospect of presiding over the White House and questioned her own abilities. Lucretia had no experience hostessing, for her religious convictions had prevented her from participating in social affairs. She did not appear to be prepared for the first ladyship, and indeed, found even the campaign challenging. She did participate in his "front porch" campaign, although she declined requests to be photographed for the campaign.

The campaign proved difficult, and the closeness of the election raised questions about the new president's credibility. Both Garfield and

Lucretia, while pleased at the victory, took these challenges personally. During the inaugural address Lucretia surprised herself by being so moved and proud of her husband that she shed tears. Once in the White House Lucretia was limited by poor health caused by bouts of malaria, but fortunately she befriended Mrs. James Blaine, wife of a cabinet member, who taught Lucretia the secrets of social hostessing and helped her. Lucretia was a quick study and discovered she had political and social abilities she was not aware of. She was interested in the history of the Executive Mansion, overseeing the historic renovation of parts of the building, and proved to be an adequate first lady in the short period of her office.

By May 1881, within two months of Garfield's inauguration, Lucretia's health had deteriorated significantly, and her high fever alarmed her husband. Distressed by his wife's illness and very attentive to her needs, he admitted to her that he could hardly function when she was sick. Lucretia remained bedridden for some time, then retired to a seaside resort in New Jersey to escape Washington's humid summer and recuperate.

While she was recovering, the president was shot on July 2, 1881, by Charles Guiteau, a disgruntled officeseeker. According to his letters, Guiteau had contemplated shooting the president only days before but hesitated because he felt sorry for Garfield's ailing wife. On hearing the news, Lucretia immediately returned to Washington by train and oversaw the efforts to save the president. She nursed him for eighty days before he lost his fight on September 19, 1881. The country admired the first lady's strength and courage and her bravery when he died.

Legacy

Lucretia Garfield lived another thirty-six years as a widow, leading a private life in Ohio. She did, however, maintain some public functions, speaking to women's groups on the subject of literature, volunteering for the Red Cross, and eventually supporting Woodrow Wilson's campaign for the presidency. She also saw to it that her husband's personal and presidential papers were preserved.

Throughout her life Lucretia retained her passion for literature. She wrote poetry, read prolifically, and even translated the works of French author Victor Hugo in her retirement. She started but did not complete a biography of her husband. Lucretia followed her children's careers and drew much happiness from their success. Her son James served as secretary of the interior under President Theodore Roosevelt, and her son

Harry became president of Williams College, the alma mater of her late husband.

Lucretia Garfield died at her winter home in Pasadena, California, in March 1918.

Bibliography

Blach, William Ralston. *The Life of James A. Garfield*. Philadelphia: J. C. McCurdy, 1881.

Brown, Harry J., and Frederick D. Williams, eds. *The Diary of James A. Garfield*. 4 volumes. East Lansing: Michigan State University Press, 1967–1981.

Peskin, Allen. *Garfield*. Kent, OH: Kent State University Press, 1978.

Shaw, John, ed. *Crete and James: Personal Letters of Lucretia and James Garfield*. East Lansing: Michigan State University Press, 1994.

Smith, Theodore Clarke. *James Abram Garfield: The Life and Letters*. 2 volumes. New Haven, CT: Yale University Press, 1925.

22

Mary Arthur McElroy

President: Chester A. Arthur (1829–1886), Twenty-first President
President's Term: 1881–1885 (Republican)

Ellen Lewis Herndon Arthur died suddenly and unexpectedly twenty months before Chester Arthur became president.

Hostess for the Widower President:
Mary Arthur McElroy (1841–1917)

When Chester Arthur assumed the presidency after the assassination of President Garfield, his only daughter, Ellen, was still a child. Arthur turned to his younger sister, Mary, to assist him with the White House's social affairs. At the time, Mary was living in Albany, New York, and had a family of her own. Hesitant to leave her family, she remained in Albany for part of the year, traveling to the capital each winter for the city's social season, where she presided over the White House social events. Mary was also shy by nature, which further contributed to her reluctance. Despite the growing temperance movement building during his tenure, Arthur and his hostess decided to serve their guests alcohol at White House social events and dinners. Because of the tragic death of President Garfield, the nation was in mourning and the White House social calendar was not as busy as it might otherwise have been. Nevertheless, Arthur was much more outgoing than his predecessors,

Rutherford Hayes and James Garfield, and the White House social events were more entertaining than the capital city had experienced since Julia Grant presided as hostess. Mary proved to be a popular and capable hostess, whose efforts were generally better received than those of the president, whose administration is remembered for very little.

23

Frances Clara Folsom Cleveland

Born: July 21, 1864; Buffalo, New York

Died: October 29, 1947; Princeton, New Jersey

President: Grover Cleveland (1837–1908), Twenty-second and Twenty-fourth Presidents

Husband's Presidential Terms: 1885–1889; 1893–1897 (Democrat)

Marriage: First: June 2, 1886, to Grover Cleveland; Washington, D.C. Second: February 10, 1913, to Thomas J. Preston Jr.; Princeton, New Jersey

Children: First marriage: Ruth (1891–1904); Esther (1893–1980); Marion (1895–1977); Richard Folsom (1897–1974); Frances Grover (1903). Second marriage: None

Early Years

Frances Folsom was an only child, born on July 21, 1864, to a wealthy couple in Buffalo, New York. Her mother, Emma Harmon, was the daughter of a prominent family, and her father, Oscar Folsom, was a graduate of the University of Rochester and an aspiring lawyer. His law partner was Grover Cleveland, future husband of young Frances and future president of the United States. Grover Cleveland came from a

Presbyterian minister's family of modest means in New Jersey; he went to Buffalo in search of employment and ended up in practice with Folsom. Because of this, Grover knew Frances from her birth.

Frances was extremely well educated for a woman of the nineteenth century, having attended such prestigious schools as Madame Brecher's French Kindergarten and Miss Bissell's School for Young Ladies. In 1873, at the age of nine, Frances suffered the deaths of three relatives to whom she was close: an uncle, an aunt, and her paternal grandmother. The following year her father died in a freak carriage accident. The young girl was sent to live with her maternal grandmother, Ruth Harmon, in Medina, New York. There Frances attended the Medina Academy for Boys and Girls from 1874 until 1879, then went to a boarding school back in Buffalo. Frances appears to have become bored with school, the city of Buffalo, and her life, and she left the academy before graduating. Young Frances, known by her family and friends as "Frank," a nickname she shared with several relatives, was a talented, popular girl who seemed destined for success, in spite of—or perhaps because of—her spontaneity and restlessness.

Frances's decision to leave school disappointed her family and Grover Cleveland. Since Oscar Folsom's death, Cleveland had overseen the Folsom finances as family executor and had also begun supervising Frances's education and functioning as her guardian. Concerned about her departure from school and her future, Cleveland obtained a certificate of completion for her; she then entered Wells College in Aurora, New York. Because Frances was not living with her grandmother by this time and her mother had moved to St. Paul, Minnesota, Cleveland increasingly became a parental figure during her college years. He often visited and wrote to her, even sending flowers on a regular basis.

Frances had a positive college experience at Wells. She was a popular student, especially among eligible bachelors. She had numerous suitors and received many marriage proposals; she was briefly engaged to a student in the seminary before ending the relationship. Meanwhile, Cleveland's career progressed well: He was elected mayor of Buffalo and in 1882 became governor of New York. The two remained close during this time. Frances visited the governor's mansion and was with her guardian a few years later at the Democratic National Convention when he received the party's nomination for president. She wanted to attend his presidential inauguration but could not because of her schedule at school.

Marriage

By the time Frances graduated from Wells College, Cleveland's affections had become romantic, despite a twenty-seven-year age difference. The Folsoms visited the president in the White House in the spring of 1885 after his inauguration. During this visit their affair appears to have commenced, and Cleveland's intention turned to marriage. By this time rumors had started to swirl in the capital about the president's love interest—though some of the rumors postulated that it was Frances's widowed mother with whom the president was smitten.

Cleveland did in fact propose to his "Frankie" in August 1885. During her visit to the capital, Frances had met Harriet Lane, the niece and former White House hostess of President James Buchanan, who instructed Frances in the art of social hostessing. Frances loved Washington and the White House and was eager to marry the president; she accepted his marriage proposal and wanted to marry immediately, but her mother cautioned against rushing into marriage and took her to Europe for an extended vacation. The trip gave the young woman time to contemplate her future but did not offer the Folsoms an escape from the growing media interest in the president's pending marriage. In Europe they were tailed by the press. When they returned to the United States, they managed to elude reporters by leaving fake luggage with their names on it as a decoy while they boarded their ship home.

The president also had a difficult time keeping the engagement out of the public eye. He and his fiancée were followed closely by curious reporters, prompting Cleveland to publish a letter in the *New York Evening Post* critical of the press's invasion of his private life. He and Frances were the first presidential couple to undergo the media scrutiny that has since become a defining characteristic of the office.

Frances was only twenty-one when she married the president on June 2, 1886, in the first presidential marriage in the White House. The president did not want to marry in Buffalo or in a church and favored a private, informal affair to avoid publicity. She, however, preferred a grand wedding, and the gala event was surrounded by much public curiosity and media pageantry. The Marine Band played the wedding march during the ceremony, and Cleveland had the word "obey" deleted from their vows. After the wedding the Clevelands honeymooned in Maryland, where they were again hounded by reporters. The newlyweds hosted two receptions at which Frances and her wedding dress were the main attraction. This was the start of a long love affair between the nation and their new first lady.

Frances's popularity was a boost to the president's own standing. During his campaign for office, a story broke that Cleveland had fathered a child out of wedlock with a woman named Maria Halprin. First reported by a preacher, the tale became even more scandalous when the public learned that Halprin's child might have been fathered by any number of men. Cleveland's political opponents developed campaign slogans about the illegitimate child and unmarried president. He did not completely deny the paternity and had apparently arranged for the child's adoption.

Family Life

Unlike most other presidential couples, the Clevelands were married in the White House and therefore began their life together during the presidency. Cleveland was the only president to serve two nonconsecutive terms, losing his bid for reelection in 1888 but regaining the office in the 1892 election.

Both during their White House years and while out of office they traveled together. Cleveland was the first president to tour the South since the end of the Civil War, and in 1887 the couple toured the West. They were greeted by appreciative crowds everywhere they went. After his defeat for reelection, they moved to New York City, and Cleveland reentered the legal profession. During his first term they had kept a home in Washington, which they sold in 1889 for a handsome profit when they left the city.

Frances's first child, Ruth (for whom the Baby Ruth candy bar was named), was born in 1891, just before Cleveland's return to the White House. Another two children were born during his second term: Esther in 1893 and Marion two years later. And in 1897, just after the end of Cleveland's presidency, Richard was born. Frances established a preschool for her own and other White House children and sought to shield them from the limelight, but despite these efforts, Frances and her children were celebrities.

After their second term in the White House, the couple was devastated by the death of their daughter Ruth at their vacation home in Buzzard's Bay, Massachusetts; Frances never returned there, spending summers in New Hampshire instead. She lost her fifth child, a daughter named for her, in 1903.

The Clevelands enjoyed a close, warm marriage, and their wide age difference was not the obstacle that might have been expected.

Presidency

Cleveland was a forty-eight-year-old bachelor when he went to the White House, only the second ever to become president. Although he had many women admirers, he seemed opposed to marrying—until Frances graduated from college. Cleveland's sister, Rose Elizabeth, nicknamed "Libbie," served as hostess for the first fifteen months of her brother's presidency. Rose was a lecturer at an exclusive girls' school and had published essays on literature. She did not enjoy her White House experience, and her strong beliefs on women's rights were at times a bit much for her brother. When he married, Rose was only too willing to turn over her social duties to her new sister-in-law.

And Frances was only too happy to accept the challenge of serving as White House hostess. The partnership between Frances and Cleveland was immediately established and proved successful in the White House. She worked with him on all family matters and the social side of the presidency, but she rarely involved herself in political affairs, though she was interested in politics. For his part, despite being surrounded by strong, capable women, Cleveland retained a rather traditional view of women, seeing them primarily as wives and mothers.

The Clevelands' White House years together were positive and productive. Together they renovated the White House and "Oak View," the home just outside the city to which they regularly escaped during the presidency. Frances took the lead in renovating the White House, and her work was applauded by the city and an appreciative public. A popular and gifted hostess as well, she was assisted in the White House by one of her oldest and closest friends, Minnie Alexander, who lived there and functioned as the first lady's private assistant. Frances used her beauty, grace, and charm to endear herself to the nation. Her socials, among the most successful in White House history, reflected the first lady's personality and were described as festive and entertaining. In addition to other parties, the first lady scheduled events after normal work hours on Saturdays to accommodate women who worked. Frances also became a fashion trendsetter, as an admiring public followed her taste in styles. Advertisers of clothing and accessories tried to use her name to market their products, both with and without her permission. When Frances declined to wear the obligatory women's bustle, she is said to have contributed to its demise.

Frances did get involved in politics during her husband's difficult bid for reelection. During the 1888 campaign a rumor was circulated by a critic, Reverend C. H. Pendleton, suggesting that the president abused his wife. The unsubstantiated report was picked up by the press, who reported that Frances was unhappy and that Cleveland was a drunkard. In a first for her office, Frances Cleveland wrote a public letter refuting the charges as baseless.

Neither the letter nor Frances's popularity was enough to return Cleveland to the White House, however; he lost the 1888 election to Benjamin Harrison in a close race. The White House staff was sad to see their beloved first lady go, but in a remark that would become famous, Frances promised them she would be back in four years. In 1892, Cleveland regained the White House after a campaign that made the most of Frances's popularity: Her likeness appeared on the Cleveland campaign literature, above that of the candidate himself.

Cleveland was a workaholic, but Frances was able to get her husband to relax and focus his energies. This was especially important during his second term. Not only was the president four years older, but he had gained weight, and during his second term he developed a cancerous growth near his jaw. To hide the seriousness of the problem from the press, Cleveland scheduled a fake fishing trip, and on board the boat a physician removed the growth. Frances was vacationing at their summer home at the same time to give the impression of normalcy.

Legacy

Frances did not want to leave the White House and wept when she departed the building and life she so loved. After his second term, Grover Cleveland's health began to deteriorate, partly from being overweight. The Clevelands moved to Princeton, New Jersey, where the former president wrote about politics and against women's participation in politics. In 1908 he became quite ill and died on June 24 at their home, the "Westland," with Frances at his side.

After her husband's death, Frances was eligible for a pension as a former first lady and widow, but because she had inherited a large amount of money, she declined the $5,000 annual pension.

In 1913 Frances married Thomas J. Preston Jr., a professor of archaeology at Princeton. Always active, she participated in university socials and the women's university club and was a popular figure around campus. She also involved herself with charities in the community. In 1887 she had become one of the first women trustees of her alma mater, Wells College—a position she would hold for a remarkable half-century—and she headed its endowment fund in 1922.

Frances maintained her interest in politics, following current events and supporting Al Smith's 1928 presidential campaign. She met many of the leading political figures of the first half of the twentieth century, including President Harry Truman. While she was visiting the Truman White House, the president's daughter introduced the former first lady to General Dwight Eisenhower, who did not know who the guest was and asked if she lived in the capital city. Frances responded humorously that she used to live in the very building in which the two were standing.

Frances Cleveland was the first White House bride and the youngest first lady. She is also remembered as one of the most popular first ladies. She enjoyed a long life, passing away in 1947 at eighty-three.

Bibliography
Carpenter, Frank. *Carp's Washington.* New York: McGraw-Hill, 1960.
Hoover, Irwin A. *Forty-Two Years in the White House.* Boston: Houghton Mifflin, 1943.
Nevins, Allan, ed. *Letters of Grover Cleveland, 1850–1908.* Boston: Houghton Mifflin, 1933.
Sadler, Christine. *Children in the White House.* New York: Putnam's, 1967.
Tugwell, Rexford. *Grover Cleveland.* New York: Macmillan, 1968.

24

Caroline Lavinia Scott Harrison

Born: October 1, 1832; Oxford, Ohio
Died: October 25, 1892; Washington, D.C.
President: Benjamin Harrison (1833–1901), Twenty-third President
Husband's Presidential Term: 1889–1893 (Republican)
Marriage: October 20, 1853; Oxford, Ohio
Children: Russell Benjamin (1854–1936); Mary Scott (1858–1930)

Early Years

Caroline Scott was born on October 1, 1832, in Oxford, Ohio, the daughter of Mary Potts Neal Scott, whose family was in the banking business in Philadelphia. Her father, Reverend John Witherspoon Scott, was a Presbyterian minister and professor who was also a founder of the Oxford Female Institute, a school in Cincinnati. Scott taught chemistry at Farmers College in Cincinnati and at Miami University in Ohio. Caroline had two sisters and two brothers.

The Scott family was of moderate but comfortable means and valued refinement and exposure to culture; it was also deeply religious. Caroline was fortunate to have been raised in a household that emphasized education. Perhaps because of her upbringing, she developed an interest in English and American literature and became an accomplished painter. She was also elegant and sophisticated and had a light, friendly disposition. She was described as a small, plump young woman with brown hair.

Marriage

Benjamin Harrison was a student at Farmers College when he met Caroline, who was several months older than her suitor. When John Scott relocated his school from Cincinnati to the town of Oxford, Harrison also moved to Oxford, transferring to Miami University to be close to Caroline. Both were teenagers when they began to court, and the young man was eager to marry his love. Near the time when the couple graduated, they became formally engaged—they had become secretly engaged earlier, in 1852. After graduation Harrison moved to Cincinnati to study law, while Caroline taught piano classes at her father's school. Their wedding was October 10, 1853, with Caroline's father performing the ceremony.

Although both were slight in physical stature, the couple's personalities were quite different. Harrison was a serious, drab, impersonal man, and from the time they began courting, Caroline was the more social of the two. Her warmth and social skills would benefit him throughout his political career.

Family Life

After marriage Harrison and "Carrie," as she was often called, resided in North Bend, Ohio, at the Harrison family home, also the site where President William Henry Harrison, Benjamin's grandfather, was buried. Harrison struggled in his initial efforts to establish a legal career, and his work took them to Indiana. But because of health problems and her husband's ongoing financial and career troubles, Caroline returned to Ohio to live with relatives. Eventually his practice began to succeed, and Caroline rejoined him.

The couple's first child, Russell, was born in 1854, and a daughter, Mary, came in 1858. Around this time Caroline became a member of the board of directors of an orphanage in Indianapolis, a position she would hold for the rest of her life. She achieved success in numerous other social and charitable endeavors and distinguished herself as one of the most socially conscious first ladies.

Harrison wanted to enter politics but waited until his law practice had become lucrative. When he turned to politics, he found quick success. In 1857 he was elected city attorney, then became a leader within the Indiana Republican Party. At the outset of his political career, however, Harrison threw himself into politics and neglected his marriage. Although he appears to have been deeply devoted to his wife, his political career demanded much of his time. Caroline often felt lonely and missed her husband. As Harrison's new career was growing, the Civil War broke out in 1861, and he joined the Union effort, which again took him away from his wife. Caroline lost a newborn child in 1861. She suffered from depression and worried about her husband's safety during the war but continued to run the Harrison household—a considerable task, as they had two children and owned a large mansion and estate. She was also very active during the war, volunteering with the Ladies Patriotic Association and Ladies Sanitary Committee, tending to wounded soldiers at hospitals, and working to get food, clothing, and medical supplies for the troops. In 1862 and 1863 Caroline visited her husband in camp in Kentucky and Tennessee. There she kept busy doing chores, mending uniforms, and generally helping out in any way she could.

Harrison was a colonel in the Indiana regiment and enjoyed modest fame in the war. During leaves in 1864 and 1865 he returned to Indiana but spent little time with his wife and family, instead speaking publicly and visiting key supporters on behalf of his political career. Near the end of the war, Caroline took her children to Pennsylvania and nearly died when all three contracted scarlet fever. This event appears to have affected Harrison greatly, for after his service he reconciled his obligations to career and family and began spending more time with his wife. The health of their marriage improved and they became nearly inseparable, attending the opera, theater, and church together and going for carriage rides. Caroline supported her husband's political career by hosting numerous social events on his behalf. Benjamin in turn supported her artistic endeavors: Caroline took art courses, and her talent was such that she exhibited her work in art shows.

Religion was an important part of their lives. They were both Calvinists, and Harrison had even considered the ministry earlier in his life. They attended a Presbyterian church near their home, where he taught Sunday school and Caroline sang in the church choir. They also prayed and read Scripture together, raising their children in a religious household. Literature was another staple of the Harrison home. Caroline was an intelligent woman who put much emphasis on education. She enrolled in literature courses and even established a club to discuss literature and the intellectual matters of the day.

Presidency

Caroline was an asset to her husband during his presidential campaign in 1888, becoming a valued adviser and political strategist. Although she was not overly fond of campaigning and found it a chore, she participated in his "front porch" campaign: Harrison basically ran from his front porch, limiting his travel schedule but making his home public property. He invited voters to the house, gave speeches from the front porch, and entertained endless visitors and reporters. The Harrison home was overrun, the furniture and the property were ruined, some furnishings even stolen. So costly was the campaign to them that at the conclusion Caroline quipped, "Well, it's the White House or the poorhouse with us now!" Although she did well in her public appearances, she begrudged the loss of her privacy, a fact of public life that would plague her otherwise impressive first ladyship. Finding humor in the face of the challenge, she joked that reporters knew more about her family than she did. She also suggested that because of the onslaught by the press, she would no longer have to write friends because they could read how she was doing in the newspapers.

Harrison won the election in the electoral college, although Grover Cleveland won the popular vote, in one of the most corrupt campaigns in U.S. history. When the Harrisons arrived at the White House, Caroline found it overrun with rats and the floors, furnishings, and walls damaged or almost completely ruined. She decided the building needed a complete renovation. To build support for her project, she invited members of Congress to the mansion to see firsthand its condition and also gave personal public tours of the building. Among her renovations were a new kitchen, new floors and curtains in much of the building, and new furniture to replace worn pieces throughout the White House. She had many of the rooms repainted and the entire building cleaned. Perhaps her most enduring contribution was the first comprehensive cataloguing of all White House furnishings and pieces. She conducted the inventory of every room and had many historic objects preserved. Caroline also modernized the building, installing a new heating system, electric lighting, and a private bath connecting to the private bedroom. On visiting the Executive Mansion after the work was completed, former first lady Frances Cleveland was quite impressed.

But Caroline had even more ambitious ideas. Shortly after entering the White House, she began drawing up plans for an entirely new mansion. Caroline hired an architect to develop the proposal, which became known as "Mrs. Harrison's house." Given the condition of the existing building, the notion was not so outrageous as it might have seemed initially. She intended its completion to coincide with the coming centennial of the city and the White House. Her renovations took place only as a backup plan when she was unable to go forward with the new building. Congress would not fund the plan, Harrison lost his bid for reelection in 1892, and she became too ill to continue promoting the idea. But she did have the architect design two new wings for the White House. In proposing a greatly expanded, more elegant presidential residence, Caroline laid the groundwork for what would become the East and West Wings of the building.

Caroline also turned her attention to the White House social calendar. With the exception of those of her predecessor, Frances Cleveland, the social affairs there had been rather drab since the Grant administration. She brought dancing back to the White House. She also enjoyed the company of her extended family who lived in the White House, including her father, children, and several grandchildren.

Caroline brought her love of painting to the White House and proposed building an art gallery in it. She took her art equipment and even a kiln to the White House and spent much of her free time working on paintings and ceramics. She also organized art classes for the wives and daughters of White House staff and other federal officials. Caroline designed her own White House china featuring scenes from around the country to celebrate the nation's abundance of natural beauty, and she established the White House china collection, preserving priceless pieces in what would become a popular feature of the mansion. Caroline found relief from the pressures of the the first ladyship not only in her art but also in gardening, working in the Executive Mansion's greenhouses and brightening the building with flowers that she placed throughout the mansion.

In spite of her many contributions, Caroline Harrison is not remembered as a successful first lady. Indeed, she was not popular in Washington's social circles, and before her husband's election there was doubt about her ability to preside over White House social events. Critics considered her rather simple and unrefined. She was also the subject of a minor controversy: In 1890 Harrison's overzealous supporters, led by Postmaster General John Wanamaker, gave the first lady a seaside home at Cape May in New Jersey. Caroline innocently and mistakenly accepted the house, which she used for convalescence. When the press learned of it, allegations of bribery followed. She tried unsuccessfully to downplay the matter and shrug it off as poor judgment, but the accusations persisted. She was greatly bothered by the criticism, apparently even more so than the president. She also took criticism of her husband harder than he did. So disturbed was the first lady by the attacks that she complained, "If this is the penalty for being President of the United States, I hope the Good Lord will deliver my husband from any future experience."

Caroline Harrison may be the most underrated first lady of all time. She was a very private individual who much preferred the comforts of family life to the busy public life of a presidential spouse. Yet she served out of a sense of civic duty, and she served ably. Part of the public's perception of her might be explained by her desire to maintain her privacy. Moreover, she suffered from poor health while in the White House and was at times unable to attend social events. The long receiving lines and demands of hostessing tired the first lady, so her daughter and her daughter-in-law, both named Mary, assisted with those responsibilities. Caroline often commented on the amount of work that went into managing White House social events. She was also surprised by the degree of scrutiny by the public and press that not only the president but the president's spouse received. Although on balance she performed admirably, Caroline seems to have been unprepared for the immense challenge of the first ladyship.

By the summer of 1891 she was quite ill, and by winter she was largely bedridden. Benjamin Harrison limited his campaign for reelection to spend time with her. Out of respect, Harrison's challenger, Grover Cleveland, also limited his campaign efforts. Caroline's health continued to worsen during 1892 as she struggled with tuberculosis and influenza. She lost her battle on October 25, 1892; two weeks later her husband was defeated at the polls by Grover Cleveland.

Legacy

Caroline Harrison was the second first lady (after Letitia Tyler) to die in the White House. Her renovation of the mansion remains one of the most comprehensive and important restorations of the building. She helped preserve and inventory many historic pieces and set the course for the expansion of the White House, yet she often receives no recognition for her role in these important matters or lesser ones. She was, for example, the first to decorate a White House Christmas tree and to make that event a public ceremony.

Caroline was also the first president general of the Daughters of the American Revolution (DAR), an organization that has devoted itself largely to preserving the nation's history. Caroline's inaugural address to the DAR in 1890 was one of the first calls by a prominent female public figure for recognizing the rights of women; in it she compared the struggle of women to that of the nation. Yet she is rarely credited for her bold speech. Her work on behalf of women can also be seen in her efforts to raise funds for the Johns Hopkins University Medical School, an institution that would become a world leader in medical research and education. She lent her prestige to the effort on the condition that Johns Hopkins admit women to the school and on an equal footing with men.

After Benjamin Harrison's defeat, he retired from politics. In April 1896 he married Mary Scott Dimmick, a well-known socialite and widow from Pennsylvania, who was also his deceased wife's niece. The Harrison children opposed the wedding. But even though Harrison had loved his first wife deeply and was devastated by her death, he seems to have found solace with Mary. There had been rumors of a love affair between her and the president during his presidency, but they cannot be substantiated. Nevertheless, the couple traveled together and were regulars in high society throughout their brief marriage until Harrison died in 1901.

Bibliography

Anderson, Peggy. *The Daughters: An Unconventional Look at America's Fan Club—the DAR*. New York: St. Martin's, 1974.

Carpenter, Frank. *Carp's Washington*. New York: McGraw-Hill, 1960.

Hoover, Irwin A. *Forty-Two Years in the White House*. Boston: Houghton Mifflin, 1943.

Sievers, Harry Joseph. *Benjamin Harrison*. 3 volumes. Indianapolis, IN: Bobbs-Merrill, 1952.

25

Ida Saxton McKinley

Born: May 26, 1847; Canton, Ohio
Died: May 26, 1907; Canton, Ohio
President: William McKinley (1843–1901), Twenty-fifth President
Husband's Presidential Term: 1897–1901 (Republican)
Marriage: January 25, 1871; Canton, Ohio
Children: Katherine (1871–1875); Ida (1873)

Early Years

The Saxtons were among the most prominent families in the town of Canton, Ohio. James Saxton was a wealthy businessman and banker whose father had owned the *Ohio Repository* newspaper. He married Katherine "Kate" Dewalt, and they had three children, a son named George followed by two daughters, Ida and Mary. Ida, their middle child, was born in Canton in 1847.

The Saxtons raised their children in the tradition of the Presbyterian Church. James Saxton emphasized a sound education for all his children, and they received a formal, thorough education in the Canton schools. Ida also attended private schools in Cleveland and Delhi, New York; after completing high school she went to Brook Hall, a presti-

gious finishing school for girls in Pennsylvania, where she was instructed in the requisite refinements and social graces necessary for a society
life. With her sister and a private tutor–chaperone, Ida traveled through
Europe for six months to fulfill her father's desire to further expose
them to culture. Although her adventurous spirit found travel agreeable,
at times she rebelled against the supervision she received, arguing with
her chaperone. Even at an early age she was an independent, strong-
willed individual with progressive views, but she could be tedious and
disagreeable over the smallest detail.

Saxton appears to have recognized young Ida's abilities, for he
encouraged her studies and her interest in having a career. Ida seems to
have enjoyed a close, supportive, and loving relationship with her
father. He even invited her to work as a clerk in his bank, an unusual
position for a young woman at the time. She liked the work and did
well in her new job, earning a promotion to cashier. Besides being intelligent and ambitious, Ida was outgoing, playful, and fun-loving; she
acted in community theater to raise money for the church. She was considered an attractive young woman, with light blue eyes and fair skin.
Rather the belle of the town, she had many suitors, including a young
man named John Wright, who courted her at the time of her trip to
Europe. While abroad, she exchanged letters with him, but he died suddenly before she returned to the United States. It was also in Europe
that she began to experience severe headaches, perhaps the precursor to
the serious illnesses and epilepsy that would plague her later in life.

Marriage

Ida Saxton was considered to be among the most eligible young women
in Canton, but she seems to have been rather selective, looking for
someone to match her potential. When William McKinley, a former
major in the Civil War, moved to Canton to start his legal career, Ida
immediately caught his eye. The two met at a church picnic and apparently fell in love quickly. McKinley was twenty-seven and Ida a few
years younger. During their courtship McKinley often visited Ida at the
bank and brought her flowers.

The two were married on January 25, 1871, in a grand ceremony
with more than a thousand guests. They were wed in the Presbyterian
church Ida had attended, but after marrying, Ida adopted her husband's
Methodist faith. As a wedding gift, Ida's father gave them a house in
Canton.

Family Life

Ida and William McKinley had a happy, successful marriage. They genuinely cared for each other, and he was very attentive to his wife. Ida called her husband "the Major," and he often referred to her as "dearest" in both their correspondence and at home. Ida supported her husband's legal and political careers and celebrated his successes.

Gradually, however, Ida's strong will and outgoing disposition were sapped by her growing illness. The headaches that had started in Europe became more severe and frequent, draining her energy and greatly limiting her ability to function. Two years after the wedding, her grandfather and mother died. That same year her second daughter died shortly after birth. Ida was never the same again. Her vivacious, determined spirit was depleted, and she began to feel that God was displeased with her. She grew somewhat paranoid and overprotective of her first child, named Katherine or "Kate" for Ida's mother, and in 1875 her fears were realized: The child died of typhoid fever at the age of four.

Ida's own condition worsened. She was diagnosed with phlebitis and epilepsy. The press for the most part ignored her physical condition, but occasionally her illness was the focus of attacks and became a minor political liability for her husband. Nevertheless, William McKinley remained very patient and caring with his wife. He took care of her during her seizures and often acted as her nurse during her weakest days. Although he was a heavy smoker, McKinley never smoked in her company, mindful both of her frail health and her disapproval of smoking and drinking.

McKinley's political career proceeded in spite of the family tragedies. In 1877 he was elected to the U.S. House of Representatives, serving until 1891. Ida was interested in politics and joined her husband at political events and in the capital, but she was never as active as she probably would have been had her illness and the deaths of her two children not occurred. McKinley secured a nurse to help his wife and to look after her when he was not home; when she did not accompany him, she turned to embroidery and crocheting, hobbies she greatly enjoyed. In 1891 McKinley was defeated for reelection to the House, but he then ran successfully for governor of Ohio.

Her illness did not prevent Ida from remaining a close companion and supporting her husband's political endeavors. She also broadened his horizons, discussing literature and current issues with him and introducing him to the theater, operas, music, and culture. McKinley himself and his aides admitted that she had a better sense of people and politics than her husband. During the early 1890s when he incurred financial difficulties, Ida used her considerable inheritance—her father had died in 1887—to save the family and fund her husband's political career.

After two terms as governor, McKinley began to pursue the presidency, winning the Republican nomination in 1896. The race would become a famous contest, pitting McKinley against William Jennings Bryan, the "Great Commoner" and well-known orator. The campaign turned nasty, and Ida became a target of Bryan's supporters' efforts to derail the McKinley bid. Among other things, she was accused of being a foreign spy and a Catholic, and of having black ancestry. The Republican Party featured Ida in their campaign literature and compiled a biography of the prospective first lady, one of the first such profiles. She also participated in her husband's "front porch" campaign and joined him in Washington.

Presidency

McKinley narrowly won the election. During the campaign there was speculation that the candidate's wife would not be up to the demands of the White House, but Ida helped her husband attain the office. Not only did she advise him and participate in the campaign, but she hosted important social events for the leading players in the Republican Party, which were designed to secure the party's nomination for McKinley.

Ida was too ill to attend the reception given in their honor by outgoing president Grover Cleveland and his wife, Frances. She also had to limit her social appearances and the McKinley social calendar. When she appeared in public, Ida often remained seated in a grand, blue velvet chair. By the time of the election, Ida was a near invalid, weakened and often under the effects of heavy medication and in serious pain. At fifty, her hair had turned completely gray and she wore it cropped, showing the signs of her affliction and aging. Public reception of the new first lady and her condition was mixed. Some criticized her and questioned her fitness to preside over the White House; others praised her for her courage in facing the ordeal.

McKinley himself also received some public support for the patience and care he demonstrated with his wife. Breaking with the practice of having the president and first lady sit across from each other at state dinners, McKinley chose to have Ida sit next to him at the table. This allowed him to care for her if she suffered a seizure. At the time epilepsy was not discussed openly, and people tended to be intolerant of the illness. Several guests at the White House reported being surprised by this practice and the first lady's condition. McKinley deserves credit for his openness in handling the epileptic seizures. Even though it might appear callous by today's standards, when Ida was having one of what they called her "fainting spells," the president would place a handkerchief over her head and excuse themselves, ushering her from the room to attend to her.

In spite of her difficulties, Ida liked being in the White House and was proud of her husband's election. Some of her old spirit even seems to have returned. She had several rooms in the mansion repainted and personally oversaw the process. Ida brought color to the building as well by placing flowers throughout the White House and ordering bouquets for the official dinners. She attempted to do what she could as first lady.

Ida closely followed the events of the day and discussed them with her husband, especially the Spanish-American War. She regarded McKinley not as a politician but as a leader and statesman. She was quick to defend him and did not hesitate to debate issues with those around her. She was one of her husband's advisers and often shared with him her views on key presidential aides. In fact, despite her weak physical condition, there were rumors that she ruled her husband and made his decisions for him.

Ida continued to suffer from personal and family tragedy. In 1898 her brother, George, was killed by his mistress in an embarrassing and painful incident. The following year she had her worst seizure to date, from which she never fully recovered. The attack left her constantly depressed, in part because she was almost completely dependent on assistance for even the most basic tasks. By 1900 she was looking forward to leaving the White House and returning to Ohio. McKinley, however, chose to stand for reelection and was returned to the White House that year. Although she was in poor health and longed for home, Ida nevertheless supported her husband's reelection campaign, although she was unable to participate in most activities. She did accompany him, however, on a multiweek tour of the country, assisted by her maid, her niece, and a physician. She enjoyed the huge outpouring of affection they received from the nation, although the travels were too much for her. Partway through the tour she became very ill, requiring surgery and nearly dying. McKinley ended the tour prematurely, and Ida returned to Canton to recuperate.

In September 1901 the president attended the Pan-American Exposition in Buffalo, New York, where he was shot by an anarchist named Leon Czolgosz. McKinley survived for a time after the shooting, and expressed concern about his wife's care after his death. Ida was able to go to her husband's side after the shooting and handled the tragedy better than most expected. The president died on September 14, 1901. At his death the first lady said, "I want to go, too."

Legacy

McKinley's presidency was limited by his own personal shortcomings, which included being a poor judge of character. He was ill served by opportunistic and corrupt aides, and his legacy was marred by scandals of financial corruption and fraud that broke after his death. Ida ignored the critics and remembered her husband as a hero and one of the country's great leaders.

After the president's death, she returned to Canton, where she regularly visited his grave. William McKinley's dying wish was granted, as Ida's sister took care of the former first lady until she died on May 26, 1907.

Bibliography

Beldon, Harry S., ed. *Grand Tour of Ida Saxton McKinley and Sister Mary Saxton Barber.* Canton, OH: Stark County Historical Society, 1869.

Hartzell, Josiah. *Sketch of the Life of Mrs. William McKinley.* Washington, DC: Home Magazine Press, 1896.

Leech, Margaret. *In the Days of McKinley.* New York: Harper & Row, 1959.

Olcott, Charles S. *The Life of William McKinley.* 2 volumes. Boston: Houghton Mifflin, 1916.

Willets, Gilson. *Inside History of the White House.* New York: Christian Herald, 1908.

26

Edith
Kermit
Carow
Roosevelt

Born: August 6, 1861; Norwich, Connecticut
Died: September 30, 1948; Oyster Bay, New York
President: Theodore Roosevelt (1858–1919), Twenty-sixth President
Husband's Presidential Term: 1901–1909 (Republican)
Marriage: December 2, 1886; London, England
Children: Theodore (1887–1944); Kermit (1889–1943); Ethel Carow
   (1891–1977); Archibald Bulloch (1894–1979); Quentin (1897–
   1918)

Early Years

Edith was born in Norwich, Connecticut, on August 6, 1861, to
Gertrude Tyler and Charles Carow. Edith's father was from an affluent,
old-moneyed family in New York. He made his mark in international
shipping but lived a hard, fast life; he was an alcoholic and squandered
much money in reckless gambling. Ultimately, Carow's lifestyle caught
up with him, and he died in 1883. Edith's mother was a paranoid,
demanding woman who suffered through her life as a hypochondriac.
Given the excesses and vices of the family, it is surprising that Edith
grew to be a well-adjusted young woman, though she was somewhat

bashful and reclusive. She rarely spoke to her mother or father beyond her childhood.

Edith's upbringing was replete with material comforts. The Carows were an active family, participating in outdoor sports and activities, society life, and cultural events. Politics was also a regular part of the household. Educated at Dodsworth and Miss Comstock's, prestigious finishing schools, Edith learned not only the manners expected of a society girl but also French, Latin, history, and music. Her favorite subject was English literature, in particular Shakespeare. She grew up with an appreciation for books and was an avid reader.

The Carows were neighbors and friends of the Roosevelts. As a girl Edith even took private school lessons at the Roosevelt home. Edith's and Theodore Roosevelt's fathers were friends, and the two children grew up as playmates. "Teddy" even named his rowboat after Edith. Both families had homes in one of New York City's most affluent neighborhoods and vacationed in Oyster Bay on Long Island. Both families also moved around the same time to upstate New York.

In their teenage years Edith and Roosevelt developed a fondness for each other that went beyond friendship. When his father died in 1878, he turned to Edith in dealing with the misfortune, and it appears that at one point he proposed marriage to her. Although they shared a common upbringing and passion for reading and the intellectual life, they had vastly different personalities. Teddy was much more outgoing; Edith was reserved. But both were headstrong, and apparently their budding romance was hindered by this trait and the arguments that resulted from it.

The chief obstacle to their courtship was Alice Hathaway Lee, a beautiful, enigmatic debutante who was only seventeen when Roosevelt met her while attending Harvard University. Although he and Edith continued to exchange letters during this time and she had visited him at Harvard, he became instantly enamored with Alice and pursued her with resolve. Edith was crushed to learn of their marriage plans, but she attended her former beau's wedding on October 17, 1880.

The young couple's few years together were happy. Roosevelt enrolled in law school at Columbia University and began his political career rapidly, getting elected to the New York state legislature right after earning his law degree in 1882. He enjoyed his time in Albany, but two tragedies greatly affected him. Weakened by the birth of their daughter on February 12, 1884, Alice died of kidney failure two days later. And within days his mother succumbed to typhoid fever.

Marriage

Unable to cope with these deaths, especially his beloved Alice's, Roosevelt retired to his ranch in the Dakota Territory to find solace. The infant child, named for her mother, was left in the care of Roosevelt's older sister, Anna. He never wanted to fall in love again and rarely spoke of his deceased wife, but shortly after he returned from the West, he and Edith began a passionate love affair. The courtship moved quickly, and they became engaged on November 17, 1885.

They kept the engagement a secret, for Edith planned to travel to Europe with her family. The Atlantic Ocean separated the two for a difficult year, but eventually Roosevelt went to Europe, and they were married in London in December 1886. During that year, he ran for mayor of New York and came in third.

Family Life

Roosevelt and Edith lived at his estate at Oyster Bay, which they renamed Sagamore Hill. They also kept a home in New York City. Edith had their first child, Theodore Jr., after a difficult childbirth in 1887. She became deeply depressed afterward and the following year suffered a miscarriage. She eventually gave birth to Kermit in 1889, Ethel in 1891, Archibald in 1894, and Quentin in 1897. Edith also helped her husband raise Alice, his daughter from his first marriage. The Roosevelts enjoyed the benefits of their status: Edith had a nursemaid to help with her firstborn and subsequent children, and they also could provide their children with many material comforts.

Edith often joked that in addition to her five children and Alice, she had a big child: her husband. Their marriage was strong, regardless, and Edith emerged as a powerful force in her husband's life. Both agreed that Edith was the only one who could control Roosevelt. He was a workaholic and could be impulsive, but she kept his vast energy focused on the task at hand and was patient with his idiosyncrasies. He, in turn, acknowledged his selfishness and recognized his wife's role in his career. Indeed, he held her opinions and intelligence in high regard and admitted that he trusted her instincts about people better than his own. Behind the scenes the two frequently discussed politics and were known to disagree on many points. Edith was not beyond using the president's senior advisers to help get her points across to him. She also ran the Roosevelt household, including the family finances. They called each other "Theodore" and "Edie."

When Roosevelt campaigned for Benjamin Harrison's bid for the presidency, Edith joined him. To her surprise she found campaigning agreed with her, although in general she tended to avoid public attention. Harrison rewarded Roosevelt by naming him civil service commissioner. After the birth of their second child, the family moved to Washington, where Edith reaffirmed her affinity for politics and delighted in the city's busy social season. The intellectual conversation at the many functions she attended was a highlight of her Washington experience. In fact, Edith preferred Washington over New York. The couple socialized frequently and also toured the West.

After a brief stint as civil service commissioner, Roosevelt returned to New York to run for police commissioner of the city. Edith supported her husband's bid, even though his schedule was grueling and she rarely saw him at home during the campaign. Things remained hectic after he won the election. During this time Edith was often lonely and suffered from mild depression and headaches. Over the Christmas season in 1894, she took a two-week private vacation in New Jersey at the home of her sister-in-law and former childhood friend. While her husband was serving as police commissioner, Edith's sister moved in with the Roosevelts, and her company seems to have eased Edith's loneliness, as did a return to the nation's capital, the city she loved. The charismatic Roosevelt gained fame as a reformer and attracted the attention of President William McKinley, who named him assistant secretary of the navy in 1897. Pregnant at the time, Edith was pleased with her husband's new position and their move back to Washington, even though the pregnancy and childbirth were difficult and left her physically exhausted. Adding to her troubles was Alice, her stepdaughter, a highly selfish and unappreciative child, who resented her stepmother. Edith had difficulty controlling her, but taking frequent, personal vacations seemed to help her mental and physical health.

Theodore Roosevelt watched the onset of the Spanish-American War with eagerness and decided to personally participate in it. Although Edith was against this, as in the case of his big-game hunting excursions to Africa and the American West, she was unable to talk him out of it. Fulfilling his overwhelming sense of patriotism, adventure, and self-promotion, Roosevelt resigned his cabinet post and organized with Leonard Wood a volunteer cavalry unit to aid U.S. troops already engaged in combat. In Texas Roosevelt brought together an eclectic mix of former cowboys and Native Americans from the West, policemen from New York City, and his classmates from Harvard. Held together by the glue of their leader's charisma, the Rough Riders would become famous. Edith saw her husband off to Texas, then joined him in Florida for their departure to the front. Roosevelt's star had been rising, but the fame he would attract as a hero of the Spanish-American War helped propel him into the national spotlight. Not leaving anything to chance, he ensured his status as a war hero by taking along his own public relations and press corps to chronicle his exploits.

After the war Edith volunteered at a hospital in New York, working with wounded veterans. His war exploits positioned Roosevelt for his next goal, the New York governorship, which he won in 1898. Edith did not participate in the public aspects of the campaign, preferring to remain out of the public eye, although she helped in his mail room and with his correspondence. She also advised him in private. Edith was proud of her husband's success but dreaded the loss of privacy. This was apparent at his inauguration, where she found the long receiving lines tiring and held flowers to avoid shaking hands with well-wishers.

In the governor's mansion Edith asserted herself, renovating the building and converting one room into a recreation area for her active brood. She proved to be a gifted hostess and joined her husband in his busy schedule. She also belonged to a women's club that met on Friday mornings to read and discuss literature and current affairs. The degree of Edith's activism in her husband's governorship is evident in her famous response to a reporter's question: "*We* like being governor very much, thank you."

Presidency

Edith grew to enjoy her time Albany, gradually getting used to the publicity. Even though Roosevelt remained a workaholic, she was pleased that he was home with the family. Moreover, her beloved home in Sagamore Hill was close enough for the family to continue to vacation there. About the time she had adjusted to the office, however, Roosevelt's name was put forward for vice president in President McKinley's reelection bid. Edith was not happy about the prospects of a national campaign and office. She was concerned about the low pay of the vice presidency and the enormous costs of entertaining during the campaign and once in office. She also worried that being vice president might end her husband's political career. Nevertheless, the McKinley-Roosevelt ticket was elected in November 1900.

Theodore Roosevelt served only a few months as vice president, for McKinley was assassinated in September 1901. Edith went to Washington to attend the funeral, then returned to New York to bring her children to the White House. On September 21, 1901, Roosevelt moved into the White House, at forty-three the nation's youngest president to assume office. Edith arrived with the children four days later. The living quarters in the White House, which Edith separated from the office, were too small for the family and the many guests the Roosevelts received. The White House basement was used for roller skating, and the entire building became a playground for games of hide-and-seek. Edith eliminated the mansion's housekeeper position and took care of the building herself with the assistance of the usher, who managed the staff and reported directly to the first lady. Building upon the traditions of her predecessors, Edith selected new china and organized the growing collection in the ground-floor hallway of the building. She also gathered portraits of the first ladies into a collection near the ground-floor entrance of the White House, which has since become a popular portrait gallery.

Because the nation was in mourning for McKinley, Edith at first did not hold social affairs. To assure private time with her husband and to assist him with his schedule and workload, she arranged to have access to an office next to the president's. She continued her role of presidential supporter, protector, and adviser, scheduling a private hour with him every day at eight in the morning. The first lady ordered the president's security officers to accompany him at all times. This supportive role became increasingly important as the president's health declined. Even though Teddy Roosevelt gave the impression of a "bull moose," he was in poor health from a weak heart and being overweight, and he had impaired vision in one eye. Edith regularly read several newspapers, clipping articles that she felt her husband should read. She also briefed him on what she read, and when the president was run-down, she made sure he set work aside at a reasonable hour in order to sleep.

After the period of mourning, Edith offered a full social calendar, including weekly musical performances in the White House. She also organized meetings on Tuesday nights for the wives of Roosevelt's cabinet members. Edith became the first first lady to have a paid staff member, when Isabelle Hagner was transferred from her position as clerk in the federal government to help the first lady with scheduling, social affairs, and miscellaneous jobs.

Edith Roosevelt saw the White House as a national treasure and historic museum and took her charge over the building very seriously. She restored much of the mansion to its eighteenth-century style and procured antique furnishings for it. She hired the well-known architectural firm of McKim, Mead, and White to draw up blueprints for the task and to oversee the renovations. Congress was impressed with her plans and appropriated the necessary funds for the ambitious overhaul. So extensive were the renovations that the Roosevelts had to move out of the building in 1902. Edith oversaw all facets of the project, such as selecting new carpet, wallpaper, and furnishings, including paintings. She also ensured that the refurbishments would produce a more practical and livable building by emphasizing modern features such as new plumbing and lighting, as well as enlarging heavily used areas such as the cabinet and state dining rooms. She also had the old greenhouses torn down.

Edith unveiled the new White House to the nation in 1903, hosting a large reception to mark the event. She received praise from political leaders and the public alike. Edith was a popular first lady who managed to retain a degree of private life despite the public and press fascination with Roosevelt's presidency. Her socials were hugely popular, and the White House buzzed with action during her tenure, especially during the wedding of her stepdaughter, Alice, to Nicholas Longworth and the society debut of Edith's only daughter, Ethel.

Legacy

Edith looked forward to leaving the White House and returning to private life in 1909. As they prepared to vacate, however, a minor scandal erupted: She attempted to take with her a sofa she had purchased, but the press reported it as if the first lady was stealing White House furniture. Edith left the sofa behind but felt bitter about the incident.

Roosevelt, in turn, was reluctant to leave the White House and regretted an earlier pledge that he would not seek a third term. To satisfy his need for adventure in retirement, he went on safari to Africa and explored remote regions of the Brazilian jungles while Edith traveled to Europe. The former president also went on a speaking tour, and Edith helped him by editing his speeches. Roosevelt ultimately did run again, challenging his own party's president, William Howard Taft, in 1912 by helping form the Progressive or Bull Moose Party and running as its candidate. While campaigning in Milwaukee, he was shot in the chest by John Shrank Jr. In typical fashion, he did not want to see a physician or stop his campaign. It took the intervention of Edith, who had been attending the theater in New York when the shooting occurred, to change his mind. Rushing to his side, she announced, "I am the only one who can manage him"; after her arrival he finally followed the doctor's orders.

The campaign and a 1913 trip down the Amazon River nearly killed Roosevelt; by the outbreak of World War I his health was fading. Still, he sought permission to raise and command a volunteer force in the war, but President Woodrow Wilson denied his request. Edith opposed most of her husband's decisions and actions after he retired, from his safaris to his third-party campaign to his attempt to join the war.

Although Roosevelt never participated in the World War, his sons did, earning their father's approval. Archie Roosevelt was injured and in 1918 Quentin was killed in action. The former president died not long after his son, on January 5, 1919. Edith escaped her sorrow as she had done many times before, by traveling extensively and often alone to Europe and the Orient.

As a widow, Edith spent much of her time reading and participating in charitable activities, including the Needlework Guild, which made clothing for the needy. Back home at Sagamore Hill she was active in her local church and stayed involved in politics by joining a women's Republican club, later delivering a speech to the Women's National Republican Club that was carried on radio. She opposed prohibition, which had nothing to do with alcohol and everything to do with what she thought was a violation of personal freedoms. She also spoke out against Franklin Roosevelt's presidential campaign in 1932, despite his distant relation to her deceased husband. Edith did not approve of FDR's New Deal programs, which she saw as misguided and involving unnecessary government intervention. When Senator Vic Donahey of Ohio favorably compared the two Roosevelts, she publicly disagreed, stating that her husband was a true progressive because his "liberalism was in accord with our theories of democracy and personal liberty, and in no way resembled the politics of the present administration." Her words about the other Roosevelt were equally strong four years later, when she supported Alf Landon's 1936 campaign: "We expected Franklin Roosevelt to take us out of the mud when he went into office, but he has led us into the mire."

During Edith's active retirement, she wrote two books, *Cleared for Strange Ports,* a 1927 travelogue, and *American Backlogs,* a history of her family. In her last years three events slowed the former first lady: a broken hip; her son Kermit's suicide in 1943, which caused her great personal pain; and the death of Theodore Jr. in 1944. Edith Roosevelt died September 30, 1948, at the age of eighty-seven. *Life* magazine paid tribute to her as one of the "strongest-minded and strongest-willed presidential wives."

Bibliography

Morris, Sylvia Jukes. *Edith Kermit Roosevelt: Portrait of a First Lady.* New York: Coward, McCann & Geoghegan, 1980.

———. "Portrait of a First Lady." In Natalie A. Naylor, Douglas Brinkley, and John Allen Gable, eds., *Theodore Roosevelt: Many-Sided American.* Interlaken, NY: Interlaken, 1992.

Morrison, Elting E., and John Blum, eds. *Theodore Roosevelt's Letters.* 8 volumes. Cambridge: Harvard University Press, 1951–1954.

Roosevelt, Nicholas. *TR: The Man as I Knew Him.* New York: Dodd, Mead, 1967.

Roosevelt, Theodore. *Autobiography.* New York: Macmillan, 1913.

27

Helen Herron Taft

Born: June 2, 1861; Cincinnati, Ohio
Died: May 22, 1943; Washington, D.C.
President: William Howard Taft (1857–1930), Twenty-seventh President
Husband's Presidential Term: 1909–1913 (Republican)
Marriage: June 19, 1886; Cincinnati, Ohio
Children: Robert Alfonso (1889–1953); Helen Herron (1891–1987); Charles Phelps (1897–1983)

Early Years

Helen Herron was born on June 2, 1861, in Cincinnati, Ohio, into a wealthy and highly political family. Both sides boasted leading political figures and impressive political connections. Helen's mother, Harriet Collins, was the daughter of a congressman from New York. Helen's father, John Herron, was a member of the Ohio senate and a U.S. attorney who had been a college roommate of future president Benjamin Harrison. Helen grew up accustomed to politics as an intimate part of daily life and developed a strong attraction to political affairs.

Although few young women of affluent families in the mid-nineteenth century aspired to a career, Helen always dreamed of being a politician or lawyer and contemplated pursuing a career as a writer or as an art and music critic. She frequently read the legal books at her father's law office, but after visiting the White House with her family when she was seventeen, she knew she wanted to be a first lady. Helen was bold and restless, unconventional in her beliefs, and especially ambitious and aggressive for women in her day. She wanted a great deal from life, and this affected her choice of potential spouses; few suitors measured up to her high standards.

The fourth of eleven children, Helen was raised in Cincinnati and developed a fondness not only for politics but also classical music. She went to Miss Nourse's School, a prestigious school for girls also attended by William Howard Taft's sister. Then she enrolled in Miami University in Oxford, Ohio, where she studied literature, history, science, and German. Helen was always attracted to challenges and intellectual pursuits. With a few friends, she established a club for discussing politics and current issues. Among the guests she invited was William Taft, a graduate of Yale University and a friend. The young lawyer was impressed by his intelligent hostess.

Although the Tafts and the Herrons knew each other, William and Helen had not met until the winter of 1880 during a sledding party. Helen was eighteen at the time and Taft was beginning his legal career. They had also performed together at a community theater company. After coming together again in the discussion group in 1884, Taft and Helen began to date.

Marriage

Their courtship went through good times and bad. Taft was remarkably unperturbed by his sweetheart's opinionated ways and criticism of traditional roles for women. Still, in spite of Taft's relative open-mindedness, Helen balked at marriage, worrying that he would not take her views and intellect seriously, and she declined his initial proposal. It is hard to say why Helen was so reluctant, possibly because of her natural assertiveness or Taft's apparent lack of that quality.

Regardless, in 1885 she accepted his marriage proposal. Their friends and families were pleased with the union of this capable couple who showed so much promise. Recognizing his potential and pursuing her own ambition, she often encouraged him to consider a career in politics, even the presidency. Taft joked that one day they would make it to the White House because Helen would most likely end up with a presidential cabinet post. They married on June 19, 1886, and honeymooned in Europe. While in London, Helen wanted to attend a session of the House of Commons; using their impressive family connections, they asked a U.S. diplomat in London to secure tickets for them. When the diplomat instead obtained permission for them to see the Royal Mews, the horse stables and lands of the royal family, she was highly displeased. To Helen Taft, attending a political session was certainly appropriate for a honeymoon.

The marriage between "Nellie" and "Will" would be a happy, successful one. Taft not only tolerated but embraced his wife's seemingly limitless ambition, intensity, and outspokenness, all traits commonly viewed as undesirable for a wife in the late nineteenth century. He also appreciated her intelligence, and the two became intellectual partners. He came to rely on her advice and decisiveness, and she often directed their home life and finances and her husband's career moves.

Family Life

The Tafts had three children: a son named Robert, born in 1889, followed by a daughter, Helen, in 1891. In 1897 a third child, Charles, arrived. Helen found happiness in her children and her husband's successful career. His legal talents earned him several appointments, including justice on the Ohio Superior Court in 1887. William Howard Taft was content with his career progression; his only ambition was to remain a judge with the eventual possibility of a seat on the U.S. Supreme Court. Helen had loftier plans for his career.

She seems to have talked Taft into accepting the position of U.S. solicitor general in the Harrison administration. In fact, it was Helen who made the necessary political connections and promoted her husband to President Harrison. The position, reasoned Helen, would better permit Taft to enter the national political spotlight. In 1890 they moved to the capital city, and Helen was in her element. She loved Washington and became a star at its social and political events. She attended Harrison's New Year's Day reception in 1891 at the White House and often listened to House and Senate proceedings from the Capitol visitor's gallery. All the while she was making important political contacts for her husband.

Politics was a part of the Taft household despite Will Taft's coolness on the issue. The letters he and Helen exchanged always included political discussions, usually ending with his deferring to Helen. Helen worked with her husband to improve his public speaking skills and helped him overcome some of his natural shyness and nervousness. In 1892 President Harrison nominated Taft to the federal circuit court in their home state of Ohio. Taft seemed interested, but Helen opposed the position, believing it would remove him from the important political circles of Washington. She also seems to have been hesitant to leave the city she loved and all the intellectual and political stimulation it offered. Taft took the position, marking one of the few times Helen was not able to sway him in a career move. But she made the most of it, continuing her political activism. Helen became one of the most prominent women in Columbus, helping found a hospital, joining a women's book club, and becoming a leader in the city's orchestra by raising funds for the organization, promoting it, and even managing much of its operations. Helen also kept up her intellectual pursuits, attending lectures and the theater, taking art classes, and reading prolifically.

When William McKinley assumed the presidency, he offered his fellow Ohioan the governorship of the Philippines, with the understanding it would be followed by an appointment to the U.S. Supreme Court. Taft was charged with helping the new territory develop democratic institutions and retain its loyalty to the United States in the period after the Spanish-American War in 1898. Taft accepted with serious reservations, but was motivated by the enticement of the highest court of the land. Helen supported going, apparently because of the adventure the position promised. True to her expectations, the Philippines proved to be stimulating, challenging, and exotic. She loved her time there, especially the exposure to another culture, and read all she could on the country. She helped educate her husband on Filipino history and culture and also made sure the experience was an educational one for her children. Helen joined her husband on trips to China, Japan, and Hong Kong during his governorship, and she also traveled without him during this period. The Tafts lived grandly in the Malacanan Palace, supported by servants and ample public funding.

With his wife assisting him, Taft oversaw the construction of a system of roads and schools, a Western-style police force, and a civil service system modeled in part after the new system in the United States. His governorship was widely seen as a big success, and Helen Taft was partly responsible for this. Considering the times, she was impressively open to the local inhabitants, sharing her home with the public, visiting many Filipino villages and the other islands, and attempting to learn the local dialect and Spanish as well. She seems to have been rather nonchalant about the dangers and civil unrest surrounding the U.S. mission in the Philippines and accepted the challenges of her husband's post with enthusiasm, confidence, and optimism. Helen's strong exterior did, however, show signs of stress because of her parents' health problems during this time and her worry over her husband's condition. The governor's health had deteriorated, and for this and other reasons he resigned his post in 1901. Back in Cincinnati Taft was treated for numerous health problems, not the least being his considerable weight, well over 300 pounds.

When Theodore Roosevelt assumed the presidency after McKinley's assassination, he sent Taft to the Vatican as a presidential envoy. Although many political wives did not travel with their husbands, Helen Taft was an exception. Because their son Robert had scarlet fever, however, Helen was unable to join him until Robert recovered. Once in Italy, she visited Rome and had an audience with the pope. After Taft's business was concluded, the couple toured Europe, then revisited the Philippines, which was in the midst of an economic crisis and a severe cholera epidemic. Helen immediately went to work to help improve the country's social and public health conditions.

William Taft's easygoing manner was frequently taken advantage of by his aggressive, ambitious wife. Periodically throughout his life, Helen talked him out of job offers in the legal or judicial professions because she favored a political career for her husband. In 1902, for example, Taft was offered a seat on the Supreme Court, his career goal, but Helen dissuaded him from accepting it. He was eventually offered the position of secretary of war under Theodore Roosevelt in 1904. Helen liked the political power that came with the position, and she assumed the role of Taft's chief adviser. But she grew bored and frustrated with the hostessing and social calls expected of a Washington wife. Her boredom and longing to return to the Philippines were momentarily eased later that year when she accompanied Taft on a diplomatic mission to Panama, and the following year she summered in England with her children, without her husband. In 1907 she joined him on a diplomatic mission to Japan, where President Roosevelt had earlier negotiated the end to the Russo-Japanese War.

All this time Helen had been courting Roosevelt's favor, pushing her husband as his successor in the White House. The president had announced he would not seek another term, and Helen seized the opportunity to rally public and political support for her husband. Again, she talked him out of accepting a seat on the Supreme Court and met secretly with the president to gain his endorsement of Taft. For his part, Taft was not interested in the office or the rigors of a campaign. He had neither the ambition, demeanor, nor energy for a presidential campaign.

Taft golfed while Helen organized the campaign, taking it upon herself to draft and edit his speeches, and she pushed her reluctant husband into the race. She worried that his passivity would undermine his bid and the president's confidence in his chosen successor. Recognizing that the public was more supportive of Roosevelt and his legacy than it was of Taft, Helen worked to tie her husband politically to the president and to keep Roosevelt interested. The president even took to discussing matters with Helen rather than with Taft.

Presidency

William Taft won the 1908 presidential campaign, in no small part because of his wife's efforts and the popularity of the sitting president, who chose him as his successor. Taft recognized the role of "his Nellie" in his political career and credited her with being his top adviser and strategist. He was tolerant of her ambition, restlessness, and even her criticism of him. They agreed on many issues, but when they disagreed, as in the case of his support for prohibition and her opposition to it, she confronted her husband about his views. Taft never wanted to be president, and perhaps no better example exists of a spouse acting to put her husband in the White House than the case of Helen and William Taft. Helen hoped to be first lady and a part of the presidency much more than Taft ever wanted the office for himself. She was the politician in the family.

Throughout Taft's political career, Helen remained passionate about politics. Although she enjoyed serving as White House hostess and always found political socials appealing, Helen was bored with the company of political wives and the social gossip of political receptions. She preferred debating the issues of the day with the men and freely joined the fray while in the White House. Unlike many of her predecessors who were equally influential in their husbands' lives and presidencies, Helen did not attempt to mask her influence. She spoke of it publicly with reporters and in an article published in the *Ladies' Home Journal* around the time of the inauguration.

Not surprisingly, her gruff manner and unconventional ways became fodder for Taft's political enemies. It did not take her long to anger the Washington establishment and the nation: She helped plan the inauguration, then chose to break tradition and ride alongside her husband on inaugural day. Because of weather, the Tafts were forced to move the festivities inside to the Senate chambers, and at one of the receptions Helen's hat caught fire after brushing against a gas lamp.

The firestorm of Helen Taft's first ladyship began quickly. She was eager to move into the White House and immediately made her presence known in staffing changes there. Helen had the mansion cleaned and rearranged, hiring women to do the work because she felt they were better at it than men. The first lady was famous for excessive demands on the staff.

Helen's first ladyship was struck a blow, however, when, only months into the Taft presidency, she suffered a stroke while taking a ship down the Potomac to Mount Vernon. The first lady lost the use of her right arm and leg and some of her facial muscles; her speech became limited. The president was severely shaken by his wife's failing health; they were close, and he had come to rely on her. During her long rehabilitation, her husband was by her side. He spent many hours reading to her and was patient and caring while helping to nurse her back to health. She eventually regained her speech. During her convalescence her daughters and sister assisted her by presiding over White House social events, but Helen wanted to resume her role, and did so roughly one year after her stroke. By 1911 she had returned to an active schedule and hosted many events, including the Tafts' silver anniversary, celebrated in the White House with more than a thousand guests.

Helen Taft had always been a hard worker, and the demands she placed upon herself probably contributed to her condition. The stroke not only depleted the first lady's energy, for she never fully recovered her strength and drive, but it also affected Taft's presidency. Without his wife, Taft's indecisiveness and passivity undermined his effectiveness, and he found it difficult to focus on his work during Helen's ordeal.

In spite of her stroke, Helen retained her interest in politics. She attended her husband's political meetings, including cabinet meetings; made sure she was briefed by his aides; and regularly attended sessions of the House and Senate. Helen was perhaps the first presidential spouse to court the media openly, granting reporters interviews and freely answering their questions, largely unheard of for women of the day, much less first ladies. In particular, she worked with female reporters, both to gain their support and to promote the progress of women in that profession. A strong supporter of women's rights and access to higher education, the first lady made her positions known.

Helen obtained the first automobile fleet for the presidency, replacing horses and buggies, and she brought many theater performances to the White House, starting the custom of having such entertainment at the conclusion of formal dinners. Her support of the arts carried over into her visibility in the Washington arts community; she attended many plays, operatic performances, and the symphony and helped establish a bandstand in the city. She redecorated the mansion, filling the building with flowers and plants and offering a regal touch to her first ladyship and White House social affairs. Her botanical interests also led to her promoting the planting of cherry trees along the Potomac. So committed was the first lady to this beautification plan, a gift from a Japanese scientist, that when the first group of two thousand trees succumbed to disease, she had three thousand more delivered and planted.

Helen Taft also played a role in her husband's political staffing decisions and cabinet appointments. But for all her intelligence and genuine interest in politics, Helen Taft could be petty and vindictive. These traits often clouded her political judgment and tainted the advice she offered the president. For instance, she was prone to firing or refusing to appoint individuals with whom she did not get along. One particularly fateful example of this was when Helen blocked the diplomatic appointment of Nicholas Longworth, Alice Roosevelt's husband, because of her hatred of Alice. This act was one factor that contributed to former president Roosevelt's disenchantment with his successor. Ultimately, Roosevelt would oppose his onetime political ally and seek the presidency as the Progressive Party candidate, which split the Republican vote, cost Taft the election, and helped Democrat Woodrow Wilson into office in 1912. The rift between Roosevelt and Taft tore the Republican Party apart, further limiting Taft's effectiveness in the latter stages of his presidency.

Although her husband was content to step down after a single term, Helen Taft loved the presidency, the White House, and the first ladyship. She did not want to leave office and pushed him to run for reelection. Before leaving office, Helen donated her inaugural gown to help support the now famous first lady gown exhibit in the Smithsonian's Museum of American History.

Legacy

In retirement William Howard Taft found happiness in New Haven, Connecticut, teaching law at Yale. Helen quickly emerged as one of New Haven's leading citizens. She remained active in the arts and theater and continued to read on a wide variety of subjects. She was also keenly interested in the events of World War I and volunteered her time to the Red Cross. In 1914 she published her memoirs, *Recollections of*

Full Years, the first presidential spouse to do so. Because of Helen's successful management of the Taft finances and her wise investments of the proceeds of her book, they enjoyed a comfortable retirement, indulging Helen's passion for international travel with trips to Bermuda, Panama, England (where Helen and her husband met King George V and Queen Mary), and Rome to meet the pope.

The presidency of Warren Harding finally allowed Taft to fulfill his dream of joining the U.S. Supreme Court, when he was appointed chief justice in 1921. Having achieved her goal of putting her husband in the presidency, Helen by this time supported his decision to accept a seat on the Court. During this time she remained active in politics and joined the Colonial Dames, a society dedicated to historic preservation and the nation's patriotic legacy. In 1925, two years after joining the organization, she served as its honorary vice president. She was also named honorary vice president of the Girl Scouts of America.

Although being chief justice brought him great pleasure, Taft's health continued to decline partly because of his ballooning weight, which resulted in two heart attacks. Helen's efforts to get her husband to lose weight were unsuccessful, and his health finally failed in 1930; he died in March that year.

The widow moved back to Washington, where she followed politics (opposing Franklin Roosevelt's New Deal legislation in the 1930s) and remained close to her children. Her son Robert had a successful political career, becoming a U.S. senator from Ohio, and her daughter and namesake earned a law degree from George Washington University and a Ph.D. from Yale and became president of Bryn Mawr College.

Helen Taft died on May 22, 1943, at her home in Washington. She was the first presidential spouse to be buried at Arlington National Cemetery. Other than Helen, only Jacqueline Kennedy has received this honor. Helen Taft was a most nontraditional woman and was the first woman to attend the swearing-in ceremony of a Supreme Court justice. She traveled widely, insisting on being at her husband's side in all his political tasks and trips. She was also remarkably open about her political ambition and views. Taft recognized his wife's role in his career and attributed his success to her. Indeed, had it not been for Helen, it is doubtful he would ever have become president. And had she not been limited by a stroke, she would almost certainly have been one of the most active and influential first ladies in history. Nevertheless, she left behind a rich legacy, including the capital city's cherry trees; their blossoming has since become a famous annual spectacle in the city.

Bibliography

Butt, Archie. *Taft and Roosevelt: The Intimate Letters of Archie Butt, Military Aide.* 2 volumes. New York: Doubleday, 1930.

Manners, William. *TR and Will: A Friendship That Split the Republican Party.* New York: Harcourt Brace Jovanovich, 1969.

Pringle, Henry F. *The Life and Times of William Howard Taft.* 2 volumes. New York: Farrar & Rinehart, 1939.

Ross, Ishbel. *An American Family: The Tafts—1678 to 1964.* New York: World Publishing, 1964.

Taft, Helen H. *Recollections of Full Years.* New York: Dodd, Mead, 1914.

28

Ellen Louise Axson Wilson

Born: May 15, 1860; Savannah, Georgia
Died: August 6, 1914; Washington, D.C.
President: Woodrow Wilson (1856–1924), Twenty-eighth President
Husband's Presidential Term: 1913–1921 (Democrat)
Marriage: June 24, 1885; Savannah, Georgia
Children: Margaret Woodrow (1886–1944); Jessie Woodrow (1887–1933); Eleanor Randolph (1889–1967)

Early Years

Ellen Axson was born in Savannah, Georgia, on May 15, 1860, but grew up in the town of Rome, Georgia. Her father, Reverend Samuel E. Axson, was a Presbyterian minister who also served as a chaplain during the Civil War for a Confederate unit from Georgia. Ellen's mother, Margaret Jane Hoyt Axson, was the daughter of a Presbyterian minister and had attended the Greensboro Female College. She died in 1881 while giving birth, and Ellen took care of the newborn child and her other, younger siblings after her mother's death. Her father took his wife's death harder than the rest of the family and seems to have suffered a breakdown from which he never recovered.

In spite of this tragedy, Ellen's youth was rather normal, defined by religion and the conventions of southern etiquette. As a young woman she seems to have been refined and easygoing. Ellen was also very bright and an independent thinker, traits her father did not approve of fully. As a student at the Female Seminary in Rome, Ellen befriended like-minded young women who reinforced her views. Although she remained religious, she questioned some of the teachings of the Bible and the Presbyterian faith and showed interest in women's equality. In fact, as a student she was so critical of mankind's oppression of women that her friends nicknamed her "Ellie the manhater." The young woman also grew increasingly ambitious and expressed a desire for a career, which was considered rather unbecoming for a southern lady. Throughout her life Ellen would demonstrate a unique blending of ambition and independent thought with southern tradition and Christianity. In 1884 Ellen pursued her passion for painting by enrolling in art classes at the New York Art Students' League.

Marriage

Ellen had become reacquainted with Woodrow Wilson, who was practicing law in Atlanta, when he visited the small town in April 1883 and attended Axson's church. Wilson's uncle was an elder of the church, and in fact, Woodrow and Ellen had first met when they were children.

Wilson apparently was immediately attracted to the young woman. The two became engaged later that year, but Ellen nearly ended the engagement when her father died suddenly; he may have committed suicide. Her fiancée talked her out of breaking the engagement and consoled her as she mourned.

Although he encouraged Ellen to remain committed to the engagement, Wilson was attending graduate school at Johns Hopkins and wanted to wait until he had earned his degree before marrying. While he was completing his education, they exchanged frequent letters that reveal the closeness of their relationship. Wilson referred to Ellen as "Miss Ellie Lou" and was very much in love with her. Ellen called her fiancée "Tommy" (his first name was Thomas). The two eventually married in 1885, and with her inheritance from her father, the young couple was comfortable financially.

Family Life

Ellen Wilson's married life was filled with the demands of a growing family. They had three daughters within five years: Margaret, born in 1886; Jessie, born the following year; and Eleanor, in 1889. Ellen's two younger brothers also lived with them for a while.

After earning his Ph.D. from Johns Hopkins, Wilson joined the faculties of Bryn Mawr in Pennsylvania and Wesleyan in Connecticut. During his academic tenure, Ellen proofread her husband's articles and books and discussed intellectual matters with him; later, during his political career, Ellen would continue her supportive role by editing his speeches and serving as his sounding board. She frequently gave him advice, helped him learn German, and translated academic texts for him. In her free time she participated in a host of activities. Ellen was an avid gardener, took cooking classes, and pursued her love of painting, enrolling in the Lyme Summer School of Art in Connecticut. Wilson enrolled her in 1908 in an effort to lift her spirits after the 1905 death of her beloved brother Eddie (and Wilson's affair with another woman in 1907). She painted landscapes and portraits, among them famous political leaders such as William Gladstone and George Washington. A member of Pen and Brush, an artistic guild in New York, and a group of women artists, Ellen entered numerous art shows and received positive reviews. In her fifties she participated in an exhibit in New York in 1911, had a one-woman show in 1912 in Chicago, and another in 1913 in Philadelphia that featured fifty landscapes—of which she sold twenty-four. At times she concealed her identity, showing her work under an assumed name.

Like her husband, Ellen was a complex individual with a multifaceted personality. Although she had been rather progressive in college, she was a somewhat traditional wife. She sewed her family's clothing and was responsible for raising the three Wilson girls, instilling in them the value of an education and a love of reading. Yet she remained a southerner at heart. Ellen was not fond of Yankees and did not want her children to be born north of the Mason-Dixon line. Both Wilsons were segregationists, and Ellen even traveled back to Georgia to give birth to her first two children, although she was unable to leave Connecticut in 1889 for the birth of her last child, in part because of health problems.

Woodrow Wilson admired intelligent women and took great comfort in the strength of his mother, wife, and daughters. During his political career he often excused himself from the expected postdinner conversation with men, preferring the company of his wife. Yet the social reformer who felt that women were intellectually equal to men also believed that women were fundamentally different in emotional ways. He opposed equal rights for women while seeking his wife's advice on the most pressing political and social issues of the day. It was also Ellen who exposed him to art and cultural refinement.

Wilson's career took him from Bryn Mawr and Wesleyan to Princeton, where he became a leader on the faculty and, in 1902, was elected president of the university. In 1890 Wilson had received offers from both Princeton and the University of Illinois; Ellen advised him to take the Princeton position but to use the Illinois offer to improve his salary and contract benefits at the elite New Jersey school. Wilson would later credit her for his success at Princeton. He initiated a series of sweeping reforms that enhanced the reputation and quality of the institution. For her part, Ellen was a reluctant first lady of the university, but she rose to the challenge, emerging as a respected public figure on campus and a highly capable hostess. She renovated the presidential home at Princeton and established a garden on the grounds.

In 1912 William Jennings Bryan visited the university on a speaking tour. Ellen recognized the potential benefit of having her husband host the leader of the Democratic Party and immediately telegraphed him at the Atlanta conference he was attending, urging him to return in time for Bryan's arrival. The two men began an important political relationship, and Bryan was impressed with Ellen as well.

Although Wilson's public life was not necessarily difficult for her, Ellen was a somewhat private woman who was never completely comfortable with public attention. In 1905 her brother and his wife and child drowned, and that same year she suffered through an illness, one of many that caused her health to decline. But perhaps most painful to Ellen was her husband's infatuation with Mary Allen Hulbert Peck, a recently separated married woman. This affair represented a pattern in Wilson's life and a recurrent problem in the Wilson marriage.

Wilson's success at Princeton launched his political career, and in 1910 he ran for governor of New Jersey. The race and ensuing demands of the office drained Wilson, as he was prone to overwork, and his health began to wane around this time. Ellen was her husband's strength during his governorship and took care of him during his illnesses. She was surprised to find that she liked being first lady of the

Garden State, granting interviews and becoming an active, visible first lady. She functioned as the honorary leader of New Jersey's charity aid society, headed numerous women's groups, and was a patron of the arts. As her husband's political adviser, Ellen toured and inspected public institutions. When a minor scandal erupted in 1912 over her supposed support for women's right to smoke, she published a rebuttal of the allegations.

Presidency

In 1912 Wilson campaigned for the Democratic nomination for president; he won on the forty-sixth ballot, aided by William Jennings Bryan's support. The split in the Republican Party ensured his election. When the couple assumed the White House in 1913, Ellen immediately made her presence known, refurbishing the living quarters and other parts of the Executive Mansion. Although she found her new home rather unspectacular and gloomy, sprucing it up with flowers, she was not intimidated by the challenges of the first ladyship or the capital. As she had done in New Jersey, Ellen found that she liked being first lady, in contrast to her earlier tendencies toward introversion.

Unlike many of her predecessors, Ellen Wilson did not offer a full social calendar. Neither she nor her husband was fond of social events, and they downplayed them in the White House. The Wilsons were notoriously tight when it came to such activities, and they were fiscally conservative. The first lady held a limited round of teas, dinners, and receptions, and she observed the Sabbath, not permitting any entertaining on Sundays. Even though she was uninterested in the latest fashions and Washington social scene, Ellen proved to be a competent hostess. She also planned her daughter Jessie's wedding in 1913 but was growing weak by the end of the year. The first lady had Bright's disease, a degenerative kidney condition, and the following year she injured herself in a fall. With that injury, her worsening kidney disorder, and tuberculosis, Ellen was confined to bed for a time. By the middle of 1914, her personal physician moved into the White House. Her illnesses affected her husband's presidency, as he found himself unable to focus during her ordeal. The president spent much time by her side; so deeply had he come to depend on her that he ignored many of the pressing duties of the office, including the rising hostilities in Europe.

Despite her declining health, Ellen undertook many activities as first lady and planned another daughter's wedding. She was the honorary president of the Southern Industrial Association, and as she had done in New Jersey, she toured and inspected public institutions. The first lady championed improved working conditions for employees of the Postal Service and Government Printing Office and advocated a range of humanitarian issues, including educational opportunities for poor and rural children and some women's issues. Ellen pushed to have women's restrooms installed in public buildings and offices; however, she did not support the most prominent women's issue of the day: the right to vote. Although Ellen was progressive in her thinking, she was also very much the product of her upbringing and retained many traditional views. Because her husband did not support women's suffrage, even if Ellen had believed in it, it is doubtful she would have stated so publicly.

She also joined the District of Columbia's national Civic Federation, an organization that worked to promote better conditions for poor blacks living in the capital city. Ellen soon emerged as a leader in this cause, touring the city's slums and building support in Congress for addressing the issue. She wisely invited members of Congress along on her tours of Washington's worst neighborhoods and was the mother of a bill nicknamed in her honor to improve the city's housing conditions. The slum clearance bill she championed was passed by Congress on the day of her death, August 6, 1914.

Legacy

On her deathbed, Ellen asked her attending physician, Cary Grayson, to take care of the president for her. She also wanted her husband to remarry. The president was at her side when she died, and he fell into a deep depression after her death. In his grief he poured himself into his work, admitting he would not have been president had it not been for Ellen. She was a close partner in her husband's political career and was perhaps the first of the first ladies to directly initiate public policy on several issues. She remains one of the foremost humanitarians to hold the office.

Bibliography

Elliott, Margaret Randolph. *My Aunt Louisa and Woodrow Wilson.* Chapel Hill: University of North Carolina Press, 1944.
Link, Arthur S., ed. *The Papers of Woodrow Wilson.* 69 volumes. Princeton, NJ: Princeton University Press, 1966–1994.

McAdoo, Eleanor Randolph Wilson, ed. *The Priceless Gift: The Love Letters of Woodrow Wilson and Ellen Axson Wilson.* New York: McGraw-Hill, 1962.

McAdoo, Eleanor Randolph Wilson, and Margaret Y. Gaffey. *The Woodrow Wilsons.* New York: Macmillan, 1937.

Saunders, Frances Wright. *First Lady Between Two Worlds: Ellen Axson Wilson.* Chapel Hill: University of North Carolina Press, 1985.

29

Edith Bolling Galt Wilson

Born: October 15, 1872; Wytheville, Virginia
Died: December 28, 1961; Washington, D.C.
President: Woodrow Wilson (1856–1924), Twenty-eighth President
Husband's Presidential Term: 1913–1921 (Democrat)
Marriage: First: April 30, 1896, to Norman Galt; Wytheville, Virginia
    (widowed 1908). Second: December 18, 1915, to Woodrow Wilson;
    Washington, D.C.
Children: None

Early Years

Edith Bolling was the seventh of eleven children born to Sallie White and William Holcombe Bolling. The Bollings were a well-to-do southern family, and Edith had a privileged upbringing in her plantation home. The family's lineage could be traced to Pocahontas, who married the English colonist John Rolfe.

Her parents were overly protective of their daughter, and Edith rarely left the family home. This was somewhat unusual for the household: Her other sisters were sent away to school, whereas she was educated at home until age fourteen, when she went to Martha Washington

College to study music. Edith did not do well in school, however, returning home after one year. In 1889 Edith attended Powell's finishing school in Richmond. A belle by sixteen, she was courted by many suitors. Edith was a tall, buxom woman who was known more for beauty than for educational pursuits.

Marriage

Edith's sister, Alice Gertrude Gordon, lived in Washington and had married into the Galt family of prosperous jewelers. One of the Galt sons, Norman, became romantically interested in Edith. After a four-year courtship, they were married in 1896. Norman Galt's business succeeded and made the couple very wealthy; however, Edith never felt close to her husband and the marriage was not a loving one. Seven years into the marriage Edith became pregnant, but her infant son died only days after birth. She never had another child. Norman Galt died suddenly a few years later, in 1908. Edith inherited the family jewelry business; she hired a manager to run the operations but remained involved personally in the business.

After Galt's death, Edith toured Europe, then returned to Washington where she became rather well known and visible driving her new automobile around town. Her sister knew Cary Grayson, President Wilson's personal physician, and among Edith's friends was Helen Bones, the president's cousin. Wilson's wife, Ellen, had died a few months earlier and the president was still grieving when he was formally introduced to Edith in March 1915 at a White House tea. Given his loneliness and his tendency to gravitate toward strong women, he immediately became interested in the wealthy, independent-minded widow. He invited her back to the White House for dinner later that month. When they were together, they talked happily for hours and Wilson read his guest poetry and literature. The president also took her for rides around the capital in his presidential carriage.

Only two months after their meeting, Wilson proposed to Edith. She declined, apparently feeling it was too sudden (and it was not uncommon at that time for a woman to turn down a suitor's first proposal). Some of the president's aides tried to dissuade him from marrying, concerned that the public would think it was too soon after Ellen Wilson's death, and they were looking as well toward his reelection campaign in 1916. Also looming was the specter of a world war; only two days after Wilson proposed to Edith, the Germans torpedoed the *Lusitania* and the United States was pulled ever closer to the conflict.

The president was also trying to put behind him his affair with Mary Peck shortly before Ellen's death.

Even during their engagement, Woodrow Wilson told Edith war secrets, and she quickly emerged as his leading adviser and closest confidante. Her surviving letters reflect her intimate knowledge of the details of the war. After a longer delay than he wished, the couple married on December 18, 1915. The marriage proved not to be the political liability his aides had feared, and Edith's company improved the president's spirits greatly.

Family Life

Throughout their short life together, Edith and Wilson were inseparable. His letters and poetry reflect the deep love they shared; after her cool first marriage, Edith found happiness in her partnership with Wilson. They regularly discussed current issues, the war, and matters pertaining to his presidency. Wilson, who had been opposed to women's suffrage, changed his position during the course of their marriage. Edith calmed him during the most tense hours of the war, nursed him through his declining health, and improved his diet as well as his public appearance and image. Edith also managed the family and White House mail and the Wilson household.

To assist her in the White House, the first lady hired a personal secretary, Edith Benham (later succeeded by E. B. Helm). She surprised herself with how much she enjoyed politics, for as a young woman and in her first marriage, she had shown no interest in politics.

Presidency

It had been customary in the White House for the president and first lady to have separate bedrooms; Wilson continued this practice with his first wife. With Edith, however, Wilson broke tradition, and the two shared a bedroom. Wilson admitted that he needed Edith with him during his presidency. Edith was often at her husband's side and was part of Wilson's inner circle, known as "the Inquiry." She was also an important part of his 1916 reelection campaign, although she was targeted for criticism by his rivals in the Republican Party.

The United States entered the war in April 1917. Edith helped him decode military messages and gave him advice on dealing with Congress. The Wilsons purchased thrift clothing in a gesture to encourage the nation to save for the wartime effort, and Edith organized a Red

Cross unit at the White House. The first lady grazed sheep on the White House lawn to control the grass and donated the wool to the U.S. cause. She was a well-known figure during the war, raising money, sewing uniforms, and becoming a symbol of support. Edith even joined her husband on his trip to Paris for the peace talks that resulted in the signing of the Treaty of Versailles on June 28, 1919. While in Europe, she toured France, Italy, and England with him and is thought to have advised Wilson on the peace accords.

During the war Edith was asked by the shipping board to name eighty-eight ships confiscated from Germany, along with some new ships. She accepted the challenge and chose a variety of appropriate names for the ships, naming, for instance, the largest ship *Leviathan* and the smallest *Minnow*. She named ships after rivers, lakes, and mountains, as well as for cities and presidents. She even consulted a Native American reference book in selecting Indian names for some of the ships.

Because of the war, the White House was not expected to offer a full social calendar; moreover, Woodrow Wilson did not enjoy entertaining, so Edith did not do as much hostessing as many of her predecessors. When she did preside over White House social events, however, she did so successfully (although she raised eyebrows when she failed to curtsy properly upon meeting the queen of England). She also worked to preserve many artifacts and pieces in the White House.

Edith could be quite demanding and critical of her husband's aides. She made it known that she did not care for Joe Tumulty, Wilson's personal secretary, and worked behind the scenes to limit his influence. She could also be spiteful toward those she perceived as her enemies, such as the aides who had tried to persuade the president not to marry her; she even pushed her husband to fire some. She was somewhat overprotective of the president as well. In all fairness, however, Wilson had a tendency to overwork and his health was fragile, as he was ill from influenza and other maladies in the White House; her efforts were thus both good and bad in this respect.

Wilson had fathered the League of Nations, but in spite of his success in Europe, he was unable to gain Republican support in the Senate to ratify the treaty and U.S. membership in the League. Wilson refused to compromise by adding provisions to protect U.S. sovereignty and set off in September 1919 on a nationwide, whistle-stop tour to rally public support for the League. During the tour Edith was unable to get him to rest. After a speech in Pueblo, Colorado, only a few weeks into the trip, the president experienced headaches, fatigue, and a physical breakdown. The tour was canceled and the president returned to Washington, where he suffered a stroke on October 2.

The full extent of Wilson's incapacitation remains a point of contention, but the president's doctors, backed by his wife, felt that the president's mental faculties were strong enough that he should stay in power. From October until the new year, Woodrow Wilson remained largely bedridden, out of sight and reach of the public, press, and even his staff. During this time Edith served as his liaison, meeting with top aides and department heads, relaying messages back and forth, and seeing that the president's decisions were assigned and carried out. She carried documents and information between the president and his staff and screened his visitors. The secretary of state, Robert Lansing, chaired the cabinet meetings without the president; Edith, apparently for personal reasons, failed to work with or support Secretary Lansing. The situation created quite a stir among the press and especially the president's critics. Republicans and journalists complained of "Mrs. Wilson's regency" and the "petticoat government" and spoke critically of the Wilsons as "presidentress" and "first man."

The full extent of Edith Wilson's actions may never be known, but she certainly acted with considerable discretion and power. At the time, the Constitution lacked a clear provision for presidential disability, and both Wilsons felt that the vice president, Thomas Riley Marshall, was a political liability and too weak to take over. In her memoirs written in 1939, however, Edith claimed she "never made a single decision regarding the disposition of public affairs. The only decision that was mine was what was important and what was not." Edith referred to her functions during the president's recuperation as her "stewardship." Nevertheless, both the first lady and the president were too restrictive in permitting access to him during the crisis, and much of the business of government went unattended.

The motion to ratify the Treaty of Versailles failed in the Senate, and in 1921 the United States simply declared the war with Germany over. Wilson, bitter and disillusioned, never fully recovered from his stroke; he was often highly emotional and disturbed and unable to think coherently. Although Edith wanted him to remain president and even to seek a third term, he was not renominated in 1920.

Legacy

Woodrow Wilson presided over the close of the "war to end all wars" and is still considered one of the nation's greatest presidents. Yet he left office in 1921 damaged by his stroke and the scandal surrounding his final years in office, and angry with the U.S. failure to support the League of Nations. He died three years later, in 1924. Edith remained so bitter over the foundering of the League of Nations that she refused to permit Henry Cabot Lodge, the Republican who led the fight against ratification of the treaty, to attend Wilson's funeral.

Edith remained active in politics and a visible force in the nation's capital for years to come. In 1928 she spoke at the Democratic National Convention in Houston and again attended her party's convention in 1932. Although she campaigned for Democratic nominee Franklin D. Roosevelt, she remained cool to his New Deal plan for moving the country out of the Great Depression. Many years later, in 1961, she was invited by John F. Kennedy to join his inaugural procession. She was eighty-nine when she died later that year, on December 28, 1961, the anniversary of her husband's death.

Edith Wilson is remembered as one of the most controversial and powerful of all first ladies. She has been called the "secret president" and "the first woman to run the government." Ironically, her pivotal position in her husband's presidency during his incapacitation occurred one year before the passage of the Nineteenth Amendment of the Constitution, granting women the right to vote. Edith was ahead of her time and continues to generate controversy over the role she played. Regardless, she was a gifted and capable woman who was her husband's closest political ally during their nine years of marriage.

Bibliography
Hatch, Alden. *Edith Bolling Wilson: First Lady Extraordinary.* New York: Dodd, Mead, 1961.
Ross, Ishbel. *Power with Grace: The Life Story of Mrs. Woodrow Wilson.* New York: Putnam's, 1975.
Shactman, Tom. *Edith and Woodrow.* New York: Putnam's, 1981.
Wilson, Edith Bolling. *My Memoir.* Indianapolis, IN: Bobbs-Merrill, 1938.

30

Florence Kling Harding

Born: August 15, 1860; Marion, Ohio
Died: November 21, 1924; Marion, Ohio
President: Warren G. Harding (1865–1923), Twenty-ninth President
Husband's Presidential Term: 1921–1923 (Republican)
Marriage: First: 1880 to Henry DeWolfe; Marion, Ohio (divorced 1886). Second: July 8, 1891, to Warren Harding; Marion, Ohio
Children: First marriage: Eugene Marshall (1880–1915). Second marriage: None

---

Early Years

The Klings were the leading family of Marion, Ohio. Amos Kling, originally from Lancaster, Pennsylvania, was a wealthy banker with ample real estate holdings in town. His wife, Louisa Bouton Kling, also came from a prosperous family; she was a sickly woman who became incapacitated by her weakness. She had had a formal education and encouraged the same for her daughter, but Florence's father was her mentor. A strict and demanding businessman, Amos Kling could be difficult. He pushed his daughter to succeed and tutored her in business practices, taking her to his bank and offering her opportunities to work in the financial field. This was unusual training for a young girl of the times, but Florence appears to have both enjoyed and had a knack for business.

Florence was also less than typical in her appearance and pastimes. She took after her father and was fiercely independent; a physically strong and imposing young woman, she was a skilled equestrienne who even won a riding contest. She also loved skating, bicycling, and—much to the chagrin of her father—the company of the town's mischievous and poor boys. But Florence had another side to her. Her musical talent, which she appears to have inherited from her mother, took her to the Cincinnati Conservatory of Music, where she distinguished herself in piano and developed a love of opera.

Marriage

One of Florence's friends was Henry "Pete" Atherton DeWolfe, by whom she became pregnant at age nineteen. She eloped with young DeWolfe in March 1880 against the wishes of her family, and Florence and Pete moved to a nearby town, where she gave birth to a son named Marshall. The marriage did not work out; Florence had no patience for DeWolfe, who was an alcoholic and a failure as a provider. On June 12, 1886, Florence filed for divorce and left her husband. In another bold move, she did not return to her family's home but chose to live alone with her young son and earn her own living. She moved back to Marion and supported herself as a piano instructor. When the divorce was granted, she took back her maiden name. Florence's tyrannical father remained furious with his "wild" daughter and refused to reconcile with her, but her former father-in-law, Simon DeWolfe, felt compelled to provide her with financial support during this difficult time.

Warren Harding had moved to Marion as a teenager. It is unclear how and when the two met because Florence burned much of their correspondence after Harding's death. One account suggests that they met at a Methodist church (although the Hardings were Baptists); another story has them passing by chance on the street. In both accounts, however, it is Florence who wanted to date the younger Warren, five years her junior. The two were an unusual match in more ways than their age difference. Harding was somewhat undisciplined and dated many attractive women. Florence was a hardworking woman not known for her physical attractiveness. What they shared was ambition. Harding had purchased a newspaper, the *Marion Star,* and Florence had plans bigger than what her first husband or her current life offered.

Florence's father objected to their union. He worked against Harding's business interests and at one point even threatened to kill his daughter's beau. The two went ahead with their plans for marriage, but Amos remained a problem, calling Harding epithets in reference to a rumor the Hardings had a black ancestor and labeling his daughter a "floozy." Warren's father, too, opposed the marriage, apparently because of Florence's age and divorce. The couple were married on July 8, 1891, in spite of the troubled courtship, and moved into Warren's home. Amos Kling did not attend the wedding.

Family Life

Florence and Harding never had children of their own, and Marshall, her son from the previous marriage, was often with relatives who helped raise the child. Kling eventually reconciled his differences with his daughter some fifteen years after the wedding. The marriage was more of a business partnership than a loving relationship; it always lacked warmth, and Harding grew tired of what he saw as his wife's constant nagging. This complaint appears to be valid, as Florence was excessive in trying to control and mother her husband. But Harding's affairs contributed to their difficulties as well. Saying that she found the tradition too limiting, she even refused to wear her wedding band.

An adventurous, outgoing individual, Florence Harding lived a nontraditional life. Donning helmet and goggles, she was among the first civilians to fly in an airplane. She regularly attended the theater, loved musicals, and developed a taste for a new form of entertainment: the movies. A lover of animals, she participated in an animal rescue charity and supported organizations working for animals; her dog, Laddie Boy, was usually at her side.

Despite the problems in their marriage, "the duchess," as her husband called her, devoted much of her life to her husband's career. At first it was his newspaper, where she worked as circulation manager. Florence handled the business end of the paper, leaving Warren to focus on the editorial aspects. She initiated a new delivery system, using young newspaper carriers, and was prudent with finances. Many of the surviving documents about the newspaper are written in her hand, and it appears she was a competent, efficient manager. Under her leadership the paper's circulation increased markedly, and the *Star* went from a weekly to a daily. The paper's success helped launch Harding's political career.

Florence had mixed views about her husband's budding career in politics. On the one hand she was ambitious, but on the other she questioned her husband's intellectual ability to succeed in the field. Florence, possibly before anyone else, recognized Warren Harding's limitations. He was lazy, continued to cheat on his wife, and had a fondness for the bottle. One object of Harding's affection was Carrie Fulton Phillips, a friend of Florence's who accompanied the couple on a trip to Europe. Several of Harding's love letters to Carrie surfaced after his death. Moreover, neither Florence nor Harding had good health. Florence had kidney problems throughout her life and may even have had a kidney removed shortly after the turn of the century; she also had a weak heart.

Despite these problems and the rumors that Florence was behind all her husband's successes, Harding's career advanced. He was elected to the Ohio senate in 1899 and became lieutenant governor in 1904. Florence was active in his political career, helping manage his campaigns and advising him on issues. In 1910 he lost his bid for governor of Ohio and contemplated leaving politics, but Florence talked him out of it, pushed him back into the political scene, and even courted important contacts for him. Her work paid off when Harding was elected to the U.S. Senate in 1914. Once again, however, Florence was concerned about her husband's marginal abilities and her lack of exposure to society and political hostessing. She also worried about the cost of living and entertaining in the nation's capital.

Florence accompanied her husband to Washington in 1915. She had the good fortune to befriend Evalyn Walsh McLean, wife of the owner of the *Washington Post* and *Cincinnati Enquirer* who was a skilled hostess and one of the city's foremost socialites. The two became good friends; Evalyn introduced Florence to Washington society and taught her how to entertain. This did not prevent the "duchess" from committing a serious faux pas when meeting European royalty: She failed to curtsy, then extended her hand in greeting. The incident created a minor stir in the capital, but the senator's wife defended herself by saying that when in America the monarchs ought to adhere to American customs. Florence and Evalyn shared a love of animals and a fascination with the occult and even vacationed together. Both went to Madame Marcia Champrey, an astrologer who did readings for them. Apparently, however, the astrologer predicted Harding's untimely death, and the already anxious Florence became even more protective of her husband.

During the war, because of the anti-German mood of the nation, Florence denied her German heritage, claiming Dutch ancestry. She joined other wives in the Ladies of the Senate Club in working for the war cause, participating in the Red Cross, and working at Union Station along with other leading women of Washington such as Alice Roosevelt, Eleanor Roosevelt, and Edith Wilson. At this time Florence discovered what would become her main interest for the remainder of her life: working with wounded veterans. She began volunteering at Walter Reed Hospital, where she became a favorite of the vets, whom she called "my boys."

Presidency

In 1920 Warren Harding emerged as a leading candidate for the presidency despite a lackluster Senate career marked more by missing votes than by legislative leadership. Again, Florence expressed concern over her husband's limited abilities, but she became his campaign leader and manager. Warren Harding was clearly not fit for the job, and he had spent time in the Battle Creek Sanitarium, supposedly to recuperate from exhaustion. His supporters also paid his mistress a huge sum of money for her silence during the campaign. Apparently, Florence was unaware of this.

She participated in his "front porch" campaign and was a major force behind her husband's image as a common man. Florence pushed the idea that the Hardings were just plain folks, a theme that played well with the public. She allowed herself to be photographed often and encouraged her husband to do the same, stating, "I want the people to see these pictures so that they will know we are just plain folks like themselves." As first lady, Florence would be one of the most photographed women of her time, regularly appearing in newsreels and allowing almost anyone to take her picture.

When the story emerged that Harding was part black, she issued a public denial. Her previous marriage and divorce also dogged the couple during the campaign. Florence's approach was to remind critics that her first husband had passed away, giving the impression that she was widowed, even though her first husband did not die until several years after their divorce and her remarriage to Harding. Florence was more active than her husband and, despite her initial hesitancy, appeared to pursue the office more aggressively than he.

With the passage of the Nineteenth Amendment, Florence became the first woman to vote for her husband for president. On hearing of his election, Florence reportedly told her husband that *she* had won him the presidency. After the election she continued to play a central role in his administration, quickly becoming his leading adviser. She helped draft his inaugural address and participated in selecting appointees, including senior staffers such as his military adviser, secretaries of the treasury and interior, attorney general, and surgeon general (Charles Sawyer, who had been her personal physician). She was a regular at cabinet meetings, and because of her, Harding appointed several women to positions in his administration. Her influence extended throughout his presidency. It appears that Florence persuaded him not to support the League of Nations, and she prevented him from proposing a longer presidential term. The first lady continued to write and edit his speeches, even selecting the individuals the president pardoned. An oft-quoted remark of hers to an aide was, "[The president] does well when he listens to me and poorly when he does not."

Harding spent much of his time playing poker with his cronies, with Florence serving them drinks. To the president's supporters and aides, she was known as "Ma" or "the boss." But she limited her own effectiveness by trying to control those around her and letting her darker side get the best of her. The first lady could be vengeful. She treated Vice President Calvin Coolidge and his wife with contempt and, because of her personal feelings toward them, tried to stop the establishment of an official residence for vice presidents. Most of Harding's staff considered her to be trouble, and the White House staff despised the first lady. Alice Roosevelt, daughter of the former president, wrote that Florence was a "slob," while former first lady Edith Wilson questioned whether Florence was up to the challenge. The Executive Mansion's housekeeper, Elizabeth Jaffrey, whom Florence would later fire, joined the first lady's many detractors in calling her uncouth and unsophisticated.

Harding managed little better. He continued having affairs, at times using the Secret Service to cover up his dalliances. Another of Florence's friends, Nan Britton, was the object of the president's affections and became pregnant with his child. By the end of his presidency, a series of ugly scandals had begun to be exposed, leading the president to utter his famous line, "In this job I am not worried about my enemies. It is my friends that are keeping me walking the floors nights." Several of Harding's staff were caught up in illegal activities, the full extent of which came to be known only after his death.

The first lady did preside over numerous White House social events, and though many in politics and inside the presidency detested her, she was popular with the general public. She opened the White House to the people and often spent so much time greeting guests in receiving lines that her hands and feet were swollen and sore by the end of the day, an affliction she called "White House feet" and "White House hands." She initiated the practice of placing a wreath at the Tomb of the Unknown Soldier on Memorial Day, hosted parties for veterans, visited and inspected veterans' hospitals, and took a personal interest in the federal government's Veterans' Bureau, to the extent that she functioned as unofficial director of the agency. Florence also managed her husband's public image, getting him to stop chewing tobacco in public, to make appearances at church, and to promote their small-town values. She was a leading advocate for women. The first lady encouraged women to vote, hosted the first all-women's tennis tournament at the White House, championed the establishment of all-female prisons, advocated creating memorials dedicated to women's achievements, and joined the National Women's Party. She assumed leadership positions in the Campfire Girls and the Girl Scouts and promoted physical fitness for women.

In spite of growing health problems for both, Florence and Harding toured the country in the summer of 1923, although at times one or the other was unable to appear in public and on at least one occasion the first lady fainted. After a trip to Alaska, Warren was so weak he could not complete his scheduled appearance. Shortly after, he became unable to speak and his health deteriorated rapidly. In San Francisco on August 2, 1923, the president died of heart failure and a cerebral hemorrhage.

Legacy

The widowed first lady oversaw the president's burial in Marion, Ohio, but after the funeral she moved back to Washington. There were mounting ethical and financial scandals associated with the Harding administration—including the Teapot Dome scandal, named for an oil reserve in Wyoming, that involved bribery and kickbacks to members of the administration in return for attractive leasing arrangements for petroleum companies. Possibly because of the growing scandals, Florence burned many of her husband's papers. The circumstances around this act are suspicious, and in light of the charges of corruption, she seems to have acted improperly in an attempt to avoid embarrassment and worse. In 1927 Nan Britton, the president's mistress, published a book titled *The President's Daughter,* the story of Harding's alleged illegitimate daughter. A flurry of books followed, one written in 1930 by Gaston B. Means even suggesting that the circumstances surrounding the president's death were questionable. Many presidential scholars rate Harding as the worst president ever to serve.

Florence's own health declined after her husband's death, and she died only a year later, on November 21, 1924. She is remembered as an active, assertive, nontraditional woman but also as a failed first lady, largely because of the scandals associated with Harding's staff, her burning of the Harding papers, and her spiteful acts against those she disliked while in the White House. Still, this ignores the accomplishments of a strong, independent woman who was in some ways ahead of her time.

Bibliography

Adams, Samuel Hopkins. *The Incredible Era: The Life and Times of Warren G. Harding.* Boston: Houghton Mifflin, 1939.

Britton, Nan. *The President's Daughter.* New York: Elizabeth Ann Guild, 1927.

Daugherty, Harry M. *The Inside Story of the Harding Tragedy.* New York: Churchill, 1932.

Johnson, Willis Fletcher. *The Life of Warren G. Harding.* New York: John C. Winson, 1923.

McLean, Evalyn Walsh. *Father Struck It Rich.* Boston: Little, Brown, 1935.

Means, Marianne. *The Woman in the White House.* New York: Random House, 1963.

Murray, Robert K. *The Harding Era: Warren G. Harding and His Times.* Minneapolis: University of Minnesota Press, 1969.

31

Grace
Anna
Goodhue
Coolidge

Born: January 3, 1879; Burlington, Vermont
Died: July 8, 1957; Northampton, Massachusetts
President: Calvin Coolidge (1872–1933), Thirtieth President
Husband's Presidential Term: 1923–1929 (Republican)
Marriage: October 4, 1905; Burlington, Vermont
Children: John (1906–2000); Calvin (1908–1924)

Early Years

Grace Goodhue was born in Burlington, Vermont, three days into the new year in 1879. The Goodhues were a respected and somewhat well-off family in the state. Grace was the only child of Lemira Barrett and Andrew Goodhue, an inspector for a steamboat company on Lake Champlain who had been appointed to his position by President Grover Cleveland. The Goodhues had been affiliated with both the Methodist and Episcopalian denominations but, apparently at their daughter's urging, switched to Congregationalism.

Grace was an outgoing young woman who liked the theater and music; she both sang and played the piano. She also enjoyed ice skating and hiking, preferred to be outdoors, and loved animals. When she was first lady, her collie, Rob Roy, was constantly with her.

When Grace was four years old, she was sent to live with friends of the Goodhues, possibly because her father had been injured at work. While staying at the home of John Lyman, a prominent figure at Yale, Grace befriended his daughter June, whom she idolized. June eventually worked at the Clarke School for the Deaf in Northampton, Massachusetts, and Grace would follow in her footsteps, developing a lifelong interest in education for the deaf. June Lyman's aunt was the founder of the school, which taught "oralism," or lipreading.

Grace attended the University of Vermont from 1898 to 1902, becoming one of the first women to graduate from the institution. Although she did not particularly like her educational experience, she thoroughly enjoyed the social side of college, developing many friends and helping to found the school's chapter of Pi Beta Phi sorority. After graduation she became a teacher at the Clarke School, where she worked for the next three years.

Marriage

Grace met Calvin Coolidge in Northampton, where they attended the same church. They shared the same circle of friends, who often went on picnics or boating excursions and held parties. One story says that she first saw him as he stood at the window of his house wearing only his underwear—a union suit—and a bowler hat while shaving.

Coolidge at the time was a lawyer and city solicitor starting his legal and political career. He was unsociable and almost incapable of showing warmth, although it seemed he put a little passion into wooing Grace—perhaps all that he could muster. Coolidge did take Grace to dances and parties, but he simply sat there and neither danced nor talked. For their first date, he invited her to a Republican Party rally. Even his marriage proposal was bland and lacking in emotion. He proposed by stating, "I am going to be married to you."

Grace and Calvin were complete opposites, perhaps the most unlikely husband and wife in the history of presidential couples. Coolidge was seven years her senior and was dour, temperamental, and described as unattractive and physically frail. His bride, in contrast, was charming, popular, outgoing, and noted for her beauty. Grace's friends were mystified at her quiet, aloof suitor, and her mother disapproved of her future son-in-law. But Grace was attracted to Coolidge, and the two were wed on October 4, 1905. The honeymoon appears to have set the tone for the marriage: The newlyweds went to Montreal, but without asking his new bride, Calvin canceled the last week of the honeymoon to save money and because he had tired of Montreal and wanted to return home to campaign for the school board.

Family Life

In spite of their different personalities and Coolidge's stodgy, controlling manner, the two got along well, largely because Grace was so agreeable and deferred to her husband on all matters. His political career advanced after the wedding. After losing the school board election in 1905, Coolidge attained a position the following year on the Massachusetts general court, which took him to Boston. Grace remained in Northampton, and the next year gave birth to their first-born, a son named John. In 1908 her second child, named for his father, was born. During this period they lived apart during the week, but Calvin visited his family on weekends.

Coolidge's political career was taken from a textbook. He was elected mayor of Northampton, then to the Massachusetts statehouse, followed by the Massachusetts senate, lieutenant governorship, and finally the governorship. Throughout his service in the governor's office, Grace stayed home and he commuted on weekends. Grace did not participate in the political side of her husband's career, and he neither requested nor valued her opinion on matters political. In fact, on occasion he declined to let her join him at political events or when he was speaking. Yet it has been suggested that without Grace, Coolidge never would have succeeded in politics. Grace's contribution was her popularity. Although her husband seemed not to care and often failed to take full advantage of her impressive social skills and likability, Grace was a social asset, a vivacious woman who won over most people she met. At political and social events she carried the conversation and made up for her husband's antisocial behavior.

Throughout her life Grace remained active in her college sorority, Pi Beta Phi. In 1910 she was selected president of the alumni chapter in western Massachusetts. Two years later she became vice president of the alumni organization and in 1915 was elected president. She was also an avid fan of baseball, in particular the Red Sox. When baseball games began to be carried on radio, she loved to sit and follow the games. Grace's other passion remained deaf education, although she stopped teaching at the Clarke School after marriage. In 1921, however, she was chosen for the board of the American Association to Promote the Teaching of Speech to the Deaf. But Coolidge did not permit her to participate in many of the activities she had enjoyed before marriage. Moreover, he often took advantage of his wife's charity and honesty by making fun of her and playing hurtful pranks at her expense. He could be mean-spirited and often curtly dismissed her questions and opinions.

Calvin Coolidge was extremely controlling and led a strict, disciplined life; he followed a meticulous routine and retired at the same time every night. Coolidge was often irritable and had a glum outlook on life; he suffered from chronic asthma and indigestion and was physically weak, all of which seem to have contributed to his disposition.

Coolidge became prominent nationally in 1919, when he used the militia to end the Boston police strike; as a result he was added to the Republican presidential ticket opposite Warren Harding in 1920. Grace and Coolidge seemed swept up in the campaign, neither one actively seeking the office and both expressing apprehension at the prospect of being elected. After the election Grace immediately emerged as one of the most popular women in Washington. As "second lady" she assumed the customary presidency of the Senate wives' club. Her beauty and charm were much discussed in the capital's social circles. Perhaps the only luxury Calvin Coolidge allowed—for he was notoriously frugal—was clothing for Grace. He spent relatively freely on the latest fashions for her and wanted her to look attractive, but he was downright cheap when it came to all other money matters.

Grace liked meeting new people in the capital city and found the social life there most agreeable. While she was well liked and enjoyed the experience, Coolidge was unimpressive as vice president and did not like the office. Their two boys were sent to the Mercersburg Academy in Pennsylvania but visited their parents in Washington.

Presidency

The Coolidges were vacationing in Vermont when the news came that President Harding had died. Coolidge filled out the term and was easily reelected on his own in 1924. As might be expected, Grace soon distinguished herself as a talented first lady and remains one of the most popular White House hostesses in history. She had a knack for remembering everyone's name, and her charm caused many guests to comment that they felt good in her presence. The new first lady benefited from the unpopularity of her immediate predecessor, Florence Harding, and the controversies that had surrounded her and first ladies Helen Taft and Edith Wilson, as well as the necessarily limited social calendars during the war. Grace was also much younger, much more attractive, and in better health than the three first ladies who preceded her.

In addition to these fortunate circumstances, Grace brought her own special talent to the White House, where she continued to help her husband's popularity by winning admirers who were otherwise turned off by him and generally compensating for his deficient social graces. Even Alice Roosevelt, known for criticizing everyone, spoke highly of Grace, who was nicknamed "Sunshine" by an admiring White House staff. Ike Hoover, the mansion's longtime chief usher, commented that Grace accounted for "90 percent of the Coolidge administration." The first lady became a fashion trendsetter, and her social events were glamorous and successful. Grace played host to the prince of Wales and entertained the leading public figures of the day, including Will Rogers and Charles Lindbergh, the stage and screen star John Barrymore, and Hollywood legends Douglas Fairbanks, Mary Pickford, and Tom Mix.

Grace presided over the renovation of parts of the White House and worked to secure historic pieces and original furnishings that had been removed from the Executive Mansion over time, including Abraham Lincoln's bed. She also pushed a measure in Congress to encourage historic donations of such properties to the White House. Grace had the foresight to use top curators to assist with her renovations, and under her tenure the White House's European decor was replaced with a more authentic Americana style. Although the president rejected many of Grace's planned renovations and she was able to accomplish only some of her goals, she did have a sunroom built and expanded the White House gardens, planting some of her favorite flowers and trees from New England and constructing a pond with water lilies. While the roof of the residence was being replaced in 1927, the Coolidges lived in a home on Dupont Circle.

Even though it undercut his political capital, Calvin Coolidge limited his wife's public appearances, refused to let her speak in public despite her impressive oratory skills, and forbade her from dancing, horseback riding, and driving a car. When Charles Lindbergh offered to take an eager Grace flying, Coolidge would not allow it. Even Grace's habit of taking long walks was not immune to his control: On a 1927 trip to the Black Hills of South Dakota, Grace took her usual lengthy hike with her Secret Service attendant, Jim Haley, and returned shortly after she was expected. The president had Haley reassigned and would not allow Grace to go on walks for some time.

The president also unwisely amended her plans for White House social events and overrode her guest lists. He also did not keep her informed of his day-to-day schedule and activities. When she offered to help with minor tasks like travel plans and correspondence, he declined her services. Grace did not attempt to influence her husband, nor did she try to participate in any political matters facing the president; Coolidge would have rejected any such effort. He did not hold women in high regard and felt that their participation in society would impede their primary roles as wives and mothers. Very few women worked in the Coolidge administration.

Grace was incredibly tolerant of her husband's demeaning and controlling tendencies. She did occasionally feel confined, but it had more to do with the demands of the White House and press than with the limitations he set. The presidency was too much for Coolidge, and he is remembered as one of the least industrious presidents in history, trying to do as little, talk as little, and meet with as few people as possible. He held short working days and slept ten to twelve hours a night. He deserved his nickname of "Silent Cal." Even Grace joked about a bet that a woman could get the president to say more than two words: Coolidge said, "You lose."

Grace appears to have held some political views even if she never shared them with her husband. For instance, she urged women to vote and often invited professional women, female college students, and women's organizations to meet with her in the White House; in allowing herself to be photographed with them, she lent her political support to these groups. Grace was a regular in the Senate galleries, where she followed the issues of the day. A good conversationalist, the first lady frequently discussed issues like health care and the status of the disabled with her guests. Grace hosted disabled guests, including Helen Keller, at the White House, raising awareness of their causes and bringing about a rush of financial contributions for them. The first lady also supported the Camp Fire Girls, the American Legion, the Red Cross, and the American Lung Association, as well as children's hospitals.

The low point of the Coolidge presidency for both was in 1924, when their son Calvin Jr. died of blood poisoning from an infected blister he got while playing tennis. Coolidge blamed himself for his son's death and lost what little enthusiasm he had for governing. Grace also took the death of her younger son hard, and with her other son away at school in Amherst, she was lonely and depressed. Four years later Calvin Coolidge stunned his wife and the country when he offered a one-sentence statement: "I do not choose to run for president in 1928."

Legacy

After the White House, the couple traveled to Georgia and Florida, then returned to Northampton. They had grown tired of Washington and the press and were eager for a quiet retirement; they even tired of visitors at Northampton. Calvin Coolidge died on January 5, 1933. After his death Grace sold their home and moved to a smaller place; always the philanthropist, she donated part of the proceeds to the Red Cross. She also seems to have asserted her independence after a lifetime of control by her husband. She traveled to Europe, vacationed in North Carolina, cut her hair short in the style of the day, and finally did what she had wanted to do so many years before: fly in an airplane and learn to drive a car.

Grace enjoyed her privacy and spent much time reading, doing needlepoint, and listening to baseball games on the radio. She also was happy in her close relationship with her surviving son, John, who married the daughter of Connecticut's governor. The former first lady became involved in politics, speaking out for U.S. participation in World War II and raising money for war refugees and the children of Germany. She also wrote articles on her husband's life and career that were published in popular magazines, as were her memoirs, which she submitted as a series of pieces in *American Magazine* and *Good Housekeeping*.

Grace Coolidge died on July 8, 1957, of heart failure. History has been much kinder to her and her service than to her husband and his presidency. In 1929 the former first lady received an honorary degree from Smith College, which was followed by similar recognition from the University of Vermont and Boston University. In 1931 she was voted as one of the nation's twelve greatest living women. She was also awarded a medal for her service by the National Institute of Social Sciences and was recognized by the Women's National Press Club.

Bibliography

Coolidge, Calvin. *The Autobiography of Calvin Coolidge*. New York: Cosmopolitan Books, 1929.

Coolidge, Grace Goodhue. *Grace Coolidge: An Autobiography*. Edited by Lawrence E. Wikander and Robert H. Ferrell. Worland, WY: High Plains Publishing, 1992.

Randolph, Mary. *Presidents and First Ladies*. New York: D. Appleton-Century, 1936.
Ross, Ishbel. *Grace Coolidge and Her Era*. New York: Dodd, Mead, 1962.
Stoddard, Gloria May. *Grace and Cal: A Vermont Love Story*. Shelburne, VT: New England Press, 1989.

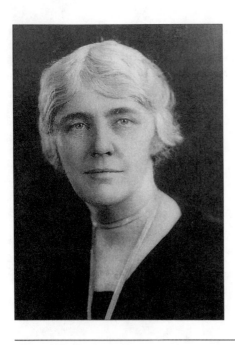

32

Lou
Henry
Hoover

Born: March 29, 1874; Waterloo, Iowa
Died: January 7, 1944; New York, New York
President: Herbert Hoover (1874–1964), Thirty-first President
Husband's Presidential Term: 1929–1933 (Republican)
Marriage: February 10, 1899; Monterey, California
Children: Herbert Clark (1903–1969); Allan Henry (1907–1993)

Early Years

Lou Henry, the elder of two daughters, was born on March 29, 1874, in Waterloo, Iowa. Her mother, Florence Weed Henry, had a college education; her father, Charles Delano Henry, was a banker. When Lou was a girl, the family relocated to California because of her mother's severe asthma, living first in Whittier, then moving to Monterey in 1890.

Lou was a vigorous, athletic young woman. She liked outdoors activities such as camping, hiking, fishing, skating, and horseback riding and excelled in baseball, basketball, and archery. After attending public school in Whittier, she went to the Los Angeles Normal School and San Jose Normal School, where she earned a teaching certificate in 1893. After college she worked as a substitute teacher in Monterey and

212

as a clerk in her father's bank. When she attended a public lecture on geology at Leland Stanford Junior University, she became so intrigued by the topic that she enrolled there in 1894 to pursue a degree in geology. At Stanford Lou performed as well as her male classmates and became one of the first women in the United States to earn a geology degree.

Marriage

It was at Stanford that Lou met fellow geology student Herbert Hoover, who was working as a laboratory assistant for John Casper Branner, the professor whose lecture had inspired Lou to enter the field. Hoover, a quiet upperclassman, developed an interest in the freshman student; he was impressed with Lou's engaging blue eyes and her intelligence. She and "Bert" began dating and were courting seriously when Hoover graduated in 1895. They continued their relationship long distance when he accepted a job working with a gold-mining operation in Australia. Hoover proposed marriage to Lou by cable.

Lou graduated and the two were married at her family home in Monterey on February 10, 1899. Hoover was in high demand as a mining engineer, and after their wedding he accepted a position in China. Lou did not hesitate to join her new husband. She also switched her religious affiliation from Episcopalian to her spouse's Quaker faith.

Family Life

During the time the Hoovers worked in China, the Boxer Rebellion broke out. The rising tide of nationalism spilled over into hostilities directed at Americans and other foreign citizens living in China. Hoover tried to get his wife to leave because of the threat to their lives, but Lou would not hear of it. When the compound where they lived was attacked, the Hoovers helped organize its defense. Lou emerged as a courageous leader among the international community living in China, helping tend the wounded, organizing a rationing campaign, and stoically going about her business on her bicycle after the tires had been blown out by gunfire. Both also learned the language during their time in China, and Lou became fluent in Mandarin, the tongue they would later use in the White House when they needed to talk privately in public settings.

After the Boxer Rebellion Hoover was transferred to London. His career progressed and he became partner in the worldwide firm of

Bewick, Moreing, and Company. Later, as an independent mining consultant, he earned millions. During this time Lou was her husband's personal assistant in all his business dealings, and she joined him on travels to Asia, the Pacific, North Africa, and Europe. The Hoover family was growing, with Herbert Jr. born in 1903 and a second son, Allan, in 1907. Both sons joined their parents on their international travels. Lou and Hoover also worked together on a five-year book project, translating the sixteenth-century text *De re metallica* (Of metals) by Georgius Agricola from Latin into English. As was the case in all facets of their lives together, Lou was a full partner in the project, and their efforts earned them the gold medal of the Mining and Metallurgical Society of America in 1914.

While living in England, the Hoovers witnessed the outbreak of World War I. They put their fortune to good use, helping U.S. citizens stranded in London by establishing a credit agency to float affordable loans, making it possible for them to return home. Lou organized hospital and relief efforts, raised money for wartime charities, and was involved in the Women's Committee for Economic Relief. The couple also worked for the Commission for Relief in Belgium and donated money to establish a hospital in Belgium. For her efforts, King Leopold of Belgium awarded Lou the Cross Chevalier, Order of Leopold, after the war. She had also established a knitting factory to aid the war effort and provide work for women.

In 1917, after the United States entered the war, the Hoovers returned and Herbert was named director of the U.S. Food Administration. Again, Lou assisted her husband in his job promoting food conservation. She also volunteered with the Red Cross and organized women's groups to assist in war and relief efforts. Lou became a troop leader of the Girl Scouts in Washington, then was selected national director of the organization in 1922. Under her tenure the Girl Scouts enjoyed an increase in their membership and began their now famous cookie sales. Later, as first lady she invited Girl Scout troops to the White House. Always interested in outdoor activities and the physical fitness of young women, she became vice president of the National Amateur Athletic Federation in 1923 and chaired its women's division, as well as the first National Conference on Athletics and Physical Education for Women and Girls.

The Hoovers were so identified with conservation that later their name became synonymous with the effort. To "Hooverize" was to conserve—although the word had mixed connotations. After the war, Herbert Hoover returned to Europe to coordinate efforts to rebuild war-torn areas; Lou remained home but continued to help raise money and lead relief efforts. When she hosted dinners, she adopted the practice of leaving a chair empty at the table to remind guests of hungry children. When the Teapot Dome scandal broke after the Harding presidency, Lou boldly spoke out for ethics in government. She also encouraged women to go into public service.

Presidency

Lou was an active force in her husband's 1928 bid for the presidency, joining him in the campaign but rarely speaking in public. Her life of international travel and her many accomplishments had prepared her for the challenges she would face in the White House. She knew Mandarin, Spanish, Latin, and some German and had organized relief and social organizations around the world. But Lou would struggle in her relations with the press. She was the first first lady to give national radio addresses, and she spoke to the Daughters of the American Revolution and other groups. Yet she distrusted the media and alienated them by documenting inaccuracies in reporting and sending them to journalists. Lou seems also to have had a poor public image. Not only did she fail to court favorable reporting, but she did not promote her many successes and accomplishments. The first lady was regarded as unattractive and unfashionable by a critical public and the Washington social crowd, and although the Hoovers were among the leading philanthropists of the time, they were perceived as uncaring and aloof.

As first lady, Lou brought musicians to perform in the White House, covering the costs out of the Hoover fortune. She was a patron of the arts and an advocate for women. Lou was behind her husband's decision to hire several women for his administration, and in 1932 she supported Executive Order 5984, a presidential directive to mandate civil service hiring without regard to the applicant's sex. The practice of excusing pregnant women from postdinner festivities in the White House seemed unnecessary to Lou, who invited her pregnant guests to participate in her receiving lines and social functions. One of her most criticized actions in the White House was to invite Jessie DePriest to tea in 1929. After the visit of DePriest, the black wife of Illinois congressman Oscar DePriest, several southern states, including Georgia, Florida, and Texas, passed resolutions in their state legislatures condemning the first lady. The Mobile, Alabama, newspaper stated that Lou "offered to the South and to the nation an arrogant insult." The *Memphis Commercial Appeal* even suggested that the country should "drop the 'white' from the White House." Lou was stung by the criticism but remained steadfastly behind her decision; she later invited the all-black Tuskegee Institute choir to perform in the White House.

Lou undertook several refurbishing projects in the White House and brought artwork from around the world into the presidential residence. With the assistance of experts, she cataloged the building's possessions, worked to locate historic furnishings for the White House, and wrote a book on the building, its history, and furnishings. She approached this task as she did all endeavors: with great energy and dedication. Both Lou and her husband were workaholics—so much so that she ended many of the time-consuming customs of protocol, including the practice of calling on and returning the social calls of cabinet wives. She found such activities to be a waste of time.

The Hoovers worked hard at all they did and often used their own money for official events because of the crisis of the Great Depression. When the first lady looked for a place where her overworked husband could escape the pressures of office, both ended up undertaking yet another charitable campaign: She found the ideal vacation site at Rapidan River in rural Virginia and purchased fourteen acres for their use. But when they saw the impoverished living conditions of the area's children, they replaced their plans for relaxation with efforts to alleviate the residents' poverty. They invested their own time and money to establish a school and hire a teacher for the children and later donated Camp Rapidan to the National Park Service.

The Great Depression undermined Hoover's effectiveness as president, and he was never able to overcome its disastrous economic conditions or effectively employ his considerable organizational skills and intelligence to the problems it spawned. Nor was he able to connect with the public. Both Lou and Hoover were victims of circumstances beyond their control. This was perhaps most apparent when a group of war veterans gathered in Washington to protest hospital conditions and to seek early payment of bonus certificates given them for their service. Although Lou provided the "Bonus Marchers" with food and the president covered their transportation costs to return home, he unwisely called in federal troops to disperse the remaining demonstrators. The incident proved a public relations disaster for an already maligned president and first lady.

Legacy

Herbert Hoover was overwhelmingly defeated by Franklin Roosevelt in 1932. Lou took the loss even worse than her husband, feeling that he deserved another term and that the voters had made a huge mistake. For all their formidable intellectual and organizational powers, the Hoovers never mastered the art of politics and personal celebrity. Lou Henry Hoover lived one of the most remarkable lives of any woman of her time, yet her life's achievements have been overshadowed by the economic crisis during her husband's presidency. After traveling around the country, they retired to both Palo Alto, California, and New York City.

With the specter of another world war looming, Lou again took action, organizing relief efforts for the victims of war and the citizens of Belgium. She also retained her interest in the Girl Scouts. On January 7, 1944, she died suddenly at their apartment in New York. She was survived by twenty years by her husband, who continued his public service under Presidents Truman and Eisenhower.

Bibliography

Burner, David. *Herbert Hoover: A Public Life*. New York: Knopf, 1979.

Furman, Bess. *Washington By-Line*. New York: Knopf, 1949.

Lambert, Darwin. *Herbert Hoover's Hideaway*. Luray, VA: Shenandoah Natural History Association, 1971.

Pryor, Helen. *Lou Henry Hoover: Gallant First Lady*. New York: Dodd, Mead, 1969.

Smith, Richard Norton. *An Uncommon Man: The Triumph of Herbert Hoover*. New York: Simon and Schuster, 1984.

33

Anna Eleanor Roosevelt

Born: October 11, 1884; New York, New York
Died: November 7, 1962; New York, New York
President: Franklin D. Roosevelt (1882–1945), Thirty-second President
Husband's Presidential Term: 1933–1945 (Democrat)
Marriage: March 17, 1905; New York, New York
Children: Anna Eleanor (1906–1975); James (1907–1991); Franklin (1909); Elliott (1910–1990); Franklin (1914–1988); John Aspinwall (1916–1981)

Early Years

Anna Eleanor Roosevelt was born on October 11, 1884. Although hers was a very wealthy and prominent New York family, Eleanor's childhood was often painful. Her mother, Anna Hall Roosevelt, was from a prosperous family also and was a well-known, attractive socialite, but she was deeply unhappy in her marriage and personal life. She was harsh with her daughter, ridiculing her as "Granny" because of her "old-fashioned" manner and "plain" appearance, and Eleanor never seemed to meet her mother's expectations or standard of beauty. Elliott Roosevelt, Eleanor's father, was a wealthy investor and the younger brother of President Theodore Roosevelt; he was a weak man with passions for alcohol and gambling and was frequently absent from home. The young girl nevertheless adored her father, who returned his "little Nell's" love.

When Anna Hall Roosevelt died in 1892, Eleanor was sent to live with her maternal grandmother, who was as stern with her as her mother had been. Two years later Elliott's vices caught up with him, and he died when Eleanor was only ten years old. As a child she had been tutored at home, but a defining event occurred that allowed her to overcome the traumas of her early years: She was sent to London to be educated at the Allenwood Academy. Her teacher there, who would become her mentor and inspiration, was Mademoiselle Marie Souvestre, a bold, free-thinking woman who recognized vast potential in the socially awkward girl. During the three years Eleanor studied under Souvestre, she gained a degree of poise and self-confidence, although she was still somewhat shy and uncomfortable about her pending society debut in 1902.

Marriage

Eleanor's friendship with her distant cousin Franklin Delano Roosevelt blossomed when he was a student at Harvard. In many ways it was an unlikely romance: Roosevelt was as confident as Eleanor was insecure, and he was a popular, sociable young man. He was also ambitious, and he idolized his relative, Theodore Roosevelt, who by this time was in the White House. In fact, the president gave away his favorite niece at the March 17, 1905, wedding.

Their courtship and marriage were opposed by Franklin's domineering mother, Sara Delano Roosevelt, who never approved of her son's choice and would never warm to her daughter-in-law. The early years of Eleanor's marriage were difficult for her because Sara constantly intervened in their life. She even selected the newlyweds' home and furniture and moved in next door.

Family Life

Although Eleanor's legendary social and political activism had already begun to manifest itself before marriage, it was necessarily curtailed because of family obligations, stemming from the birth of six children. They arrived over a ten-year period, beginning a year after marriage: first Anna, followed by James in 1907, Franklin (who died in infancy) in 1909, Elliott (1910), Franklin Jr. (1914), and John in 1916. This was not a happy period in Eleanor's life. She was frequently lonely and felt limited both by the challenges of motherhood and the presence of her invasive mother-in-law. During this time Roosevelt, who had studied law at Columbia, began his political career, which included a seat in the New York senate in 1911 and serving as assistant secretary of the navy from 1913 to 1920 under President Woodrow Wilson.

In Washington the Roosevelts were part of an administration that downplayed social hosting. This freed Eleanor to pursue charitable work and later become involved in wartime relief activities with the Red Cross and other organizations. These activities were part of several key factors—along with moving away from her mother-in-law and marital problems caused by her husband's affair with Lucy Mercer—that reinforced Eleanor's sensitivity to the underprivileged and her affinity for leadership.

Roosevelt's star was on the rise, and in 1920 he ran with James M. Cox on the Democratic ticket for vice president. Eleanor participated in his election and even gave speeches, gaining valuable experience that would mark her years as first lady. But the Democrats lost, and shortly after the defeat Roosevelt contracted polio, losing the use of both legs. This was understandably a devastating time for him, and he responded initially by withdrawing from politics. While Roosevelt struggled with his affliction, Eleanor entered the political void, becoming a recognizable force in New York politics. Because of her visibility, she kept her husband's name in the forefront of both New York and Democratic Party politics, making it possible for his eventual return to public life. The 1920s marked another major period for Eleanor, and she grew increasingly confident and independent. Her relationship with her husband became more distant after his affairs, contributing to her sense of self and to her commitment to social and political activism. Even though she contemplated divorce, she stayed with Roosevelt and nursed him through his painful, long recovery, although he remained crippled. Franklin's mother wanted him to return to the family home and abandon political life; for perhaps the first time in her married life, Eleanor stood up to her mother-in-law and urged her husband to reenter politics.

During this crucial period and in the ensuing years, Eleanor would participate in an impressive array of public and political endeavors, including the Women's City Club, where she served on the board; the Women's Division of the Democratic State Committee; the National Consumers League; and the League of Women Voters, where she chaired the Legislative Affairs Committee, tracking bills and gaining an understanding of the political process, and rising to the position of vice chair. This position offered her the opportunity to write league reports. She also wrote for the *Women's Democratic News, Redbook, Current History, Good Housekeeping,* the *North American Review,* and the newsletter of the Women's Trade Union League. Eleanor thus honed both her public speaking and writing skills. She also campaigned for Al Smith in 1928, the Democratic nominee for president. Over the course of the decade, she became an advocate for workers' compensation, child labor laws, the settlement movement, and electoral reforms, emerging as a progressive thinker and leader in the state of New York and in the Democratic Party and strengthening her desire for social justice and connection with the public.

Eleanor had also become involved with two projects that would occupy a very special place in her life. She helped lead the Todhunter School for Girls, where she taught courses in current issues, history, and literature, and the Val-kill Furniture Factory, an experiment in social charity and employment. Although she had grown increasingly fond of politics, these two projects provided passion in her life. In 1928 Franklin Roosevelt returned to politics, winning the governorship of New York. Even though she was the force behind his successful return to public life, Eleanor viewed the governorship with mixed feelings. She was concerned that as first lady of New York she would lose her independence, and she dreaded the social responsibilities of her new office.

Presidency

Four years later, when FDR ran for the presidency, Eleanor again expressed concern about the loss of her much-valued independence, but she was a visible and helpful part of the campaign. Once in the White House, she continued to be savvy in her dealings with the press corps and cultivated positive relations with female journalists. By granting them exclusive interviews, the popular first lady helped advance the cause and careers of women in journalism and, at the same time, assured herself favorable coverage in the nation's newspapers. Eleanor complemented these interviews with formal press conferences, the first first lady to do so, and opened them to female reporters. The first lady's relations with the press also included radio broadcasts and writing her own columns. On New Year's Eve 1935, she started her column "My Day," which was syndicated in hundreds of newspapers around the country. She also had a column in *Woman's Home Companion* and in

1942 began writing "If You Ask Me" for the *Ladies Home Journal,* which was picked up by *McCall's* magazine in 1949. Eleanor's writings made her immensely popular; the first lady's personal mail flooded the White House mail room. The columns also allowed her to advance her personal views and favorite issues. Although she offered frank advice, over the years her writings became increasingly political. In 1940 Eleanor even represented her husband by speaking on his behalf at the Democratic National Convention.

Perhaps Eleanor's main contribution to her husband's presidency was her function as his eyes and ears. Even though the president sometimes was annoyed with his wife's "nagging" on various issues—and this increased throughout his tenure in office—the president did respect her opinion, and the first lady felt free to disagree with him and offer her frank appraisal of political questions. Because polio had left the president dependent on a wheelchair or leg braces, he came to rely on Eleanor to travel for him. In this capacity Eleanor became the most-traveled first lady in history, visiting hospitals, government offices, and even the troops during the war, all without her husband. She conducted many fact-finding missions in a quasi-official capacity. Additionally, as so many first ladies had before her, Eleanor clipped newspaper articles she felt the president needed to read.

Eleanor's influence extended to nearly all areas of Roosevelt's presidency, including policy decisions. As testament to the respect in which she was held, she was invited to testify before Congress during committee hearings on workers and the poor. She was successful in getting the president to hire many women, including Frances Perkins as secretary of labor, the first woman to hold a cabinet position. She was also far ahead of Roosevelt on the issue of civil rights and pushed him to do more in his New Deal programs for social welfare. Eleanor's influence is evident in many facets of the National Industrial Recovery Act and other key components of the New Deal such as the National Youth Administration, the Civilian Conservation Corps, federal emergency relief operations, and public works programs. She led the effort in 1935 to include art among the New Deal's Works Progress Administration initiatives. Unemployed artists were hired to create art for public buildings, and the Federal Writers Project and Federal Theater Project owe their existence to her tireless lobbying. The first lady even arranged for some of the art produced through these projects to be displayed in prominent museums.

Eleanor was not always successful in influencing her husband. They disagreed on many topics, and she was often frustrated with what she perceived to be the slow progress of the New Deal. A case in point was civil rights. Although Eleanor was pleased with such decisions as FDR's executive order precluding discrimination in military contracts, she thought he was much too cautious in his concern about alienating important southern Democrats over civil rights. One such instance was the antilynching cause, advocated by the first lady but avoided by the president because of opposition in the South. Eleanor began crusading for such measures, independent of the president. She used travels, her syndicated columns, and public appearances to forward her own platform. The first lady's work on behalf of civil rights included membership in the Urban League; accepting a position on the board of the NAACP, the country's leading civil rights organization, and attending its conventions; campaigning tirelessly to end segregation; hiring an all-black domestic staff in the White House; making high-profile visits to poor black communities; and helping raise money for Howard University, the country's most prestigious black institution of higher learning. She even showed up unannounced to fly with the Tuskegee Airmen, an all-black air unit that was grounded during the war because of racism, boldly displaying her confidence in and support for their cause.

In 1939, when the Daughters of the American Revolution refused to allow Marian Anderson, the black contralto, to perform in Constitution Hall, which they owned, the first lady resigned from the organization. Eleanor followed this by criticizing the DAR in her column and scheduling a concert performance for Anderson at the Lincoln Memorial in the capital. Then she invited visiting royals from London to attend a concert by Anderson in Richmond, Virginia, the capital of the old Confederacy, on July 4. Such bold, public actions became Eleanor Roosevelt's trademark. No first lady before or since has been willing to risk such public condemnation or the president's political standing through such acts. For this, she was condemned in the southern press and even received death threats from the Ku Klux Klan.

Eleanor also took on powers inside the Beltway. She criticized the Gridiron Club's annual dinner, a well-known Washington institution, because the Washington Press Corps did not include women at the event. Eleanor parodied the traditional party by hosting the "Gridiron Widows Dinner." Her crusade for civil rights for minorities and women included formal activism within the White House as well. As first lady she convened a White House Conference on Negro Women and pushed the appointment of a black friend, Mary McLeod Bethune, to a leadership position in the National Youth Administration. At the Southern

Conference on Human Welfare in Birmingham, Alabama, in 1938, when Eleanor was not allowed to sit next to Bethune because of the city's segregation ordinance, the first lady moved her chair into the aisle between the black and white seating sections.

As the first lady of human rights, Eleanor's interest extended to all persons facing oppression. During her travels Eleanor came to embrace the cause of improving living conditions in Appalachia, one of the country's poorest areas; she pushed for public health care, employment, and education assistance for the residents and even donated her own time and money to the cause. She was courageous enough to oppose the internment of citizens of Japanese descent during the difficult, tense times of World War II and argued with Congress to allow more Jewish refugees into the United States. She risked public criticism and undermining her husband's positions on the war, but history has judged the first lady, not the president or Congress, as correct in these actions. She visited U.S. soldiers at bases around the world, traveling to England in 1942 and the South Pacific in 1944, despite the dangers of the war and against the advice of those who feared for her personal safety. The first lady also visited military hospitals and personally fulfilled the requests of soldiers to contact their families.

Eleanor was easily the most nontraditional and publicly active first lady in the history of the office. Her accomplishments also distinguish her as the most powerful of all first ladies. Although presidential advisers often worried about her visibility, activism, and influence, this did not seem to deter or limit her. Nor did criticism in the press. Eleanor's marriage, however, never recovered from her husband's earlier affairs and remained more of a business partnership. When the president died at Warm Springs, Georgia, in 1945, Lucy Mercer Rutherford, the woman with whom he had had an affair beginning thirty years earlier, was with him, not his wife.

Legacy
After FDR's death, Eleanor oversaw the details of his funeral and helped brief the new president, Harry Truman, on the war and domestic policy matters. But the Eleanor Roosevelt story did not end with her husband's passing. Indeed, it merely marked a new chapter of increased autonomy and progressive activism. She appears to have felt freer to offer her opinions and pursue her own agenda once liberated from her White House obligations. On her own she became one of the leading shapers of postwar liberalism, helping found Americans for Democratic

Action, an organization espousing liberal ideals; campaigning for Adlai Stevenson in 1952 and 1956 and other Democratic candidates for office; and having the wherewithal to oppose the anticommunist witch-hunts of Senator Joe McCarthy and his House Un-American Affairs Committee.

Eleanor continued her extensive travel schedule and wrote several books. Her newspaper column, "My Day," ran until September 11, 1962, almost twenty-seven years. The former first lady of the United States became a first lady to the world when she was appointed by President Truman as a U.S. delegate to the new United Nations, where she chaired the committee that drafted the Universal Declaration on Human Rights. She also devoted herself to numerous other causes, such as housing assistance, civil rights, and improvements in health care delivery. In 1961 President John Kennedy asked Eleanor to return again to the United Nations; she was greeted by a standing ovation from the delegates. Kennedy also appointed her to chair his Commission on the Status of Women and to sit on the board of the new Peace Corps program.

In 1960 Eleanor was diagnosed with aplastic anemia, a dangerous blood disease. She stayed active even though her health and energy declined. She died of bone marrow tuberculosis on November 7, 1962, and was buried on the family estate in Hyde Park, New York. Widely considered to be *the* American first lady, she was the most active and influential individual ever to occupy that position. Her determination broke down barriers not only for first ladies but for all women everywhere. Her firsts in the first ladyship are too numerous to mention, and for more than a decade she topped the list of most admired women. Eleanor Roosevelt was no less than one of the most important figures—man or woman—of the twentieth century.

Bibliography

Black, Allida, ed. *What I Hope to Leave Behind: The Essential Essays of Eleanor Roosevelt.* Brooklyn, NY: Carlson, 1995.
Lash, Joseph P. *Eleanor and Franklin: The Story of Their Relationship, Based on Eleanor Roosevelt's Private Letters.* New York: Norton, 1971.
MacLeish, Archibald. *The Eleanor Roosevelt Story.* Boston: Houghton Mifflin, 1965.
Roosevelt, Eleanor. *On My Own.* New York: Harper, 1958.
———. *The Autobiography of Eleanor Roosevelt.* New York: Harper, 1961.

34

Elizabeth "Bess" Virginia Wallace Truman

Born: February 13, 1885; Independence, Missouri
Died: October 18, 1982; Independence, Missouri
President: Harry S. Truman (1884–1972), Thirty-third President
Husband's Presidential Term: 1945–1953 (Democrat)
Marriage: June 28, 1919; Independence, Missouri
Children: Mary Margaret (1924–)

Early Years

Elizabeth "Bess" Wallace was born in the farming community of Independence, Missouri, on February 13, 1885. The Wallace family was by no means wealthy, but relative to the simple standards of their neighbors they were comfortably well-off. Her mother was Margaret "Madge" Gates Wallace, and her father, David Wallace, was a farmer and businessman. Bess was raised in both the Episcopalian and Presbyterian faiths and had a solid education, attending school in her hometown, then Barstow Finishing School in Kansas City.

Bess was both an outstanding student and a talented athlete. She liked riding horses and ice skating and also played baseball and tennis. She was both the town's belle and a tomboy, an athlete and a star student. In 1903 her father committed suicide, apparently because of his perceived failure to live up to his and his family's expectations; Wallace was in debt, and alcohol was also a factor. The Wallace children were sent to Colorado Springs for a brief time after the tragedy.

Marriage
Bess Wallace and Harry Truman were classmates and friends in school, growing up in the same hometown. Whereas Bess was athletic and the pride of her teachers, Harry was a small, frail, shy boy whose family was poor. Harry admired Bess from a distance and hoped to impress his popular friend but did not think she would like him. They graduated together and some time later began to court. His letters to her speak of his deep affection for Bess and appreciation of her blue eyes and curly, blond hair. After a long courtship, which Bess's mother never supported, feeling her daughter deserved much more than Truman had to offer, they discussed marriage but, because he was about to begin a wartime tour of duty, decided to wait until after the war to marry. The wedding finally took place on June 28, 1919, after he returned home from the military; Harry was thirty-five and Bess thirty-four. Bess's mother still disapproved of Harry and expressed concern over his Baptist faith.

Family Life
After his return, Harry Truman opened a haberdashery in Kansas City with a friend from the military. Initially the store did well, but hard times befell their operation, and it went out of business in 1921. In spite of his later image as an independent-minded reformer, Truman found his way into politics as a county judge through Kansas City's Democratic political machine. He also attended the Kansas City law school from 1923 to 1925.

In many ways Bess was the archetypal homemaker. She had little interest in politics, and after suffering a few miscarriages, she had a daughter, Margaret, in 1924. Bess's mother lived with the Truman family but still thought little of her son-in-law.

Truman's political career brought him an opportunity to run for the U.S. Senate in 1934. Bess was not very active in the campaign and only marginally interested in the office. When Truman was elected, the family moved to Washington, though neither Bess nor her mother liked the city, and the high cost of maintaining two residences drained their finances. Bess not only disliked moving from Independence, but she minded the loss of her privacy. She had no desire to host or attend political and social events in the capital, doing the absolute minimum required of her. Harry Truman nevertheless idolized his wife and valued her opinion, so while Bess was a most reluctant public figure and offered her husband little support, she did serve as his confidante. She also worked in his Senate office as a secretary, causing a minor controversy, even though she was competent in her clerical duties and Truman defended her employment.

Truman rose from obscurity into the national limelight during World War II, when he led high-profile investigations into possible wrongdoing and waste in military procurement. His work caught the president's attention, and in one of the century's most surprising political success stories, Truman was added to the Roosevelt ticket as vice president in 1944. President Roosevelt was in poor health and occupied with the war, so Truman carried much of the campaign burden for the Democrats. Bess reluctantly joined her husband, traveling with him around the country, from one stump speech to another. Both the U.S. public and the Democratic Party elders were unfamiliar with Truman's spouse, even mistakenly listing her as a former schoolteacher in their official biography. During the campaign Truman would occasionally introduce his wife as "the boss," a playful tag that became a well-known part of his presidential campaign a few years later. Bess held a single meeting with the press, in which she said she was "reconciled" to her husband's bid for office—not a ringing endorsement, to say the least. She exhibited her characteristic candor and brevity, traits for which she would be both admired and dismissed in later years.

Presidency

Only months after assuming office, Truman was thrust into the presidency when President Roosevelt died suddenly in April 1945. Bess Truman did not like the White House, the presidency, or the first ladyship. She saw herself primarily as a wife and mother and only distantly as a ceremonial official. She did as little as possible and even returned to Missouri during some of the most critical times of her husband's tenure, such as when he made the decision to drop the atomic bomb on Japan. Yet in private Bess was an invaluable part of Truman's presidency; he would later admit he never made an important decision without consulting her. She helped edit her husband's speeches as well and, perhaps most important, was able to calm his temper and control his use of foul language.

Bess seems to have been ill prepared for many of her new duties. In her first public event she was asked to christen a military ship, but after several forceful swings by the first lady, the bottle of champagne refused to break. The embarrassment seemed to set the tone for her tenure in office. She was not well traveled and had little experience with social hosting. She also had the misfortune of following the most active, well-known first lady in history and often came up short in comparisons to her and other predecessors. The first lady was labeled "unsophisticated" by the Washington social crowd, and when Clare Booth Luce, one of its leading figures, dismissed Bess as common and drab, the president removed the socialite from the White House guest list. Bess did not present herself well in terms of appearance or attitude. She was rather gloomy in outlook, and her disdain for her duties was often apparent. She was fortunate that the busy times following World War II and later the demands of the Korean conflict and rise of the Cold War precluded her offering a full social schedule in the White House. Also, the need to refurbish the mansion's deteriorating frame required the first family to live at Blair House for an extended period.

The first lady did involve herself in a few causes. She supported the Daughters of Colonial Wars, the Red Cross, the Women's National Farm and Garden Association, and the Daughters of the American Revolution. Yet when black leaders asked Bess to boycott a DAR tea because of the organization's support for segregation, she refused to do so and was criticized and compared unfavorably to Eleanor Roosevelt. One critic, New York congressman Adam Clayton Powell, even suggested she was the "last" rather than the first lady. And her disdain for the press did not help her relations with Washington journalists, who were already upset with the first lady's low profile and unwillingness to grant interviews.

Although she opposed her husband's bid for reelection in 1948, she again went along reluctantly on his nationwide, whistle-stop tour aboard the *Ferdinand Magellan*. She was an unexpected hit on the campaign, as her homespun, ordinary image was appreciated by the residents of the small towns where the train stopped. When the president introduced his wife by saying, "I want you to meet the boss," the gesture and the first lady were met by much applause. Truman won reelection, against most predictions. Bess Truman had mixed feelings about the outcome, as it meant she had to endure the office for another four years.

Legacy

After leaving the White House, the Trumans toured Europe, then retired to Independence where they enjoyed many more years together. Their retirement was warm and largely uneventful, with the exception of Bess's mastectomy in 1959. Truman died the day after Christmas in 1972. Bess became the longest-lived first lady, dying at ninety-seven on October 18, 1982. Because of the volume of letters they exchanged, we know much about the Truman marriage, including the vital role Bess fulfilled in private, where she was involved in all her husband's decisions. Her reluctant yet central role in her husband's political career can perhaps best be seen in her comment to a reporter, who asked if she had ever held a job. Bess responded, "I've been in politics for more than twenty-five years."

Bibliography

Daniels, Clifton. *Lords, Ladies and Gentleman: A Memoir.* New York: Arbor House, 1984.

Ferrell, Robert H., ed. *Dear Bess: The Letters from Harry to Bess Truman, 1910–1959.* New York: Norton, 1983.

Robbins, Jhan. *Bess and Harry: An American Love Story.* New York: Putnam's, 1980.

Truman, Harry S. *Memoirs.* 2 volumes. New York: Doubleday, 1955–1956.

Truman, Margaret. *Bess Truman.* New York: Macmillan, 1986.

35

Mary Geneva "Mamie" Doud Eisenhower

Born: November 14, 1896; Boone, Iowa
Died: November 1, 1979; Washington, D.C.
President: Dwight D. Eisenhower (1890–1969), Thirty-fourth President
Husband's Presidential Term: 1953–1961 (Republican)
Marriage: July 1, 1916; Denver, Colorado
Children: Doud Dwight "Icky" (1917–1921); John Sheldon Doud (1922–)

Early Years

Mary Doud was known as "Mamie" (and also "Mimi") when she was a child. The second of four Doud daughters, Mamie was born on November 14, 1896, in Boone, Iowa. Her mother's family, the Carlsons, had recently immigrated to the United States from Sweden, and Swedish was spoken at home when Mamie was growing up. John Sheldon Doud, Mamie's father, earned a prosperous living in cattle trading and meatpacking. The Doud family moved to Colorado when Mamie was a girl, apparently because of the fragile health of her mother and her oldest sibling, Eleanor. They lived in Pueblo, Colorado Springs, and then Denver; the family escaped Colorado winters in San Antonio, Texas.

Mamie was a fun-loving, outgoing girl with a fondness for jewelry and clothing. She had a comfortable upbringing and, through her family's travels, visited such exotic locales as New Orleans and the Panama Canal. She attended public and private schools near her home but did not excel. Although school did not hold her attention, she learned about managing money and the art of business from her father, skills that interested her. She also liked dancing and social functions and was sent to Miss Wolcott's, a finishing school, whose curriculum was more to her taste than the classics. Mamie grew into a well-liked, well-adjusted young woman.

Marriage

Charming, popular, and from an affluent family, Mamie had many suitors, but it was a young military officer who captured her heart. In 1915, while her family was visiting a friend at Fort Sam Houston in Texas, she met Dwight Eisenhower, then a second lieutenant and six years her senior. Eisenhower was interested in the nineteen-year-old belle, and she in him. The two toured the fort together. The young officer, who grew up in relative poverty, admired John Doud's success and business acumen. They became engaged on Valentine's Day in 1916. Mamie's family approved of Eisenhower, but her father was concerned about Eisenhower's plans to enter the air corps, thinking it would be too risky. As a condition for his support, Doud asked that his future son-in-law avoid air service. The request was granted, and Mamie and "Ike" were married on July 1, 1916, at the Doud home in Denver.

Ike's career would be the centerpiece of their lives together. He made this clear, stating, "Mamie, there's one thing you must understand. My country comes first and always will. You come second." Although she was not always happy with the arrangement, Mamie faithfully supported her husband's career and repeatedly endured long separations and bouts of loneliness.

Family Life

Eisenhower's career caused them to move often, sometimes more than once a year, and they called more than thirty houses home in several states as well as in Panama, France, and the Philippines. Most of these houses were smaller and much less than what Mamie was accustomed to, for Eisenhower's military pay could not match what Mamie's father had made (although her father assisted the couple by lending them money). The moves and separations took their toll on Mamie, who suffered from loneliness and serious bouts of depression. Contributing to this was Ike's habit of spending time with his military pals, sometimes missing dinners and staying out late at night gambling or playing cards. Their marriage was lukewarm at times, and Eisenhower was often inattentive to his wife's needs. Mamie dealt with her loneliness by returning home to Denver to console herself with her family. Eisenhower's career kept him from home when their first child, Doud Dwight (known as "Icky") was born in 1917. Mamie suffered further when the little boy died in 1921 of scarlet fever. A second son, John, was born a year after Icky's death, which helped her heal the loss of her firstborn. She also had a number of maladies, including a weak heart, insomnia, and an inner ear problem that caused dizziness; she had spells of ill health throughout her life.

During World War II Eisenhower rose to the rank of supreme commander of the allied forces, serving in Europe for over three years, during which time Mamie saw her husband only once. Her son, John, was at West Point, so Mamie lived alone in Washington during the war. She was lonely and worried about Ike's safety; she was also greatly disturbed by rumors of Eisenhower's relationship with his British driver, Kay Summersby.

But in spite of the difficult times, the two experienced many high points in their life together. When Eisenhower was on General Fox Connor's staff, Connor's wife apparently recognized the problems in the Eisenhower marriage and encouraged Mamie to be more conscious of her appearance and to take more interest in her husband's career. Mamie seems to have heeded the advice. Although Eisenhower did not solicit his wife's counsel and she appears to have had little if any influence over him, her presence and actions nevertheless benefited her husband's career. She became the epitome of the supportive military wife and always stood by her husband, entertaining military brass at their home. She managed the family's finances and handled all family and social matters. Although Eisenhower was rather narrow-minded and interested in little more than the military, Mamie helped broaden his perspectives and introduced him to cultural experiences. During the war she served food to soldiers at a USO canteen and worked with the American Women's Voluntary Services. Mamie was never a full partner in her husband's military or political career, like so many first ladies before her, but she was unwavering in her support of all he did and was a well-liked hostess during his rise to fame.

After the successful conclusion of World War II in 1945, Eisenhower continued his duty in Europe for two years, as chief of staff of the U.S. Army. After the war the Eisenhowers purchased a farm in Gettysburg, Pennsylvania, where they longed to retire to what was the first place they could truly call their own home. In 1948, however, Eisenhower resigned and became president of Columbia University in New York City, a post he held until 1950, when he took a leave of absence to become supreme commander of the Allied Powers in Europe and organize NATO's defense forces.

Presidency

By the end of World War II, Eisenhower was a national hero. His stature remained high, and both parties sought him to run for the presidency in the 1948 election. Although he turned them down, he accepted the Republican nomination in 1952. Both Ike and Mamie were in many ways reluctant to seek office, but they campaigned diligently. Mamie, who originally opposed the idea, joined her husband on his nationwide campaign. Although she had never liked or felt comfortable in crowds and had formerly disliked traveling, she came to enjoy campaigning and was a smiling, popular figure among the crowds who turned out to see the war hero and his wife.

Once in the White House, unlike her immediate predecessors, Mamie took pleasure in hosting social events, and she provided a complete social calendar. She also found all the pomp and pageantry that surrounds the White House rewarding and fun. Not only did she like entertaining, but she was good at it, having gained experience as a hostess during Ike's long career as an officer. She had several rooms redecorated featuring pinks and greens, her favorite colors. She took great pride in her ability to manage a household; even the president was impressed with the tight ship she ran. She could be demanding of the White House staff, but Mamie remembered all their names and bought them presents during the Christmas holidays, one of her favorite times of the year. The Christmas season in the Eisenhower White House always found the building decorated and in a festive spirit; Mamie held additional social events and entertained many guests at that time.

The first lady's active participation did not extend beyond the social sphere of the presidency. Mamie took no interest in politics and did not attempt to influence her husband's decisions. She almost never asked him about what he did or his policies. She attended no political meetings and rarely even entered the Oval Office, nor did Eisenhower involve his wife in any of the political aspects of his presidency. Mamie did not advocate any social issues during her first ladyship, and when offered the opportunity by the *New York Herald Tribune* and other papers to write a column similar to Eleanor Roosevelt's, she declined. She also did not hold press conferences.

The first lady's uninvolvement in political matters does not mean she was not a valuable part of her husband's presidency. Mamie was enormously popular during Eisenhower's two terms and came to embody the symbol of traditional womanhood during the 1950s. Her trademark matching pink gloves, purse, and accessories and her short bangs initiated a minor fashion trend known as the "Mamie look." Addressing the first lady's popularity during the election, the *New York Times* even suggested that she was worth "fifty electoral votes." But perhaps her biggest contribution was in caring for her husband when he had a heart attack in 1955. Mamie was protective of Ike and worked to create a sense of normalcy or "home" in the White House as he recuperated. She altered and reduced the president's work schedule, improved his diet, and established a quiet room upstairs for him to practice his therapeutic hobby, painting. Another heart attack and intestinal surgery during his second term greatly diminished his energy level, but Mamie nursed her husband through each ordeal and can be credited for keeping his spirits high and helping him overcome his waning enthusiasm for the office. Her efforts become all the more impressive when one considers that her own health was far from optimum: She was frequently weak, and her recurring health problems affected her social schedule and left her exhausted during much of her first ladyship.

Legacy

After the limited social calendar during the Great Depression, World War II, and the immediate postwar era, combined with the general disinterest in entertaining by first ladies Hoover, Roosevelt, and Truman, Mamie Eisenhower's readiness to entertain was well received by the capital city. She is remembered as one of the most popular social hostesses in the twentieth century. But she also was perhaps the least political first lady of the century, and unlike most of her predecessors, she had no political influence with the president. Still, Mamie steadfastly supported Eisenhower's career—to which she often took second place—throughout their long life together.

After the White House the Eisenhowers eagerly retired to their home in Gettysburg, Pennsylvania, where they enjoyed several happy years. The general died in 1969. Mamie suffered a stroke in 1976 and died three years later, on November 1, 1979.

Bibliography

Brandon, Dorothy. *Mamie Doud Eisenhower: Portrait of a First Lady.* New York: Scribner's, 1954.

Brendon, Piers. *Ike: His Life and Times.* New York: Harper & Row, 1986.

David, Lester, and Irene David. *Ike and Mamie: The Story of the General and His Lady.* New York: Putnam's, 1981.

Eisenhower, John S. D. *Letters to Mamie.* Garden City, NJ: Doubleday, 1978.

Eisenhower, Susan. *Mrs. Ike: Memories and Reflections on the Life of Mamie Eisenhower.* New York: Farrar, Straus & Giroux, 1996.

36

Jacqueline Lee Bouvier Kennedy Onassis

Born: July 28, 1929; Southhampton, New York
Died: May 19, 1994; New York, New York
President: John F. Kennedy (1917–1963), Thirty-fifth President
Husband's Presidential Term: 1961–1963 (Democrat)
Marriage: First: September 12, 1953, to John Kennedy; Newport, Rhode Island. Second: October 20, 1968, to Aristotle Onassis; Skorpios, Greece
Children: First marriage: Caroline Bouvier (1957–); John Fitzgerald Jr. (1960–1999); Patrick Bouvier (1963). Second marriage: None

Early Years

The Bouviers were a fixture in the network of moneyed families in New York City and Long Island, New York. On July 28, 1929, the elder of two daughters was born in Southhampton, to Janet Lee and John "Jack" Vernon Bouvier III. Jacqueline Bouvier led a privileged childhood that included all the trappings of luxury. She was an active child who was an accomplished horseback rider, and her hobbies included ballet, art, and poetry.

But the Bouvier marriage left much to be desired. Jackie's father was often away from his family and was prone to infidelity and excessive partying. Jackie's mother was a dignified, image-conscious woman who soon tired of her husband's dalliances; the two divorced in 1940. The event crushed their impressionable, emotional older daughter. Janet Lee then married Hugh D. Auchincloss, a wealthy stockbroker who was twice divorced and had three children from his previous marriages; Auchincloss and Janet would have two additional children together. The family moved to Washington and summered at his estate in Newport, Rhode Island. Regardless, the young girl missed her father and longed for the times she occasionally spent with him.

Jackie grew into a sophisticated young lady. She was educated at the best schools and at age fifteen attended Miss Porter's, a well-known finishing school in Farmington, Connecticut. Her social debut was much anticipated, and her beauty and poise were the talk of society columnists. When she debuted during the 1947–1948 social season, she was named "debutante of the year." Jackie attended Vassar College in New York and won *Vogue* magazine's "Prix de Paris" essay contest; among the prizes was a scholarship to study in Paris. At the Sorbonne she studied French and French art, becoming fluent in the language. This was one of the happiest times of her life, as she loved France and her experience there. When she returned, she finished college at George Washington University, graduating in 1951.

After graduation she declined a job offer from *Vogue,* and a family friend helped her obtain a position with the *Washington Times Herald,* where she worked from 1951 to 1953. Her column, "Inquiring Camera Girl," involved photographing and interviewing people about social and political issues of the day. One of her interviews was with Tricia Nixon, the daughter of the vice president.

Marriage

Jackie's beauty invited many suitors, and she was briefly engaged. While on an assignment for the newspaper in 1952, she met John Kennedy, then a congressman from Massachusetts running for the U.S. Senate. Their romance was slow to start, and the courtship went through hot and cold periods. Jackie was not interested in politics and thought Kennedy was too ambitious. But they became engaged the following year and married on September 12, 1953, in Newport, Rhode Island.

The match seemed made in heaven. The wedding generated much attention among the media, society columnists, and political establishment because of the prominence of the two families involved, the bride's beauty and social standing, and Kennedy's status as the capital's most eligible bachelor, as well as his great potential for political success. But if it appeared to be an ideal union, the marriage had many problems and has since been a topic of much speculation. Jackie was never comfortable in political circles and, in spite of her upbringing, did not enjoy entertaining at social and political events. Nor did she like political life in Washington or the loss of privacy that went along with her husband's career. She was uncomfortable as well with the large Kennedy family, especially her husband's domineering parents, who often intruded on their married life and were not fond of their new daughter-in-law.

Family Life

Shortly after their marriage, John Kennedy was elected to the U.S. Senate, and only two years into his term, he sought the vice presidential spot on the 1956 Democratic ticket. His bid for the higher office failed, but it put Kennedy in the national limelight and on track for his own presidential ambitions. It also symbolized the central role his political career would play in the Kennedy marriage.

After a miscarriage, Jackie had a daughter, Caroline, in 1957. In 1960 she was pregnant during her husband's successful presidential campaign; John Jr. was born that year. Another son, Patrick, born prematurely in 1963, died after two days, only weeks before the assassination of President Kennedy.

Perhaps the greatest challenge of Jackie's family life was not her strained relationship with her in-laws or her reluctance to engage in public life because of the loss of privacy, but rather her attempt to raise a family away from the glare of public attention. In spite of the public's fascination with the handsome young Kennedy family and JFK's popular presidency, she was fairly successful in shielding her children from the media and, as much as could be expected, providing a degree of normalcy for them. During her first ladyship she organized a private school in the White House for her daughter and a few other children, as Edith Roosevelt had done decades earlier.

Another challenge of the Kennedy marriage was JFK's poor health. Even though he projected the image of an active, fit man, he suffered from a variety of ailments, including a recurring back problem that required serious surgery in both 1954 and 1955. The marriage was at times strained, and the two spent time alone, away from each other in the company of their own circles of friends. They even vacationed separately, and it raised some eyebrows when Jackie traveled without her husband to such destinations as Greece, India, Pakistan, and Italy. It did not help that she was disinterested in politics and, to a degree, in Kennedy's career. Moreover, he generally did not attempt to include her in his career or political decisions, except to take advantage of the benefit to his image of having an attractive young wife and family. Jackie did assist him with his book, *Profiles in Courage,* for which he won the Pulitzer Prize in 1957, which helped fashion the daring, heroic image that greatly aided his pursuit of the presidency.

Presidency

Because Jackie was pregnant with her second child for most of her husband's presidential campaign, she did not actively participate in it. She was nevertheless a positive presence, writing a weekly column titled "Campaign Wife" that was circulated by the Democratic Party. Only thirty-one years old when Kennedy was elected, Jackie was the second youngest first lady–elect and third youngest presidential spouse in the country's history. (Both Julia Tyler and Frances Cleveland were in their early twenties in the White House.)

Jacqueline Kennedy was a reluctant first lady who generally did not enjoy her experience in the White House. She did not take an active part in her husband's presidency and rarely made formal remarks, although apparently she wrote her own speeches when she did. Even though she neither cared for nor involved herself in politics, Jackie was an immensely popular first lady and a major asset to the Kennedy administration.

Jackie brought a high degree of sophistication and culture to the first ladyship. She enhanced the menu at White House dinners, once hosting forty-nine Nobel laureates. She spoke French and Spanish and had some familiarity with Italian. Her taste in fashion set off nationwide trends. Her looks played well on the new medium of television. As a former journalist and wife of a media-conscious president, she from time to time allowed herself and the children to be photographed; the White House freely released pictures of her. Her relationship with the press was an unusual one, as Jackie did not like or trust the media and often attempted to avoid them and ban them from certain White House events. Yet both she and her husband knew how to use the press to their advantage. Reporters were often frustrated at Jackie's distance and non-cooperation, especially when her press secretary, Pamela Turnure, covered for the first lady's unwillingness to grant their requests. Yet they fawned over the first lady, and she enjoyed much positive press coverage. For a first lady so loved by the general public, Jackie did not like mixing with them and was aloof and condescending in her views of the people who admired her. She was famous inside the mansion for begging out of public appearances and events.

Although she did not champion a political cause as first lady, Jackie did support organizations such as the American Cancer Society and the Girl Scouts. The first lady also became one of the most prominent advocates of the arts in White House history. She supported international exchange programs for students and artists and was a patron of the National Cultural Center, which was eventually renamed the Kennedy Center for the Arts. The first lady invited famous artists to White House socials, and her events often featured their performances, to which she invited children's and educational groups.

Arguably the most famous White House restoration and renovation were headed by Jacqueline Kennedy. The first lady inventoried its furnishings and artworks and led a drive to procure additional historic artworks and antiques, including items formerly in the mansion. She did much of the work herself, going from room to room cataloging items. Moreover, many of the ideas behind the project were hers, including her vision of the White House as a living museum of history. To assist her, Jackie obtained the services of experts in art history, including John Walker, director of the National Gallery of Art, and such politically well-connected individuals as Clark Clifford, a prominent lawyer and White House aide. The first lady's charisma greatly aided the raising of private funds, and many collectors found it hard to deny her request for donations of period pieces to the White House collection.

Her much anticipated renovations were unveiled to the nation on February 14, 1962, in a televised tour of the White House. The hour-long tour, watched by an estimated forty-two million viewers, was not only a political success for the president and first lady but won an Emmy award. The number of visitors skyrocketed after the tour. Jackie also developed the first comprehensive historical guidebook to the White House for visitors. Congress responded by passing legislation, backed by the first lady, that would encourage donations to the White House of valuable and historic pieces and forbade presidents from giving away items from the mansion as souvenirs, which several presidents had done.

Jackie was also successful in her international travels. On state visits to nations such as Colombia, Mexico, and Venezuela, the first lady addressed the crowds in Spanish, for which she received praise both there and at home. When the couple visited France, Jackie impressed her hosts, including the venerable and hard-to-please Charles de Gaulle, with her command of French and her knowledge of French art and culture. De Gaulle was nothing less than enamored of Jackie. When speaking of the first lady's popularity in France, the *New York Times* suggested that the president was simply "the man who accompanied Jacqueline Kennedy to Paris."

Legacy

Jackie Kennedy was with her husband when he was assassinated in Dallas, Texas, in November 1963. The event has become immortalized in American memory, along with the first lady's courage and strength during the ordeal. She stood beside Vice President Lyndon B. Johnson during his in-flight swearing-in ceremony, and it was Jackie who planned her husband's funeral, an epic event that helped ensure his legacy. The Kennedy legend was furthered when Jackie referred to those magical years as "Camelot," a term that has since become a central part of Kennedy's enduring popularity.

After the assassination, the former first lady lived briefly in Georgetown, then moved to New York City. She was never able to escape the gaze of the public and press, as she became an icon of popular culture and one of the most recognized women in the world. Still attempting to shun publicity, Jackie avoided public events, even those pertaining to her husband's presidency, but she is credited with selecting the famous architect I. M. Pei to design the Kennedy Library in Massachusetts. Jackie and her husband's brother, Robert Kennedy, developed a close friendship that helped both endure the loss of the president, but she was again devastated when Bobby was assassinated in 1968 while campaigning for the presidency. A few months later she stunned the country by marrying Greek shipping magnate Aristotle Onassis. Onassis was much older than his thirty-nine-year-old bride, and the marriage seemed one of convenience, driven by self-interest on both sides. Jackie binged on Onassis's considerable fortune but often spent time away from him.

After her second husband's death in 1975, Jackie lived in New York City, where she worked as an editor for Viking Press, then Doubleday. To the day of her death in May 1994, she remained a symbol of the Kennedy presidency, and she is remembered as one of the most famous first ladies in history.

Bibliography

Adler, Bill. *The Uncommon Wisdom of Jacqueline Kennedy Onassis: A Portrait in Her Own Words.* New York: Citadel Press, 1994.

Anthony, Carl Sferrazza. *As We Remember Her: Jacqueline Kennedy Onassis in the Words of Friends and Family.* New York: HarperCollins, 1997.

Curtis, Charlotte. *First Lady.* New York: Pyramid Books, 1962.

Thayer, Mary Van Rensselaer. *Jacqueline Kennedy: The White House Years.* Boston: Little, Brown, 1971.

———. *Jacqueline Bouvier Kennedy.* New York: Doubleday, 1961.

37

Claudia Alta "Lady Bird" Taylor Johnson

Born: December 22, 1912; Karnack, Texas
President: Lyndon B. Johnson (1908–1973), Thirty-sixth President
Husband's Presidential Term: 1963–1969 (Democrat)
Marriage: November 17, 1934; San Antonio, Texas
Children: Lynda Bird (1944–); Luci Baines (1947–)

Early Years

Claudia Alta Taylor was born on December 22, 1912, near the town of Karnack in Texas. When she was still a baby, the Johnson family nurse-maid and cook, Alice Tittle, declared the infant was cute as a "Lady Bird," and the nickname stuck. Lady Bird's mother, Minnie Pattillo Taylor, came from a wealthy family in Alabama but held views uncharacteristic for a woman of her time living in the South. It appears that Minnie Taylor would pass on to her daughter her support for women's rights, a love of reading, and her intelligence, refinement, and ambition. She was a big influence on the child's early years but died when Lady Bird was a young girl, in 1918 after suffering a fall while pregnant.

Minnie's sister, Effie Pattillo, moved from Alabama to take care of her deceased sister's family. Thomas Jefferson Taylor, Lady Bird's father, appears to have dealt with his grief by throwing himself into his work, leaving Effie to raise his daughter. Thomas Taylor did impart to his daughter his business acumen, and she was a quick study. While growing up, Lady Bird developed an interest in flowers and the outdoors and was as comfortable in the woods as in the classroom.

Lady Bird finished school at age fifteen and studied at Saint Mary's School for Girls in Dallas. In 1930 she enrolled at the University of Texas in Austin, where she excelled in her studies, especially history, literature, and journalism, and graduated with honors. While at the University of Texas, she wrote for the campus newspaper, the *Daily Texan,* developing an understanding of the press that would later serve both her and her husband in his political career. Lady Bird was a popular student who dated often and had high expectations for any future spouse; she wanted to have her own career as well.

Marriage

Lady Bird met Lyndon B. Johnson in 1934 in Austin, when a mutual friend introduced them. Johnson, a few years older than Lady Bird, was working as a congressional aide. Instantly infatuated, Lyndon Johnson asked her out on a date, then proposed right after their meeting, but she declined. Johnson returned to Washington and aggressively pursued the relationship, calling and writing and expressing his desire to marry. She had made quite an impression on her impulsive suitor; in fact, everything about Lady Bird impressed Lyndon, especially her intelligence. He gave her intellectual and political books as gifts. A few weeks later Johnson returned to Texas and again proposed. This time Lady Bird accepted, and the couple were married on November 17, 1934.

Lyndon Johnson was in every way a political animal. Politics was his passion and he wanted it to be hers as well; it was very much a part of their courtship and their plans for the future. Lady Bird soon mastered the basics and became Johnson's close political confidante. She even learned the names of the constituents in his congressional district.

Family Life

Lyndon Johnson came to depend on his wife. Although he was famous for not taking advice, he often listened to and even solicited her opinion. She was the only one who could keep his temper in check, and her calmness and deliberation balanced his demanding, restless nature. Lady Bird was also a quick learner who became increasingly astute in her political judgment over the course of Johnson's public career. After a number of years in politics, she was often heard saying *"we* want" or *"we* agree," reflecting their growing partnership. Lady Bird was a model political spouse who steadfastly supported her husband throughout his long public career. Even in the beginning of his career, when he ran for a seat in the Congress, Lady Bird donated some $10,000 and her father kicked in another $25,000 to the campaign. These funds helped Johnson win the election. When Johnson joined the navy during World War II and had to leave the capital for service, he refused to give up his congressional seat. Lady Bird ran the congressional office for her husband while he was away.

If Johnson appreciated his wife's role, he did not seem to show it. He was a difficult man to live with, self-serving and prone to criticizing his wife, even in public and over such matters as her clothing. Johnson had a reputation for being rude and yelling at her and his assistants. Fortunately for both the politician and the marriage, Lady Bird was a patient person. She was also a hard worker. In an effort to overcome her shyness, Lady Bird practiced her speaking and in 1959 even enrolled in a course at a public speaking club in Washington. She was aware of her limitations and worked to overcome them and to improve her public image. Another example of her energy and determination was her work with the Austin radio station she purchased in 1943, KTBC. She was not only the owner but did everything from managing to cleaning the station, turning it into a moneymaker. KTBC grew into a lucrative media business that made the Johnsons wealthy.

Lyndon's career progressed when he was elected to the U.S. Senate in 1948. During the 1950s he rose to be the Senate majority leader. Lady Bird continued to work for her husband, supporting his career and, after his heart attack in 1955, nursing him back to health. Although she had miscarried, she generally experienced good health and had two children: Lynda Bird, born in 1944, and Luci Baines in 1947. Her firstborn would eventually marry Charles Robb, who served Virginia as a U.S. senator and its governor.

Presidency

Johnson's success in the Senate positioned him to run for president, and in 1959 and 1960 he began pursuing the office. His bid failed, but he was placed on the 1960 Democratic ticket as the running mate for John Kennedy. Although Johnson hated playing second fiddle, he and Lady Bird campaigned hard for the ticket. In Dallas, they were confronted by a group of supporters of the Republican candidate, Richard Nixon. Lady Bird was heckled, spit on, and even hit with a sign, yet she was not deterred from future campaigning. The incident generated much praise for Johnson's courageous wife and generated positive publicity for the Democratic ticket.

John Kennedy won the presidency, and because the first lady sought to avoid as many public duties as possible, Lady Bird emerged as one of the most active "second ladies" the nation had ever experienced, filling in for Jacqueline Kennedy. As wife of the vice president, she honed her hosting and public speaking skills and had the opportunity to visit several states and foreign countries.

After Kennedy's tragic death, Lyndon Johnson became president and Lady Bird quickly asserted herself as first lady. In the White House Lady Bird hosted working women to celebrate their accomplishments in her "Women Doers" luncheons. Following in her predecessor's footsteps, Lady Bird continued work on the White House, initiating a few of her own renovations and, in collaboration with the National Geographic Society, producing a historic account of the mansion, "The Living White House." She was also her husband's adviser. Lady Bird helped him with his speeches and was probably the only person who could criticize him. She was one of the most visible and active first ladies in the history of the office, giving over a hundred speeches, appearing on television and radio, traveling extensively, and embracing a variety of causes; she was a valuable campaign aide and political asset for her husband.

The highlight of Lady Bird's campaigning was in 1964. Concerned over the loss of his base of support in the South because of the 1964 Civil Rights Act, the president sent his wife on a goodwill mission through the region. Lady Bird embarked on a four-day, thousand-mile trip beginning on October 5, 1964, that took her through eight southern states, including Virginia, North Carolina, South Carolina, Georgia, Florida, Alabama, Mississippi, and Louisiana. Her eighteen-car train, dubbed the "Lady Bird Special," made forty-seven stops along the way while the first lady met with governors, members of Congress, and other key political figures. As the president's emissary, Lady Bird reminded her often hostile audiences that she and the president were proud southerners and that the president needed their support. Many of the ideas on the whistle-stop tour came from the first lady. The trip was a success, and she was credited with helping to minimize the president's losses in the South over his support of civil rights.

The first lady's most famous activity was her leadership in the

Johnson administration's beautification and conservation initiative. The program started in 1964 and expanded in 1965 and each subsequent year of the Johnson presidency. Lady Bird was never completely satisfied with the term "beautification" to describe the program, because the initiative also involved environmental protection and the conservation of natural resources. Initially, the Committee for a More Beautiful Capital was convened in 1965 to clean urban areas and plant trees and flowers. Lady Bird publicized the program by speaking to numerous garden and civic clubs, inviting the wives of cabinet members to participate, and hosting a White House Conference on Natural Beauty in 1965. Wisely soliciting the participation of experts in the field, Lady Bird expanded her project nationwide to include removing unsightly billboards from scenic highways, protecting historic sites, and promoting awareness of conservation issues.

The first lady took her beautification and conservation program into the inner city, seeing it as a way to improve social conditions in troubled urban areas through revitalizing city parks, landscaping, and involving local residents in the projects. She helped build dozens of urban parks and playgrounds. On November 25, 1965, the first lady appeared on national television to promote her project and its accomplishments. The hour-long show, titled "A Visit to Washington with Mrs. Lyndon B. Johnson on Behalf of a More Beautiful Capital," featured the first lady visiting parks and projects. On a national level, she raised money for the project while raising awareness of conservation issues, including clean air and clean water. Lady Bird also lobbied Congress to expand the national park system and establish new wildlife areas.

Lady Bird's activism included advocacy of the Headstart program and other antipoverty measures. She was a recognizable figure in most aspects of her husband's famous Great Society policies. Lyndon Johnson was well known for his long workdays, but Lady Bird, too, was a tireless worker. The first lady's leadership continued long after she left the White House. In retirement she helped establish a wildflower research center in 1982 and, with Carlton Lees, published a book titled *Wildflowers Across America* in 1988.

Legacy

Lady Bird supported her husband's decision not to seek another term in the White House in 1968. The turmoil of the late 1960s and the enduring crisis of the Vietnam War had taken their toll on the president. The Johnsons retired to their ranch in Texas, but even in retirement the activist first lady remained a prominent public figure. Lady Bird had kept a detailed account of her experiences since 1963, and in 1970 she wrote *A White House Diary*. She also served on the board of regents of the University of Texas and continued to advocate conservation issues. Lyndon Johnson suffered the heart attack that took his life on January 22, 1973.

One of the most admired women of her time, Lady Bird was honored in 1977 with the Presidential Medal of Freedom. In 1981 she was the subject of a documentary film, "The First Lady: A Portrait of Lady Bird Johnson." She was awarded the Congressional Gold Medal in 1988. Lady Bird Johnson was perhaps the most well-rounded first lady in the history of the presidency. She excelled at every task, from social hosting to campaigning. She was her husband's most trusted adviser and was an effective advocate for one of the most famous social causes associated with the first ladyship. A stroke in 1993 and failing eyesight have slowed the former first lady, but as of this writing Lady Bird Johnson continues to live on the Johnson ranch near Austin, making her one of the longest-lived first ladies.

Bibliography

Gould, Lewis L. *Lady Bird Johnson and the Environment.* Lawrence: University Press of Kansas, 1987.

Johnson, Lady Bird. *A White House Diary.* New York: Holt, Rinehart & Winston, 1970.

Middleton, Harry. *Lady Bird Johnson: A Life Well Lived.* Austin, TX: Lyndon Baines Johnson Foundation, 1992.

Montgomery, Ruth. *Mrs. LBJ.* New York: Holt, Rinehart & Winston, 1964.

Smith, Marie. *The President's Lady: An Intimate Biography of Mrs. Lyndon B. Johnson.* New York: Random House, 1964.

38

Thelma Catherine "Pat" Ryan Nixon

Born: March 16, 1912; Ely, Nevada
Died: June 22, 1993; San Clemente, California
President: Richard M. Nixon (1913–1994), Thirty-seventh President
Husband's Presidential Term: 1969–1974 (Republican)
Marriage: June 21, 1940; Riverside, California
Children: Patricia (1946–); Julie (1948–)

Early Years

Thelma Catherine Ryan was born in the small mining town of Ely, Nevada, on March 16, 1912. Her father, William Ryan, was of Irish descent and worked as a miner there. Pat's mother was Kate Halberstadt Bender, a struggling widow with two children who immigrated to the United States before marrying Ryan. Because his daughter was born on the eve of St. Patrick's Day, William Ryan called his little girl "St. Patrick's babe," and the name "Pat" stuck.

When Pat was still a young girl, Ryan moved his family to the farming community of Artesia, near Los Angeles, California. He had made little money in mining, and the family continued to face difficult times. In 1925, when Pat was barely a teenager, her mother died, leaving her to take care of her father and two older brothers. This she did while balancing her domestic chores with the demands of school. Shortly thereafter Ryan's health began to deteriorate; Pat nursed him throughout his ordeal, but he died around the time she finished high school. It seems that the characteristic perseverance and courage Pat would show during her husband's political career and presidency had manifested itself early on.

Pat did well in school and was a disciplined young woman who always dreamed of something better. She longed to travel and experience new things and became quite independent and adventurous after her parents died. Although she had little money, she was willing to work in a variety of jobs, from bank teller to janitor, to support herself. After high school she enrolled in Fullerton Junior College. In 1931 an opportunity arose to drive an elderly couple across the country; Pat seized her chance not only to make some money but also to see the country. Arriving on the East Coast, she decided to stay in New York City for a few years, where she worked as a secretary. While there, she completed training at Columbia University and took a job as an X-ray technician at a hospital. She also visited Washington, D.C., in 1933. She returned to California to attend the University of Southern California. Despite working long hours in miscellaneous jobs such as a dental technician, phone operator, clothing model at a department store, and even a movie extra, Pat graduated in 1937 with honors and a degree in merchandising. She then took a job at Whittier High School in California teaching business education, including typing and shorthand. She pursued an interest in dance and theater by assisting in the school's theater productions and serving as the cheerleading adviser.

Marriage

In 1938 Pat auditioned with a community theater group in Whittier for a production entitled *The Dark Tower*. During the auditions she met Richard Nixon. Originally from Whittier, Nixon had just returned to the area after completing his law degree at Duke University in North Carolina. The two became friends and participated in theater together, but Nixon's interest was much more romantic than hers. He asked Pat out and immediately asked her to marry him. She declined, but the two continued to be friends and date for the next two years. Nixon was so intrigued with Pat that he pursued her even while she went out with other men—even driving her to her dates.

Pat eventually agreed to marry Richard Nixon, and the two were wed on June 21, 1940, in Riverside, California. She adopted her husband's Quaker faith, to which both nominally adhered. She also continued teaching after marriage, and Nixon practiced law in Whittier until 1942.

Family Life
The United States entered World War II a year and a half after the couple were married. Nixon took a position in the Office of Price Administration in Washington, then enlisted in the navy. While her husband served in the South Pacific, Pat worked in San Francisco as an economist and analyst, the only woman in the San Francisco Office of Price Administration. She also volunteered for wartime causes, including the Red Cross.

After the war, with no professional political experience, Nixon ran for the U.S. House of Representatives and was elected. Pat helped in the 1946 campaign and that same year gave birth to Tricia; two years later a second daughter, Julie, was born. For one who had never participated in politics, Pat was an asset on the campaign trail. Working more as a manager than as the candidate's wife, Pat studied campaigns and elections, analyzed the opponent's voting record, and offered her husband advice on the stump. She also assisted with mail and did clerical work for the campaign. Her support of Richard Nixon's political career and campaigns continued through his election to the U.S. Senate in 1950 and his tenure as Dwight Eisenhower's vice president from 1953 to 1961.

Pat's work on her husband's behalf had more to do with her role as a supportive wife than with any interest in politics. She never grew to like politics and was bothered by the negativity that surrounded the occupation, even referring to politicians as "vicious," ironic since her husband first gained national attention through his work on the infamous House Un-American Affairs Committee and in Senator Joe McCarthy's ugly anticommunist crusade. Nixon was ruthless in his attacks on opponents and approached politics as a battle. Pat thought little of Senator McCarthy and such tactics, and her loyalty to her husband was certainly put to the test on numerous occasions. But Nixon was often on the receiving end of destructive politics, such as the 1952 attack on his character and behavior that nearly removed him from the Republican ticket.

Through her husband's rise in politics, Pat remained a source of strength and support for him. During Nixon's 1960 bid for president,

Pat was again a central part of the campaign. The Republican Party even held a "Pat Week" rally for women voters and issued press releases and campaign literature featuring the candidate's wife. Nixon supporters used campaign slogans like "Pat for first lady," "When you elect a president you are also electing a first lady," and "The first lady has a working assignment"—testimony to her popularity. Nixon's close loss in 1960 was a bitter defeat for both the candidate and his wife. Pat wanted her husband to retire from politics, and he gave her his word he would. The Nixons moved back to California, and he practiced law in Beverly Hills. But the calling to public office was too much for Nixon to ignore, and over Pat's opposition he ran for governor of California in 1962—and lost. Nixon announced his departure from politics, and the following year they moved to New York City, where he worked as a lawyer.

Presidency

The political bug again bit Richard Nixon in 1968, and he once more ran for president, defeating Hubert Humphrey and George Wallace. Although Pat had long since tired of politics, she dutifully supported her husband's campaign and participated in the public aspects of his presidency. In fact, Pat Nixon emerged as a highly visible first lady. She traveled to Africa in 1972, visiting Ghana, Liberia, and the Ivory Coast, and went to South America as the president's personal envoy on such assignments as assisting with an earthquake relief mission.

Pat was an active hostess, putting on concerts and children's events at the White House and the city's monuments. The first lady served on her husband's Committee on Employment of the Handicapped and put her support into action by arranging special tours of the White House for physically disabled and blind and deaf visitors and making sure the building was accessible to all. She also had the White House guidebooks printed in other languages, had the building illuminated at night, and offered candlelight tours of the mansion during the Christmas holidays. The first lady refurbished parts of the building, commissioning work on the staterooms, and procured artifacts and obtained portraits of some of the previous occupants, which enhanced the presidential and first lady portrait galleries. In 1971 she opened the White House to guests for Sunday church services in the East Room.

Her personal project as first lady was promoting volunteerism on behalf of the poor and underprivileged. Dubbed the National Recruitment Program and dedicated to the "spirit of people helping people," the initiative included establishing a National Center for Voluntary Action and encouraging the public to volunteer in schools, hospitals, and other worthy enterprises. But the first lady's efforts were far from ambitious, and the program was unsuccessful in generating much public support. This appears to have been the result of the first lady's growing disinterest in politics and Nixon's tendency to control and minimize his wife's activities. The strain of public life and of being "managed" by her husband and his aides became apparent, as Pat became more remote from the office; she was criticized as "Plastic Pat" and "the robot" because of her staged, unenthusiastic public appearances. There were rumors of alcohol abuse and depression. However, even though the trials of public office took their toll on Pat, such rumors appear to have been exaggerations.

Although Pat Nixon was a strong, talented woman, her capabilities and cheerful demeanor faded over the course of the Nixon presidency. At the outset, she attended cabinet meetings, studied issues, and discussed policy with her husband. Her enthusiasm was drained, however, by the tumultuous events of the late 1960s and early 1970s, public hostility toward the president and the Vietnam War, and the poor treatment she received from her husband. Nixon failed to include his wife in his decisionmaking and showed little interest in or warmth toward her. The events of the Watergate scandal took a further toll on the couple. Even though Pat stood by her husband, his actions—especially news that he had even taped conversations with her—understandably hurt her.

Nixon's resignation from the presidency on August 9, 1974, was traumatic for Pat, who had never enjoyed being the center of publicity. She longed for privacy and a reprieve from politics.

Legacy

Pat Nixon rarely receives the credit she deserves. She was a highly able individual, a gracious hostess, and devoted supporter of her husband despite countless setbacks and difficulties. Pat was a vital source of strength for the president as he endured both the crisis of Watergate and the shame and harm to his reputation that occurred during and after the scandal.

Back in California Pat cherished her privacy, although she did attend select events with her husband. She was at the dedication ceremony when a local high school was renamed in her honor in 1975, and she accompanied the former president on his triumphant return to China; she also attended both the dedication of the Nixon Library and

Birthplace in 1990 and the opening of the Reagan Library the following year. By this time her health had declined. She had suffered a stroke in 1976 and another in 1982, from which she never fully recovered. The former first lady died on June 22, 1993, Richard Nixon the following year.

Bibliography

David, Lester. *The Lonely Lady of San Clemente: The Story of Pat Nixon.* New York: Thomas Y. Crowell, 1978.

Eisenhower, Julie Nixon. *Pat Nixon: The Untold Story.* New York: Simon and Schuster, 1986.

Nixon, Richard. *RN: The Memoirs of Richard Nixon.* New York: Grossett and Dunlap, 1978.

Oudes, Bruce, ed. *From the President: Richard Nixon's Secret Files.* New York: Harper & Row, 1989.

Safire, William. *Before the Fall: An Inside View of the Pre-Watergate White House.* Garden City, NJ: Doubleday, 1975.

39

Elizabeth "Betty" Bloomer Ford

Born: April 8, 1918; Chicago, Illinois
President: Gerald R. Ford (1913–), Thirty-eighth President
Husband's Presidential Term: 1974–1977 (Republican)
Marriage: First: 1942 to William C. Warren; Grand Rapids, Michigan (divorced 1947). Second: October 15, 1948, to Gerald R. Ford; Grand Rapids, Michigan
Children: First marriage: None. Second marriage: Michael Gerald (1950–); John Gardiner (1952–); Steven Meigs (1956–); Susan Elizabeth (1957–)

Early Years

Elizabeth Bloomer was born on April 8, 1918, in Chicago. When she was a young child, her family moved to Grand Rapids, Michigan. She preferred the name Elizabeth, but her nickname, "Betty," stuck. Betty's father, William Bloomer, worked as a salesman and was often away from home, leaving Betty's mother, Hortense Neahr Bloomer, to raise the family and run the household. William died in an accident when Betty was a teen, and the family bore the loss largely because of his wife's strength and determination. Betty apparently inherited much of these qualities from her mother.

One of Betty's passions was dancing. After finishing high school, she wanted to go to New York City to pursue dance as a career, but her mother persuaded her to wait until she was older. She delayed going east for two years, then went to Bennington College in Vermont to study dance. Betty made it to New York City, where she performed in Carnegie Hall and danced with the famous Martha Graham dance company, but she returned to Michigan, partly at her mother's urging. Betty's independence and decision to teach dancing and live in her own apartment frustrated Hortense, but she eventually remarried; Betty herself met a young man named William Warren, whom she decided to marry in spite of Hortense's disapproval.

Marriage

In 1942 Betty and Warren were married at his home in Grand Rapids. Warren sold insurance, and his efforts to secure a better position took them to several different cities. Like his career, the marriage was a failure; after five years Betty divorced him.

Shortly after leaving Warren, Betty was introduced to Gerald Ford by friends. He was a few years older, had been a football star at the University of Michigan, and had graduated from Yale Law School. Ford was seeking a seat in the U.S. House of Representatives when he and Betty became engaged, and the wedding, on October 15, 1948, occurred in the heat of the race. In fact, he campaigned right up to the date and left his new bride at home immediately after so he could campaign. Even though the marriage would become a close working partnership with many strong points, it was clear from the beginning that Ford's career was his primary interest. Later in life Betty often experienced loneliness and depression because of her husband's preoccupation with politics. After the wedding and his election, they moved to Washington, and Betty worked in her husband's office, assisting with mail and other clerical tasks.

Family Life

While Ford was in Congress, the couple built a home in Alexandria, Virginia. Four children were born between 1950 and 1957, and during this time Ford's career progressed as well. He continued to be reelected and by 1965 had become Republican minority leader of the House. Ford's absorption in his career often kept him away from home, a situation aggravated by this leadership position. Betty stayed busy with family and household responsibilities, teaching Sunday school, and working with various social and children's organizations. Although she supported her husband's campaigns, she suffered from depression and resented his neglect. Seeking solace in alcohol and counseling to aid her loneliness, Betty also became addicted to painkillers taken for a nerve problem in her neck.

As Betty struggled with addiction for many years, her self-esteem suffered. She looked forward to Ford's retirement from politics and the possibility of spending more time together. During the Nixon presidency, however, when Vice President Spiro Agnew resigned in late 1973 over a scandal, Ford was tapped to become the next vice president. Her husband's selection caught Betty by surprise.

Presidency

The following year Richard Nixon himself resigned, and Gerald Ford ascended to the presidency, the only person to achieve the office without first being elected. Ford seemed the right man for the time. He promised the country a period of healing after the trying times of the Nixon years and the Watergate scandal. But his decision within a month to pardon his predecessor undermined his initial popularity, and the new president never fully recovered politically.

A reluctant public figure who was battling addiction, Betty Ford nevertheless was a natural in office and would become one of the most well-known, popular, and capable first ladies in the country's history. Betty, who greatly admired Eleanor Roosevelt's accomplishments, herself became a source of strength for countless women. On September 26, 1974, she was diagnosed with breast cancer and underwent a radical mastectomy. Neither the operation nor chemotherapy kept her from fulfilling the duties of first lady, and she was soon presiding over White House social events. In what would become her trademark frankness, she talked openly about her breast cancer; her forthrightness and leadership stirred the national consciousness and began an important open dialogue on the disease. Her office was overwhelmed with mail, while money poured into the American Cancer Society and record numbers of women began getting checkups for breast cancer.

The sincere, open manner in which the first lady addressed personal and socially sensitive issues earned her both admiration and scorn. For instance, in 1975, during an appearance on the popular television show *60 Minutes,* Betty candidly discussed such taboo topics as her bout with breast cancer and the issues of abortion, premarital sex, marijuana, and the Equal Rights Amendment. The host, Morley Safer, ambushed the first lady with pointed and highly personal questions. In answering one, Betty conceded it was possible her daughter might have had sexual intercourse before marriage, but as a mother she would stand behind her daughter regardless of what the teenager had done. The telecast received a mixed response, but ministers and parishioners across the southern Bible Belt criticized the first lady, and the Women's Christian Temperance Union censured her.

Hate mail poured into the White House, but the president supported his wife, and Betty, undeterred, continued to discuss any issue frankly. Spontaneous, direct, and bold, Betty lobbied on behalf of the Equal Rights Amendment, spoke out in support of abortion rights and for the controversial *Roe v. Wade* Supreme Court ruling on abortion, advocated women's issues, and continued to champion breast cancer awareness. The first lady was a keynote speaker at the International Women's Year Congress in 1975 and embraced such lightning-rod issues as offering amnesty to those who had evaded the draft during the Vietnam War, promoting handgun registration, and reducing sentences for first-time offenders caught using marijuana. To her critics the first lady responded, "Being ladylike does not require silence."

Betty Ford remained popular in spite of controversy over her public comments. In 1975 she was named *Time* magazine's "Woman of the Year" and continued to be admired by many women around the country. She lived up to her early promise to be an activist first lady by supporting a full agenda of social and political causes, including public funding for the arts and day care centers and issues on behalf of the physically handicapped and mentally ill. Betty took to wearing a large ERA button and fought for the ratification of the doomed constitutional amendment. Her popularity was evident during Ford's 1976 campaign to stay in office: Campaign buttons appeared with the slogan "Vote for Betty's Husband."

Betty was also a political partner to the president. Ford valued her advice and attributed much of his success to her. She had even wisely warned him against pardoning former president Richard Nixon, an act that undermined Ford's presidency. Betty accompanied her husband to China in 1975, was the force behind his establishment of the National Commission on the Observance of the International Women's Year, and prompted the president to award her former dance instructor, the legendary Martha Graham, the Presidential Medal of Freedom. Behind the scenes Betty had the president's ear, and they frequently discussed political issues in private. The first lady seems to have influenced

Ford's decision to appoint women to such prominent positions as secretary of the Department of Housing and Urban Development and ambassador to Great Britain. She was also a successful hostess, offering more intimate White House dinners and affairs and inviting more women to these events. The first lady became a key proponent of the arts, supporting the capital's performing arts community, and she worked on behalf of the city's children's hospital.

In spite of her popularity and formidable political power and skills, Betty Ford never developed an appreciation for politics. She was an effective leader and a highly political first lady, yet politics for her was not a labor of love. The first lady continued to struggle with her addictions and longed to leave public office. But even to the end of her husband's unsuccessful campaign in 1976, the first lady served admirably. When Ford's voice, weakened from campaigning through the eleventh hour, failed him, Betty delivered the president's concession speech. With her visibly shaken and defeated husband at her side and the national media carrying the event, Betty calmly conceded victory to Jimmy Carter and closed her long life in politics.

Legacy

Betty Ford's public life did not stop when Ford's political career ended. Although she had looked forward to their retirement, Betty continued to advocate the causes she championed as first lady. She remained a leader of the Equal Rights Amendment and served in 1981 as the honorary chair of the ERA Countdown Committee. Stating that "women ought to have equal rights, equal social security, equal opportunities for education, and an equal chance to establish credit," Betty expressed frustration with prominent women like first lady Nancy Reagan who did not support women's equality. She was also recognized by the American Cancer Society for her work to promote breast cancer awareness.

In retirement the Fords moved to Rancho Mirage in California. In 1978 Betty finally addressed her long battle with addiction and checked herself into the Long Beach Naval Hospital for alcohol and drug treatment. As she had always done, she fought her personal battles in public and earned the support of the American people. After successfully handling her addiction, Betty raised public support and funds to develop a center devoted to treating substance abuse. The Betty Ford Center has become recognized worldwide and has treated celebrities such as Elizabeth Taylor, Johnny Cash, and Liza Minelli, as well as thousands of others. The same year the former first lady admitted her addictions, she wrote her autobiography.

Betty Ford is remembered as one of the most outspoken first ladies. She was a trailblazing feminist and one of the few first ladies openly to disagree with her husband, although as his close confidante, she also gave him strength and necessary support.

Bibliography

Cannon, James M. *Time and Chance: Gerald Ford's Appointment with History.* New York: HarperCollins, 1994.

Ford, Betty, with Chris Chase. *The Times of My Life.* New York: Harper & Row, 1978.

——. *Betty: A Glad Awakening.* Garden City, NJ: Doubleday, 1987.

Ford, Gerald. *A Time to Heal.* New York: Harper & Row, 1979.

Weidenfeld, Sheila Rabb. *First Lady's Lady: With the Fords at the White House.* New York: Putnam, 1979.

40

Eleanor Rosalynn Smith Carter

Born: August 18, 1927; Plains, Georgia
President: James Earl "Jimmy" Carter (1924–), Thirty-ninth President
Husband's Presidential Term: 1977–1981 (Democrat)
Marriage: July 7, 1946; Plains, Georgia
Children: John William (1947–); James Earl III (1950–); Donnel Jaffery (1952–); Amy Lynn (1967–)

Early Years

Unlike many of her predecessors, Rosalynn Smith was born into a family of very modest means, on August 18, 1927. Her parents, Frances "Allie" Murray and Wilburn Edgar Smith, struggled to make ends meet in the small town of Plains, Georgia, where her father worked as a mechanic. Her upbringing was defined by the small-town values of conservativism, religion, and hard work.

When Rosalynn was a teenager, her father died, leaving the already struggling family facing poverty. Her mother worked in a variety of jobs and sewed to support them. The oldest of four, Rosalynn helped Allie raise the three younger children, and the family managed to get by. Rosalynn graduated as valedictorian of her small high school and then attended Georgia Southwestern College. She was a simple, disciplined, and intelligent young woman.

Marriage

Rosalynn grew up near Jimmy Carter in the rural community, and one of her friends was Carter's younger sister. Even though Jimmy was a few years older, the couple knew each other in their youth.

After graduating from high school, Carter attended the U.S. Naval Academy in Annapolis, Maryland. When he was home visiting, he and Rosalynn went on a date. From their first date Carter knew he wanted to marry her, but she hesitated. They corresponded after he returned to Annapolis. A few months later he proposed marriage, but feeling it was too soon, Rosalynn delayed their betrothal. A short time later, however, she visited him at the Naval Academy, and they became engaged. The couple were married in their hometown on July 7, 1946.

Family Life

The Carters moved to Norfolk, Virginia, following Jimmy's naval assignment. As his career progressed, the family moved to various postings. Carter was often away from home, leaving Rosalynn to raise their children by herself. They had four: John ("Jack"), born in 1947; James ("Chip") in 1950; and Donnel ("Jeff"), who was born in 1952. A daughter, Amy, arrived much later, in 1967.

In 1953 Carter's father died, and he decided to resign from the navy and take over the family peanut business. Rosalynn opposed the move. She enjoyed living in different locations and did not want to go back to the small town where she was raised. Nevertheless, they did return to Plains, marking one of the few times the couple disagreed over a career decision. The Carters had become close friends and shared many similar interests, like art and poetry; they often studied new subjects and read together. Rosalynn also helped her husband run the family business and managed the records and finances. By the time Carter considered pursuing public office, they were close business partners as well.

In 1962 Carter ran successfully for the Georgia senate and was reelected in 1964. In 1966 he ran for governor but lost. Rosalynn was apprehensive about public life; the prospect of losing her privacy worried her, and she doubted her abilities. But she proved to be a skilled campaigner and a natural in politics. In 1970, when Carter again sought the governorship, Rosalynn placed her young daughter with relatives so that she could campaign full time for her husband. She was an asset to the campaign, and he won the election.

As first lady of Georgia, Rosalynn was an activist, reinventing the role of governor's wife there. She advocated a variety of social issues, including mental health reforms. She also initiated the state's wildflower program. The Carter partnership grew during the governorship; Rosalynn traveled with her husband, the two discussed policy issues together, and she became his most trusted adviser. Her public speaking prowess improved, and the Georgia first lady delivered many speeches. In 1974 Carter announced his intention to seek the presidency. A long-shot candidate, Carter traveled around the country for the next two years, getting his message out and slowly building support for his candidacy. Rosalynn worked tirelessly on the campaign stump, and Carter consulted her in all of his policy decisions. He was the Democrat's nominee in 1976 and won the election over Ford that fall.

Presidency

In the White House Rosalynn continued her close partnership with her husband. She worked from her office in the East Wing, attended presidential cabinet meetings, and even scheduled weekly "policy lunch" meetings with the president. Her role in the Carter administration extended to serving as presidential surrogate and envoy. An intelligent, hardworking first lady, Rosalynn was up to the task, and she made sure she was briefed by presidential advisers. The couple mutually trusted and respected each other; both were forthright and honest and held similar religious and ethical beliefs. They regularly discussed policy options and took a speed-reading course to improve their ability to be well informed on many topics. Rosalynn edited her husband's speeches and was responsible for getting him to rely less on facts and details and use an approach that both advocated and was based on moral principles. Like her husband, however, she was somewhat of a perfectionist and did not take criticism well.

Rosalynn stood in for Carter at several public events, including a highly publicized trip to Central and South America and the Caribbean, where she met with the leaders of seven nations: Brazil, Colombia, Costa Rica, Ecuador, Jamaica, Peru, and Venezuela. Her nearly two-week tour was a mixed success. The chauvinism of the heads of state she met limited her effectiveness in delivering the president's message, as did what appears was jealousy from the U.S. Department of State, which saw its jurisdication usurped by the first lady. Yet Rosalynn showed herself to be remarkably well informed, articulate, and capable. She even developed a degree of fluency in Spanish in preparation for her trip.

Rosalynn's diplomatic tasks also included meetings with the king of Thailand and the Secretary-General of the United Nations and a visit to a Cambodian refugee camp. The first lady went on the president's behalf to Boston to greet Pope John Paul II during the first papal visit to the United States, and she worked closely with her husband during his diplomatic retreats at Camp David, including the successful peace talks between Egypt and Israel. In only her first year in office, the first lady traveled to more than a dozen countries and nearly two dozen U.S. cities.

Rosalynn emerged as the nation's leading advocate for mental health care reform and expanding services for the elderly. In 1977 she became honorary chair of the President's Commission on Mental Health, although her role was more than honorary: She convened meetings and hearings that considered a comprehensive array of issues pertaining to mental health reform. The task force's proposal was passed into law as the Mental Health Systems Act. The act included many initiatives, such as mental health research and development, the creation of community health centers, and mental health considerations in rural areas. Rosalynn was praised by mental health experts for her work on the commission.

Rosalynn was a somewhat reluctant hostess, but she performed admirably in her various social functions. Her events were more informal than those of her predecessors, downplaying the usual pageantry of White House affairs; she did not spend all the funds available to her for hosting and refurbishments at the mansion. But the first lady showcased performing artists there and established a trust fund to generate money for future White House maintenance and renovations. She also developed a booklet about the White House for children, written from the perspective of daughter Amy, titled *The White House: It's Your House Too*.

As one of the most active first ladies ever, Rosalynn and her staff of roughly twenty worked on a wide array of issues such as children's immunization and women's rights. A confident and strong speaker, she gave numerous speeches across the country and was featured at the National Women's Conference in 1977. Because of her knowledge on mental health issues, she testified before Congress as an expert witness, the first first lady to do so since Eleanor Roosevelt. During Carter's reelection campaign in 1980, the president was preoccupied with the Iranian hostage crisis and did little campaigning himself. Rosalynn did much of it for him, traveling the country on a chartered jet, but despite her best efforts, Carter lost the election.

Legacy

Her husband's loss to Ronald Reagan was hard for Rosalynn. Reagan pushed to cut the mental health care initiatives she had worked to make a reality. She was also upset when the Equal Rights Amendment failed to be ratified in 1982. For her work, however, the first lady received awards from the National Mental Health Association and the National Organization for Women. Rosalynn Carter's legacy as a devoted human rights advocate and champion of child immunization, mental health care, and the rights of women and the underprivileged is secure.

In retirement the former first lady has taken on new challenges. Alongside her husband, Rosalynn has worked with the well-respected Carter Center in Atlanta, monitoring international human rights, hosting an annual symposium on mental health care, and serving on the board of trustees. In 1988 she convened a conference at the center with other first ladies, on "Women and the Constitution." Rosalynn serves on the board of several corporations and charities and with her husband helps build homes for low-income families through the organization Habitat for Humanity.

Rosalynn has received honorary degrees from a number of colleges and universities, including Morehouse, Notre Dame, Wesleyan, and Winthrop, and has continued her intellectual pursuits as a distinguished lecturer at Agnes Scott College in Georgia and as a fellow with the women's studies program at Emory University. She has also authored or coauthored three books since leaving office.

Bibliography

Carter, Rosalynn. *First Lady from Plains.* Fayetteville: University of Arkansas Press, 1984.
————. *Helping Yourself Help Others.* New York: Random House, 1995.

Maddox, Linda, and Edna Langford. *Rosalynn: Friend and First Lady.* Old Tappan, NJ: Fleming H. Revell, 1980.

Norton, Howard. *Rosalynn: A Portrait.* Plainfield, NJ: Logos International, 1977.

41

Anne Frances "Nancy" Robbins Davis Reagan

Born: July 6, 1921; New York, New York
President: Ronald Wilson Reagan (1911–), Fortieth President
Husband's Presidential Term: 1981–1989 (Republican)
Marriage: March 4, 1952; Riverside, California
Children: Patricia Ann (1952–); Ronald Prescott (1958–)

Early Years

Anne Frances Robbins, nicknamed "Nancy," was born on July 6, 1921, in New York City (although she would later give her birthdate as 1923). She was the only child of Edith "Dee" Luckett and Kenneth Robbins, a car salesman, who separated shortly after their daughter's birth and divorced in 1928. Dee Luckett was an actress from Washington, D.C., although she claimed to be from a prominent family in Virginia. When her marriage failed, Dee decided to return to an acting career and sent Nancy to live with her aunt and her family, the Galbraiths, for several years. The separation was difficult for Nancy, who was scarred emotionally from the experience.

Nancy's mother remarried in 1929, wedding Loyal Davis, a prominent Chicago neurosurgeon. Even though they were very different people—fun-loving, free-spirited actress and a conservative, strict, and somewhat old-fashioned doctor—the marriage worked. Nancy came back to live with them and was adopted by Davis. She adored him and liked the affluence and privilege of her new household. Davis sent his new daughter to the prestigious Girls' Latin School, where she became active in student government and theater. After graduation Nancy went to Smith College, where she studied theater and ultimately earned a degree in 1943. During college Nancy fell in love with a young man, but the relationship ended tragically when he died in a train wreck.

A successful acting career followed, including a stint on Broadway. Nancy was then signed by MGM studios in Hollywood and made roughly a dozen films, typically in minor and supporting roles.

Marriage

The final film of her career was *Hellcats of the Navy,* in which she appeared with Ronald Reagan, then president of the Screen Actors Guild and a well-known B-film star. Reagan had been married previously to actress Jane Wyman, with whom he had two children, Maureen and Michael. Nancy seems to have been enamored with the handsome Reagan from the start and pursued the relationship. The two dated, although Reagan continued to see others; his interest in Nancy was intermittent at first, but gradually they became committed and were married on March 4, 1952, in Riverside, California.

Like Nancy's parents, the two were a seemingly unlikely pair. Nancy was high-strung, nervous, and serious, while Reagan was laid-back, informal, and fun loving. But the marriage was one of the most solid in the history of the presidency. Nancy often stated that her life began when she married Reagan. After the wedding Nancy gave up her film career and devoted herself to her husband and family. Although the Reagan union appeared to be a traditional marriage, with Nancy as a model wife and mother, this was not exactly the case. Nancy was the more ambitious of the two and often the driving force behind the marriage and her husband's career.

Family Life

In contrast to the warm relationship between Nancy and Reagan was an often dysfunctional one between her and her stepchildren, as well as with her own children, Patty, born in 1952, and Ronald, born in 1958.

Throughout the 1950s, both Nancy and her father, Loyal Davis, influenced Reagan's political views. Also at that time, as his acting career began slowing, the former Democrat became spokesman for General Electric; his work for the GE Theater positioned him as a voice of conservativism and corporate America and brought him exposure in Republican Party circles. By 1964 he was a leading proponent for Republican presidential candidate Barry Goldwater and for the party. In 1966 Reagan was elected governor of California. Throughout his two terms in the governor's office his wife was a key part of his administration. Although she was not involved directly in politics or policymaking, she was highly protective of her husband and played a role in decisions that related to his image, work schedule, and senior staffing matters. Nancy distrusted the media and for good reason; she had poor relations with the press corps, who saw her as insincere and criticized her high spending and what became known as "the gaze," the infatuated way she looked up at her husband, which the press dubbed an act.

Although she was nervous about speaking in public and worried about how she would perform in public life, Nancy excelled as first lady of California. She visited state hospitals, advocated a foster grandparents program, and took up the issue of missing prisoners of war. Although she did not speak often and her campaigning role was moderate, Nancy was effective and popular when she did campaign. Reagan was reelected governor in 1970 but did not run again in 1974. By the end of the decade, however, Republicans were looking to him as the candidate to regain the presidency; he defeated Jimmy Carter in the 1980 election.

Presidency

From the start of the Reagan presidency, Nancy made her presence known within the White House and in private. She helped plan the inaugural festivities and select the Reagan team. Perhaps her central role throughout her husband's two terms, however, was that of presidential protector. The first lady was a powerful force in the administration who jealously guarded the president. She was aggressive with those she suspected of not having his best interests in mind, and she often limited his schedule. Nancy became even more controlling and protective after an attempted assassination of the president at the beginning of his term in 1981 and with the onset of Reagan's health problems, including colon cancer surgery in 1985 and prostate surgery two years later. Although she was concerned about his health, aides regularly complained about what they saw as unnecessary intervention by the first lady and feared the president would appear to be dominated by his wife.

Nancy was also very image conscious, but this worked both ways for the couple. Nancy controlled the façade of the administration seen by the public, which brought glamour to the White House, but the public also perceived the first lady as artificial and excessively materialistic. Presidential aides worried about the "Nancy problem." Stories circulated about the high cost of the inauguration and the jewelry and gown Nancy wore to the event, along with the many lavish events hosted by the first lady and the expensive White House redecorations she oversaw. Later in the administration a minor scandal erupted over the first lady's failure to return gowns provided to her by famous designers, as the law required. Although her public image suffered when she was called "Queen Nancy" and the "Dragon Lady," such criticism was not completely warranted, as much of the money she spent came from private donations. But the expenditures certainly seemed at odds with the president's cuts in social programs. When the public learned that Nancy often consulted an astrologer and then acted on the advice, her already sagging popularity sank further.

One way Nancy tried to improve her image was to discourage drug use by the country's youth. She led the administration's "Just Say No" campaign, becoming identified with the issue. The first lady initiated a nationwide dialogue on teen drug use. Appearing at many public and media events such as school rallies and parades, she became the nation's most visible spokesperson on the issue. She convened a first ladies' conference on drug abuse and addressed the United Nations. She also enhanced her public image by poking fun at what she was criticized for: her expensive tastes in fashion. Nancy humanized her seemingly cold persona by performing a skit as "Second-hand Rose" at a Gridiron Club event, dressed in mismatched old clothes.

Although she did not support other issues in public, preferring to be seen as a traditional wife and social hostess, in private, the first lady was involved in any matter that affected her husband. Although she did not discuss policy issues per se, she worked closely on Reagan's staff appointments, travel, public appearances, and ceremonial functions. The first lady appears to have been responsible for difficult and high-profile firings in the administration, acting as the enforcer for a passive president. On occasion, when he struggled with difficult questions, the first lady was seen prompting her husband with the appropriate answer. She was also ideologically conservative, opposing the Equal Rights Amendment and other women's issues like abortion rights.

Legacy

Public criticism was quite painful to the first lady. She also faced difficult times when her stepfather died in 1982 and her mother in 1987. That same year Nancy underwent a mastectomy after discovering breast cancer. But the first lady endured the trials of the presidency and, after leaving Washington, responded to her critics with her aptly named autobiography, *My Turn*, in 1989. In retirement Nancy faced perhaps her greatest challenge when Reagan was diagnosed with Alzheimer's disease in 1990. She responded as always by standing by her husband and attempting to shield him from public scrutiny.

One of the most controversial and perhaps one of the most powerful first ladies, Nancy Reagan was highly ambitious and a constant force behind her husband throughout his career. Recognizing her influence and her role in his success, Reagan's friend, actor Jimmy Stewart, once quipped, "If Ronnie had married Nancy at the time he married Jane Wyman, he would have won an Oscar. She would have made him do it."

Bibliography

Hannaford, Peter. *The Reagans: A Political Portrait.* New York: Coward-McCann, 1983.

Leamer, Laurence. *Make-Believe: The Story of Nancy and Ronald Reagan.* New York: Harper & Row, 1983.

Leighton, Frances Spatz. *The Search for the Real Nancy Reagan.* New York: Macmillan, 1987.

Reagan, Nancy, with William Novak. *My Turn: The Memoirs of Nancy Reagan.* New York: Random House, 1989.

Wallace, Chris. *First Lady: A Portrait of Nancy Reagan.* New York: St. Martin's Press, 1986.

42

Barbara Pierce Bush

Born: June 8, 1925; Rye, New York
President: George Herbert Walker Bush (1924–), Forty-first President
Husband's Presidential Term: 1989–1993 (Republican)
Marriage: January 6, 1945; Rye, New York
Children: George Walker (1946–); Pauline "Robin" Robinson (1949–1953); John Ellis (1953–); Neil Mellon (1954–); Marvin Pierce (1956–); Dorothy Walker (1959–)

Early Years

On June 8, 1925, Barbara Pierce was born in Rye, a suburb of New York City, the third of four children. A distant descendant of President Franklin Pierce, her father, Marvin Pierce, was a successful businessman and publisher who rose to the presidency of the McCall Corporation. The Pierce family enjoyed great prosperity, and Barbara's upbringing was one of privilege and comfort. Barbara was a happy child but felt inadequate in the shadow of her attractive and cultured mother, Pauline Robinson Pierce. The young girl's insecurities about her physical appearance would trouble her throughout her life.

Because politics was one of the Pierce family's interests, Barbara was exposed to it as a child; her maternal grandfather served as a judge on the Ohio Supreme Court. Barbara's formal education was at Ashley Hall, an elite boarding school in Charleston, South Carolina.

Marriage

While a student in Charleston, Barbara met George Bush during Christmas break. Barbara was only sixteen and Bush was a senior at Phillips Academy, a school in Andover, Massachusetts, for sons of the wealthy and powerful. A romance blossomed from the initial meeting, and the two began corresponding. Bush later invited Barbara to visit his family at their Kennebunkport, Maine, home; there he declared his intention to marry her. They were engaged in 1943, but Bush enlisted in the U.S. Navy as a pilot in World War II.

During the war Barbara enrolled in Smith College but was a marginal student and dropped out of school. Bush served with distinction, earning recognition when he was shot down in combat. He returned home over Christmas in 1944, and he and Barbara were married on January 6, 1945, in Barbara's hometown of Rye.

Family Life

After their marriage and his tour of duty, George Bush attended Yale University. While her husband pursued his degree, Barbara worked at the Yale Co-op. Although she preferred to settle down in New England after his graduation, Bush moved the family to Texas and worked in the oil business, striking it rich. Bush quickly rose to prominence within their community and in the Lone Star State, and he launched his political career, winning a seat in the U.S. House of Representatives in the 1960s. Although he lost a bid for the Senate, he had established himself in the Republican Party and was offered a series of prestigious political appointments in the 1970s, including UN ambassador from 1971 to 1973; chairman of the Republican National Committee (1973–1974); special U.S. envoy to China (1974–1975); and director of the Central Intelligence Agency (1976–1977).

Family life for Barbara Bush was in many ways quite conventional. She had six children, the first of whom, George, was born in 1946; her youngest, Dorothy, was born in 1959. Barbara ran the Bush household, as her husband was frequently away from home. She did not take an active role in his career, but she was supportive and, during his service in Congress, wrote a regular column for his constituents. Barbara also taught Sunday school and supported causes like the United Way. Although these were successful times, they were not always easy or happy ones for Barbara. Her mother's death in 1949 and the loss of her young daughter Robin from leukemia in 1953 caused her great grief. She also wrestled with feelings of loneliness and depression, partly because of Bush's frequent absences due to career demands and partly because of her long-standing feelings of inadequacy. Although she would become an immensely popular first lady and her public persona combined warm grandmother and strong spouse, Barbara was painfully conscious of her looks and struggled with weight problems and chain-smoking. She seems to have resented her husband's enjoyment of the political life, and it did not help that Bush frequently dined and attended events without her. During the women's liberation movement in the 1960s and 1970s, Barbara's sense of inadequacy apparently intensified because of her status as a full-time homemaker. She could also be vengeful with those she felt had crossed her, and she had a razor-sharp tongue. During the 1984 campaign, when her husband was attempting to retain his office, Barbara snapped to the press that his opponent, Democratic vice presidential nominee Geraldine Ferraro, was a word that rhymed with "rich."

Although she was displeased with his position as head of the CIA, Barbara earlier had thoroughly loved her experience in China. While there, she took many photographs that later were the basis of a slide show on the people, geography, and culture of China. Barbara was a reluctant, even apprehensive public figure, but she became a skilled speaker and hostess and would emerge as one of her husband's greatest assets. She was extremely popular on the campaign stump and was credited with helping to humanize her noncharismatic husband. Barbara developed views on many political issues, some of which, such as her support for the Equal Rights Amendment and abortion rights, were opposed to her husband's. But as a traditional spouse who was keenly aware of the political game, Barbara did not reveal these until after Bush ended his public career.

Presidency

From 1981 to 1989, as the wife of the vice president, Barbara Bush became well known and respected. She thus made a considerable contribution to Bush's 1988 presidential campaign. By the time she assumed the first ladyship, she was a gifted, politically experienced public speaker. Known as the "Silver Fox" for her grandmotherly image combined with pearls and elegant blue dresses, Barbara Bush was one of the most popular first ladies of all time. The public eagerly embraced her homespun wit and casual demeanor, especially after the calculating and controversial reign of Nancy Reagan.

The first lady's special project was literacy. In 1984 she wrote a book about her pet cocker spaniel titled *C Fred's Story;* the proceeds were donated to the cause of literacy. A few years later Barbara wrote another book, this one from the perspective of her dog Millie; its earnings went to the foundation for literacy she had started. She traveled widely, attending events on behalf of children's and adult literacy, and wrote articles promoting family literacy in a variety of publications, including *Reader's Digest.* Barbara took full advantage of her image in promoting this cause and her husband's presidency. She also skillfully deflected potential criticism of her weight and old-fashioned looks by making fun of her appearance in a disarming, endearing manner. Barbara was diagnosed with Grave's disease, a thyroid condition that affects vision and gives the eyes a bulging, puffy appearance. She stoically handled the problem, and indeed the illness only seemed to enhance her popularity and the country's empathy with her. So effective was the first lady in her public contacts that she was jokingly referred to as Bush's "secret weapon."

In 1990 Barbara was invited to deliver the commencement address at Wellesley College, but some of the student body protested, arguing that the first lady was not a good role model for young women because she had dropped out of college and did not have a career. Barbara handled the controversy masterfully, saying that she understood the protestors' criticism. She took Raisa Gorbachev, Russia's first lady, as a guest to the graduation ceremony and ended her speech by suggesting that someone in the audience might have the good fortune to follow in her footsteps as the spouse of the president, closing with the line, "And I wish *him* well!"

Barbara Bush advocated volunteerism, support for the elderly, and a more conciliatory position among Republicans toward gays, supporting legislation for hate crimes and AIDS awareness. Although she rarely spoke out on political issues, Barbara was her husband's close confidante throughout his term. She was a good judge of character, although she could be a bit petty and harsh toward those who opposed the president. She spoke at the 1992 Republican National Convention, one of the highlights of the convention and her public career, even though Bush later lost his bid for reelection.

Legacy

Barbara set up the foundation for literacy bearing her name; her interest in and advocacy of the issue and foundation have continued. Although her first ladyship did not bring any lasting changes to the office and she was one of the least politically active first ladies of the late twentieth century, her presence and popularity did contribute positively to her husband's presidency. In retirement Barbara Bush wrote her memoirs and remains highly popular.

Bibliography

Bush, Barbara. *Barbara Bush: A Memoir.* New York: Scribner's, 1994.
Kilian, Pamela. *Barbara Bush: A Biography.* Thorndike, ME: Thorndike Press, 1992.
Radcliffe, Donnie. *Simply Barbara Bush: A Portrait of America's Candid First Lady.* New York: Warner Books, 1989.

43

Hillary Diane Rodham Clinton

Born: October 26, 1947; Chicago, Illinois
President: William "Bill" Jefferson Clinton (1946–), Forty-second President
Husband's Presidential Term: 1993–2001 (Democrat)
Marriage: October 11, 1975; Fayetteville, Arkansas
Children: Chelsea Victoria (1980–)

Early Years

Hillary Rodham was born in Chicago on October 26, 1947, the oldest of Hugh and Dorothy Rodham's three children. They were a middle-class family, and Hillary's mother stayed home to raise the children, while her father operated his textile and fabric store. In the comfortable suburban community of Park Ridge, Illinois, Hillary was an active girl, participating in the Girl Scouts and sports like softball, tennis, and volleyball, and taking ballet lessons. She was an exceptional student and a leader in her school, organizing food drives and other worthy endeavors, working on the school newspaper, and serving in student government. At one time she dreamt of becoming an astronaut. After writing to NASA, however, she learned that the agency did not accept female astronauts. This appears to have made an impression on her, driving her to work even harder for her goals.

Another of Hillary's early influences came through a Methodist church youth group. The group's pastor exposed them to a variety of urban and social problems, and in 1962 they had the opportunity to hear Martin Luther King Jr. speak. Although she was raised in a Republican community and family, Hillary gradually became interested in causes associated more with the Democratic Party. She attended Wellesley College, where she continued to excel academically and where she seems to have solidified her beliefs. By 1968 she was firmly opposed to the Vietnam War, and her political views had moved to the left. As the student speaker at her graduation in 1969, she gave a strong, inspirational speech that earned national attention.

Marriage

After college Hillary went to Yale Law School, where she served as a member of the editorial board of the *Yale Review of Law and Social Action*. There she met Bill Clinton, a fellow law student, while studying at the law school library. They shared a strong interest in politics and together worked for George McGovern's 1972 presidential campaign. In 1973 she was hired as a staff attorney for the Children's Defense Fund, putting into practice her interest in children's legal issues and child advocacy. Her next political experience came in 1974, when she served on the staff of the House Judiciary Committee during its investigation into the Watergate scandal and possible impeachment of President Richard Nixon.

When Bill Clinton pursued a seat in Congress in 1974, Hillary helped manage his campaign, which, however, was unsuccessful. After dating, sharing a residence, and working together on political functions, Hillary and Bill Clinton were married on October 11, 1975, in Fayetteville, Arkansas. Hillary taught briefly at the law school at the University of Arkansas in Fayetteville.

Family Life

Politics was the central component of Clinton family life. In 1976, shortly after their marriage, Bill was elected Arkansas attorney general; he was elected governor two years later. Daughter Chelsea was born in 1980. From the beginning of his career, Bill Clinton's political partner was his wife. During the twelve years Clinton served as governor of

Arkansas, Hillary became one of the state's most powerful political figures and a well-known national leader. She joined the Rose law firm in Little Rock, one of the state's most powerful, and was honored in 1983 as the Arkansas Young Mother of the Year. A year later Hillary became the state's Woman of the Year. In 1988 she was recognized by the *National Law Journal* as one of the country's one hundred most influential lawyers. In the late 1970s, under President Carter, she had served on the board of the Legal Services Corporation.

After Clinton's first term as governor from 1978 to 1980, he was not reelected. As both of them would do later in the White House, the first lady recognized the power of public opinion and underwent a complete makeover. During Clinton's 1982 campaign for governor, she changed her style of dress and even eyeglasses, toned down her voice, literally and figuratively, and began using her married name. The Clintons were successful and returned to the statehouse in 1983. As first lady of Arkansas, Hillary was an activist and a political reformer. As her husband's close political partner, she was tapped to head state reform commissions. She also established the Arkansas Advocates for Children and Families and a home instructional program for the state's preschoolers, two of the many initiatives she helped develop for the state's children and educational system.

Presidency

Hillary's partnership role in her husband's career can best be seen and understood in her appearance on national television to defend their marriage. During the 1992 campaign, when rumors of his marital infidelity threatened to derail Clinton's presidential aspirations, Hillary came to the rescue of her husband and the campaign. On *60 Minutes,* in the attractive time slot immediately after the Super Bowl, Hillary Clinton sat by her husband and attested to the health of their marriage, thus reassuring the public about Bill Clinton's character. Hillary was a prominent force throughout the 1992 campaign, and the candidate himself did not try to mask her importance or influence, suggesting that by electing him, the country would get "two for the price of one."

One of the president's first actions after taking office was to appoint his wife to head the task force charged with health care reform. Her appointment was challenged legally by opponents to universal health care who saw it as a violation of federal nepotism statutes; thus the role and activities of the first lady became a subject of national debate and consideration by the courts. Pointing out that first ladies have functioned as de facto government employees and the office has a long tradition of public service, a federal court of appeals permitted Hillary to participate in the initiative. She impressed those she worked with, including experts she interviewed and congressional committees for whom she testified on behalf of health care reform. Although the ambitious reforms the first lady proposed were defeated in Congress, she established herself as a policy force in the White House.

In short order Hillary Clinton became one of the highest-profile, politically active first ladies in the history of the office. She played a central role in the Clinton presidency and advocated a number of causes. But her influence and activism created controversy among those uncomfortable with such visibility and power in the office of first lady. Rarely has a first lady received such hostility from the media and the president's opponents. The issue of her power and influence was in the headlines for much of Clinton's first term in office. Little about the first lady escaped criticism by Republicans and political commentators, including her hairdo and taste in clothing. When her successful legal career and liberated views came under attack, her comments about not choosing to stay home and bake cookies or to simply "stand by her man"—borrowed from the lyrics of country singer Tammy Wynette— enraged many housewives and conservatives. The first lady was implicated in improper behavior as well. Controversy surrounded her financial dealings in land investments in Arkansas, her legal writings regarding children's rights, and her role in the administration's missteps, such as the firing of employees in the White House travel office.

Consequently, the first lady assumed a lower profile during her husband's reelection campaign in 1996. Regardless of the criticism and her decreased visibility, however, Hillary remained an influential adviser to the president and a crusading advocate for women's issues and social programs such as child immunizations, education, adoption services, and health care. In 1995 she started writing a weekly newspaper column entitled "Talking It Over," the same year she spoke at the United Nations World Conference on Women, held in China. In 1997 Hillary hosted the White House Conference of Early Childhood Development and Learning and the White House Conference on Child Care and worked to ensure passage of the Adoption and Safe Family Act that year.

The first lady frequently lobbied members of Congress, participated in senior-level policy discussions within the Clinton administration, and was a powerful fundraiser at Democratic Party events, particularly among female members of the party. In many ways she was a pioneering first lady and was probably the most overtly, politically active spouse since Eleanor Roosevelt. Hillary gave numerous speeches and traveled widely for humanitarian issues.

Like Eleanor before her, Hillary Clinton was disinterested in hosting events at the White House. She much preferred politics. But she responded to duty and was a successful hostess of a number of events. Also like other first ladies, Hillary showcased the arts, particularly the White House collection of American crafts, and promoted the history of the people's White House.

Legacy

A highly intelligent woman, Hillary Clinton was the first presidential spouse to hold an advanced degree. Her decision to run for the U.S. Senate in 2000 marked yet another first for the office. During her tenure she published legal opinions in a scholarly journal and wrote an acclaimed book on raising children, *It Takes a Village*. The first lady was comfortable discussing policy issues in interviews and on the campaign stump. Yet it appears that part of the public was not ready for such a visible partnership in the presidency, especially in the areas of policy and politics.

One of the legacies of the Clinton presidency will surely be the Monica Lewinsky affair. This highly political sex scandal involving a young White House intern produced allegations of inappropriate conduct and inaccurate statements directed at the president and even resulted in impeachment proceedings in the Congress. The scandal dominated news reporting and was the most public story of the Clinton presidency. Yet, despite tarnishing President Clinton's record of achievement, the affair seemed almost to benefit Hillary Clinton. Although it was surely embarrassing for her, Hillary Clinton's public approval rating increased during and after the affair. Moreover, this occurred despite her noticeably lower profile in the wake of the scandal and the public statements made by the first lady defending her husband. The first lady was widely applauded for her stoic resolve and the poise she demonstrated in the face of scandal. The affair also seemed to reenforce the role of the first lady as wife, a role less controversial to the public than that of political activist or presidential adviser. First and foremost, the first lady is the president's spouse and the public seemed to recognize the difficulty in fulfilling this role in the most public of places: the White House. The ordeal also highlights Hillary's highly public first ladyship as one that assumed both the traditional duties of spouse, hostess, and symbol of women as well as the nontraditional role of political adviser and policy activist.

In her high-profile bid for a seat in the U.S. Senate, Hillary Clinton established yet another precedent for the first ladyship. In the most closely watched congressional race of the 2000 election, Hillary Rodham Clinton defeated her Republican opponent and was elected to represent the state of New York in the U.S. Senate. This marked the first time a former first lady was elected to public office. As was the case with Hillary Clinton's first ladyship, her bid for public office fascinated the public and the media and was defined by high points and controversy.

Such a post–White House career for a first lady or any political spouse would have been unthinkable just a few years ago. However, the reality of Mrs. Clinton's senatorial campaign in the state of New York reflected the increasingly political role assumed by first ladies and the increasingly public nature of the office. The first lady, after all, was no stranger to legislative politics during her first ladyship and even her enemies have conceded her impressive command of the issues. First ladies in general have become not only popular public figures but among the country's foremost political figures as well. Hillary's campaign further reflected the institutionalization of political roles as a fundamental component of the first ladyship.

Hillary Clinton will be remembered as one of the most visible, active, yet controversial first ladies of American history. The debates that surrounded Hillary symbolize the nature of the first ladyship in general, an office without specific constitutional mandates. The first lady's roles and duties are defined largely by public opinion and the vision for the office shared by the president and first lady themselves. Given the uncertainty and varying perspectives with which the public views the office, it is not surprising that Hillary Clinton's activism polarized public opinion. Some applauded her role; others saw her as a liability to her husband's presidency.

Bibliography

Clinton, Hillary. *It Takes a Village and Other Lessons Children Can Teach Us.* New York: Simon and Schuster, 1996.

King, Norman. *The Woman in the White House: The Remarkable Story of Hillary Rodham Clinton.* New York: Carol Publishing Group, 1996.

Radcliffe, Donnie. *Hillary Rodham Clinton: A First Lady for Our Time.* New York: Warner Books, 1994.

Warner, Judith. *Hillary Clinton: The Inside Story.* New York: Signet, 1993.

44

Laura Welch Bush

Born: November 4, 1946; Midland, Texas
President: George W. Bush (1946–), Forty-third President
Husband's Presidential Term: 2001– (Republican)
Marriage: November 5, 1977; Midland, Texas
Children: Barbara Pierce and Jenna Welch (1981–)

Early Years

Laura Welch was born in Midland, Texas, in 1946 and had a normal, comfortable upbringing. Raised in Midland, she was an only child whose father, Harold Welch, worked as a homebuilder before he died in 1995. Her mother, Jenna, has been a lifelong resident of the city. At seventeen Laura's otherwise happy life was shattered when she was involved in a tragic auto accident that took the life of her sweetheart.

After completing high school, Laura earned a bachelor's degree in education from Southern Methodist University in Dallas. She then received a master's degree in library science from the University of Texas in Austin and became a teacher and librarian, working in public schools in Dallas, Houston, and Austin from 1968 to 1977.

Marriage

Laura and George W. Bush actually grew up in the same town and attended the same junior high school for a year. At one point in their professional careers, both lived and worked in Houston, Laura as a teacher and Bush as a member of the Texas Air National Guard. In fact, in Houston they even lived in the same apartment complex. Yet they did not meet or become romantically involved until being introduced by a mutual friend at a party in Midland. While working in Austin as a librarian, Laura went back home to visit her family, and her friends Jan and Joey O'Neill invited her to a barbecue to meet Bush. Knowing he was interested in politics, which she disliked, Laura was hesitant about being "set up" and not especially eager to meet him. Nevertheless, their interest in each other was immediate and mutual.

George Bush asked Laura to marry him just three months after their meeting, and the couple wed only a month after their engagement; the wedding took place in Midland in 1977. Both bride and groom were thirty-one years old. Bush has called his decision to marry Laura the wisest of his life and frequently credits her with being a positive influence on him. "Young and irresponsible" was how Bush described his early adulthood, a time when he struggled with alcohol abuse. Laura helped provide her husband with the focus and maturity necessary for his political rise to power.

Family Life

The newlyweds lived in Midland, where shortly after marrying, he ran for a seat in Congress. Although unaccustomed to political life and concerned about the challenges of a congressional campaign, Laura did participate in his bid for office. Bush lost the campaign but continued in his father's footsteps, working in the oil business. He expanded his business interests by becoming part owner of the Texas Rangers, a professional baseball team.

Thus, Laura has been a reluctant political spouse. When she married Bush, who came from a political family and entertained his own prospects of elected office, Laura joked that she never wanted to deliver a speech. But even though she has not unconditionally encouraged her husband's political pursuits, she has cautiously participated in them and supported his public career. She also became active in the elder Bush's vice presidency and campaigned for his successful presidential bid in 1988.

In 1981 Laura gave birth to twin girls, Barbara and Jenna, named for Laura's mother-in-law and mother, respectively. The pregnancy was difficult, as Bush was often away on business, and she was diagnosed with toxemia late in her term. Her kidney problems were a serious threat, and Laura spent the final days of the pregnancy restricted to bed. During their youth the Bush twins did not take much interest in politics, even though their grandparents were in Washington at the same time. Laura worked hard to shield her children from the glare of the media associated with Bush Sr.'s public life. In an effort to have a normal family life, she tried to have family dinners at home each evening and, later, to limit events at the governor's mansion.

George W. Bush was elected governor of Texas in 1994. By the time he had assumed the governorship, Laura had become a leading advocate for reading and literacy in Texas, as Barbara Bush was nationally. She hosted seven Texas authors for a day of readings at the University of Texas, held the day before her husband's inauguration. The shy librarian apparently had overcome her hesitation about appearing and speaking in public.

Presidency

Living in the White House was not something Laura had hoped to experience. In fact, she has often talked openly about her reluctance to subject her family to the rigors of a presidential campaign and her feelings about criticism directed at her husband. Yet her straightforward, no-nonsense disposition, much like that of her famous mother-in-law, has helped her throughout Bush's public life. By the time of Bush's presidential campaign, Laura Bush had become a partner in his political life and was a visible, integral part of the campaign. Overcoming her shyness, Laura has granted interviews, campaigned, and even given speeches on behalf of her husband and literacy. She even campaigned on her own during the presidential race.

During her husband's time as governor, Laura championed reading and literacy as her personal crusades. Because she is a former librarian and avid reader who enjoys reading a variety of topics (Texas author John Graves is one of her favorites), the cause of promoting reading and libraries comes naturally to her. In 1996 Laura arranged a celebration of Texas authors known as the Texas Book Festival, which has since become an annual event to raise money for these libraries. Many of the state's libraries have received sizable grants; roughly $600,000 had been raised for Texas public libraries by 2000.

As first lady of Texas she promoted family literacy programs in conjunction with the Barbara Bush Foundation for Family Literacy and also initiated a program in 1998 to assist parents in helping their young children to read, to better prepare them for school. In addition to reading, the first lady's interests include promoting education, breast cancer awareness, and building support for adoption; she has also continued the long tradition of first ladies being patrons of the arts. The former first lady of Texas was active in the state's Community Partners program, a volunteer branch of the Department of Protective and Regulatory Services dedicated to establishing Adopt-A-Caseworker programs and arranging services such as providing diapers and clothing for abused and neglected children.

It is clear that Laura Bush came to the White House well prepared for the challenges of the first ladyship. She has stated that she admires her mother-in-law Barbara Bush, an invaluable personal resource for the first lady as she prepared for her own first ladyship and a role model for her tenure in the White House. In addition to Barbara Bush, Laura names Lady Bird Johnson, another Texas first lady, as a White House role model and a woman she admires.

Like Hillary Clinton before her, Laura Bush shares the concern of keeping her family life private. Although her daughters are older than the Clintons' daughter, Chelsea, was when she came to the White House, Laura does not want her or her daughters' personal life exposed in the press. Also like her predecessor, Laura was well educated and had served as a state first lady before coming to the White House. Like many recent first ladies, she took a favorite social cause with her and, in turn, brought it to the attention of the nation. Laura Bush joins Louisa Adams as the second woman to marry the son of a president who, in turn, would follow in his father's footsteps and become president himself.

Bibliography

Bush, George W., with Karen Hughes. *A Charge to Keep*. New York: William Morrow, 1999.

Ide, Arthur Frederick. *The Father's Son: George W. Bush, Jr.* Boston: Minuteman Press, 1998.

Minutaglio, Bill. *First Son: George W. Bush and the Bush Family Dynasty.* New York: Times Books, 1999.

First Lady	School
Abigail Adams (1744–1818)	no formal education
Louisa Adams (1775–1852)	no formal education
Barbara Bush (1925–)	Ashley Hall (SC); Smith College (MA)
Laura Bush[a] (1946–)	Southern Methodist University, 1968 (TX); University of Texas, 1973
Rosalynn Carter[a] (1927–)	Georgia Southwestern College, 1946
Frances Cleveland[a] (1864–1947)	Wells College, 1885 (NY)
Hillary Clinton[a] (1947–)	Wellesley College, 1969 (MA); Yale Law School, 1973 (CT)
Grace Coolidge[a] (1879–1957)	University of Vermont, 1902
Mamie Eisenhower (1896–1979)	public school (MO); finishing school (CO)
Abigail Fillmore (1798–1853)	New Hope Academy (NY)
Betty Ford (1918–)	Central High School (MI); Bennington School of Dance (VT)
Lucretia Garfield (1832–1918)	Geauga Seminary (OH); Hiram College (OH)
Julia Grant (1826–1902)	boarding school (MO)
Florence Harding (1860–1924)	Cincinnati Conservatory of Music (OH)
Anna Harrison (1775–1864)	Clinton Academy (NY); Mrs. Graham's Boarding School (NY)
Caroline Harrison (1832–1892)	Oxford Female Seminary (OH)
Lucy Hayes[a] (1831–1889)	Ohio Wesleyan University, 1850
Lou Hoover[a] (1874–1944)	Leland Stanford Jr. University, 1898 (CA)
Eliza Johnson (1810–1876)	no formal education
Lady Bird Johnson[a] (1912–)	St. Mary's Episcopal School for Girls (TX); University of Texas, 1933
Jacqueline Kennedy[a] (1929–1994)	Holton-Arms School (DC); Porter's School (CT); Vassar College (NY); Sorbonne (Paris); George Washington University, 1951 (DC)
Mary Lincoln (1818–1882)	John Ward's Academy (KY); Mme. Mentelle's School (KY)
Dolley Madison (1768–1849)	no formal education
Ida McKinley (1847–1907)	Brook Hall Seminary (PA)
Elizabeth Monroe (1768–1830)	no formal education
Pat Nixon[a] (1912–1993)	University of Southern California, 1937
Jane Pierce (1806–1862)	no formal education
Sarah Polk (1803–1891)	Moravian Female Academy (NC)
Nancy Reagan[a] (1921–)	Girls' Latin School (IL); Smith College, 1943 (MA)
Edith Roosevelt (1861–1948)	Miss Comstock's School (NY)
Eleanor Roosevelt (1884–1962)	Allenwood School (London)
Helen Taft (1861–1943)	Miss Nourse's School (OH); University of Cincinnati (OH)
Margaret Taylor (1788–1852)	no formal education
Bess Truman (1885–1982)	public school (MO); Barstow School for Girls (MO)
Julia Tyler (1820–1889)	Chegary Institute (NY)
Letitia Tyler (1790–1842)	no formal education
Martha Washington (1731–1802)	no formal education
Edith Wilson (1872–1961)	Powell's School (VA); Martha Washington College (VA)
Ellen Wilson (1860–1914)	Female Seminary (GA); Art Students' League (NY)

Note: Martha Jefferson, Rachel Jackson, Hannah Van Buren, and Ellen Arthur were married to men who would eventually serve as president but died before their husbands took office. None had formal education.

a. Graduated from college.

Appendix 2 First Ladies' Birthplaces (by state)

State	First Lady
Connecticut	Edith Roosevelt
Georgia	Ellen Wilson; Rosalynn Carter
Illinois	Betty Ford; Hillary Clinton
Iowa	Lou Hoover; Mamie Eisenhower
Kentucky	Mary Lincoln
Maryland	Margaret Taylor
Massachusetts	Abigail Adams
Missouri	Julia Grant; Bess Truman
Nevada	Pat Nixon
New Hampshire	Jane Pierce
New Jersey	Anna Harrison
New York	Elizabeth Monroe; Julia Tyler; Abigail Fillmore; Frances Cleveland; Eleanor Roosevelt; Jacqueline Kennedy; Nancy Reagan; Barbara Bush
North Carolina	Dolley Madison
Ohio	Lucy Hayes; Lucretia Garfield; Caroline Harrison; Ida McKinley; Helen Taft; Florence Harding
Tennessee	Sarah Polk; Eliza Johnson
Texas	Lady Bird Johnson; Laura Bush
Vermont	Grace Coolidge
Virginia	Martha Washington; Letitia Tyler; Edith Wilson
England	Louisa Adams

Appendix 3   Ages on Becoming First Lady

First Lady	Age on Becoming First Lady
Anna Harrison	65 years, 222 days
Barbara Bush	64 years, 227 days
Abigail Fillmore	62 years, 111 days
Florence Harding	60 years, 202 days
Margaret Taylor	60 years, 164 days
Bess Truman	60 years, 57 days
Nancy Reagan	59 years, 198 days
Elizabeth Monroe	58 years, 247 days
Martha Washington	57 years, 313 days
Pat Nixon	56 years, 310 days
Caroline Harrison	56 years, 141 days
Mamie Eisenhower	56 years, 68 days
Lou Hoover	54 years, 340 days
Eliza Johnson	54 years, 151 days
Laura Bush	54 years, 78 days
Betty Ford	53 years, 123 days
Ellen Wilson	52 years, 293 days
Abigail Adams	52 years, 113 days
Lady Bird Johnson	50 years, 335 days
Letitia Tyler	50 years, 145 days
Louisa Adams	50 years, 20 days
Ida McKinley	49 years, 269 days
Rosalynn Carter	49 years, 155 days
Lucretia Garfield	48 years, 320 days
Eleanor Roosevelt	48 years, 144 days
Helen Taft	48 years, 71 days
Jane Pierce	46 years, 357 days
Hillary Clinton	46 years, 86 days
Lucy Hayes	45 years, 188 days
Grace Coolidge	44 years, 212 days
Julia Grant	43 years, 37 days
Mary Lincoln	42 years, 81 days
Sarah Polk	41 years, 181 days
Dolley Madison	40 years, 288 days
Edith Wilson	40 years, 140 days
Edith Roosevelt	40 years, 39 days
Jacqueline Kennedy	31 years, 176 days
Julia Tyler	24 years, 53 days
Frances Cleveland	21 years, 226 days

Appendix 4   First Ladies' Presidential Marriages (in chronological order of the presidency)

First Lady	Her Age at Marriage	His Age at Marriage	Length of Marriage
Martha Washington	27 years, 199 days	26 years, 318 days	40 years, 329 days
Abigail Adams	19 years, 348 days	28 years, 360 days	54 years, 3 days
Dolley Madison	26 years, 118 days	43 years, 183 days	41 years, 286 days
Elizabeth Monroe	17 years, 231 days	27 years, 294 days	44 years, 219 days
Louisa Adams	22 years, 164 days	30 years, 15 days	50 years, 212 days
Anna Harrison	20 years, 123 days	22 years, 289 days	45 years, 130 days
Letitia Tyler	22 years, 137 days	23 years	29 years, 165 days
Julia Tyler	24 years, 53 days	54 years, 89 days	17 years, 206 days
Sarah Polk	20 years, 119 days	28 years, 60 days	25 years, 165 days
Margaret Taylor	21 years, 273 days	25 years, 209 days	40 years, 18 days
Abigail Fillmore	27 years, 329 days	26 years, 29 days	27 years, 53 days
Jane Pierce	28 years, 243 days	29 years, 352 days	29 years, 22 days
Mary Lincoln	23 years, 326 days	33 years, 265 days	22 years, 162 days
Eliza Johnson	16 years, 225 days	18 years, 139 days	48 years, 75 days
Julia Grant	22 years, 208 days	26 years, 117 days	36 years, 335 days
Lucy Hayes	21 years, 124 days	30 years, 87 days	40 years, 18 days
Lucretia Garfield	26 years, 206 days	26 years, 357 days	22 years, 312 days
Frances Cleveland	21 years, 316 days	49 years, 76 days	22 years, 22 days
Caroline Harrison	21 years, 19 days	20 years, 61 days	39 years, 5 days
Ida McKinley	23 years, 231 days	27 years, 361 days	30 years, 232 days
Edith Roosevelt	25 years, 118 days	28 years, 36 days	32 years, 35 days
Helen Taft	25 years, 168 days	28 years, 277 days	43 years, 262 days
Ellen Wilson	25 years, 48 days	28 years, 177 days	29 years, 43 days
Edith Wilson	43 years, 64 days	58 years, 354 days	8 years, 47 days
Florence Harding	30 years, 327 days	25 years, 248 days	32 years, 25 days
Grace Coolidge	26 years, 274 days	33 years, 92 days	27 years, 93 days
Lou Hoover	24 years, 318 days	24 years, 184 days	44 years, 331 days
Eleanor Roosevelt	20 years, 157 days	23 years, 46 days	40 years, 26 days
Bess Truman	34 years, 135 days	35 years, 51 days	53 years, 181 days
Mamie Eisenhower	19 years, 229 days	25 years, 260 days	52 years, 270 days
Jacqueline Kennedy	24 years, 46 days	36 years, 106 days	10 years, 71 days
Lady Bird Johnson	21 years, 330 days	26 years, 82 days	39 years, 66 days
Pat Nixon	28 years, 97 days	27 years, 163 days	53 years, 1 day
Betty Ford	30 years, 190 days	35 years, 93 days	
Rosalynn Carter	18 years, 323 days	21 years, 279 days	
Nancy Reagan	30 years, 242 days	41 years, 26 days	
Barbara Bush	19 years, 213 days	20 years, 208 days	
Hillary Clinton	27 years, 359 days	29 years, 42 days	
Laura Bush	31 years, 1 day	31 years, 122 days	

Appendix 5

Martha Wayles Skelton Jefferson

Born: October 19, 1748; Charles City County, Virginia
Died: September 6, 1782, nineteen years prior to her husband's presidency; near Charlottesville, Virginia
President: Thomas Jefferson (1743–1826), Third President
Husband's Presidential Term: 1801–1809 (Democrat-Republican)
Marriage: First: November 20, 1766, to Bathurst Skelton; Charles City County, Virginia (widowed 1770). Second: January 1, 1772, to Thomas Jefferson; Williamsburg, Virginia
Children: First marriage: infant son (1767–1771). Second marriage: Martha Washington (1772–1836); Jane Randolph (1774–1775); infant son (1777); Mary (1778–1804); Lucy Elizabeth (1780–1781); Lucy Elizabeth (1782–1785)

Early Years

Martha Wayles came from a wealthy family. Her parents, John and Martha Eppes Wayles, owned a large plantation in Charles City County, near Williamsburg, Virginia. Although very little is known about her youth, she appears to have had a privileged upbringing, typical for daughters of the Virginia gentry. It is probable she was educated in her family's home, assisted by occasional tutors. She was fairly well schooled for a girl of her day and age, although that, as for most eighteenth-century girls, seems to have been mainly in the domestic realm—learning to cook, sew, and manage a household. Reading, literature, Bible study, and French possibly were part of her education as well, and because of Martha's musical abilities, it appears she was taught to sing and play instruments.

Several accounts describe Martha as a striking young woman with hazel eyes and auburn hair; along with her family's prominence, her beauty made her a much sought-after bride among Virginia's leading young men. At age eighteen, on November 20, 1766, she married Bathurst Skelton, a powerful, successful lawyer, apparently also from Virginia. A year after their marriage, Martha gave birth to a son. In 1770 Skelton died; the following year Martha lost her young son. Not much is known about her first marriage.

Marriage

Around the time of her child's death, Martha began to be courted by Thomas Jefferson. She was only twenty-two and was most likely one of the wealthiest women in Virginia. In the 1700s it was not uncommon for a young widow to begin a relationship with another man not long after her husband died, especially if she had children. After a very short engagement, Thomas and Martha were married on New Year's Day 1772, at her plantation home, known as "the Forest." Thomas Jefferson was twenty-nine and Martha twenty-three. It seems to have been a perfect marriage between two wealthy members of Virginia's gentry, and they appear to have been truly in love. Both were proficient musicians—Jefferson an accomplished violinist and Martha excelling at the harpsichord. Soon after their marriage, Jefferson purchased a fortepiano for his new bride.

Jefferson's plantation home, Monticello, was in a sparsely populated area of rural Virginia, unlike the community in which Martha was raised. She seems to have been apprehensive at first but grew to enjoy her husband's beloved Monticello.

In nine years of marriage to Jefferson, Martha gave birth to six children, four of whom died in infancy. The tragedy of their deaths along with the physical strain of frequent pregnancies and childbirth weakened an already fragile woman. The marriage was a happy one, despite the loss of their children and Martha's frail health. Only two Jefferson children, Martha and Mary, survived past their teen years. Martha (nicknamed "Patsy") was an exceptionally bright young woman, who reportedly took after her father. Mary (nicknamed "Polly") lacked her sister's intellect but was said to have her mother's beauty and mannerisms.

Family Life

In addition to being an intellectual well versed in numerous fields, Jefferson was a complex man. Despite his belief that "all men are created equal" and his humanitarian advocacy of the "common man," he did not support such rights for women. A liberal and reformer, he held traditional views on women, believing they should first and foremost function as wives. Women should concentrate on being good homemakers, dress well and have good manners, and, according to the father of the Declaration of Independence, aim to please their husbands. Jefferson even counseled against women involving themselves in politics, and it appears that Martha did not advise her husband or play any role in supporting or promoting his political career.

The couple lived a life typical of wealthy plantation owners. But the onset of the Revolutionary War and Jefferson's central role in forwarding the ideals of liberty and independence posed a great challenge to them. Jefferson often had to be away from his delicate wife and young children, and shortly after New Year's Day in 1781, a British invasion near Monticello forced her to escape to Richmond with them. Near the end of the war, she became very ill. The birth of another child in 1782 was too much for her, and she died a few weeks later.

Jefferson kept locks of his wife's hair, just as he had done with each child he and Martha lost. He went into a deep state of mourning and depression, burning their correspondence and remaining in seclusion for some three weeks after her death. As Martha lay dying, Jefferson is said to have made a vow to her never to remarry.

Presidency

Martha Jefferson died approximately nineteen years before Thomas Jefferson's election to the presidency. His older daughter, Martha, served as his primary hostess, staying at the White House with her family and presiding over its social affairs during the winters of 1802–1803 and 1805–1806 (see Chapter 3).

Legacy

Martha Jefferson's contribution to her husband's career was negligible. Although they shared a warm marriage, her poor health always limited her and eventually ended her life at a young age. Even if she had lived, it is doubtful she would have played a vital role in his presidency, not only because of her health but also because of her husband's traditional views on women. It is safe to say that Martha did not influence her husband's political opinions or career directly. Yet given that Jefferson was the author of the Declaration of Independence, a founding father of the country, and the patriotic pen behind the Revolution, history owes Martha Jefferson some consideration. It was she who was beside him during the critical years of these momentous deeds.

Jefferson appears to have felt deeply for Martha, as evidenced by the sorrow that overcame him after she died. He was frequently absent from political business in Virginia to be at her side, even turning down an appointment by the Continental Congress to be commissioner to France because of her frail health and choosing to remain with her at Monticello. But Jefferson recorded little of their life together, and after her death he found it too painful even to talk about her. She remains one of the least well known presidential wives.

Bibliography

Betts, Edwin, and James A. Bear, eds. *The Family Letters of Thomas Jefferson.* Columbia: University of Missouri Press, 1966.

Brodie, Fawn M. *Thomas Jefferson: An Intimate History.* New York: Norton, 1974.

Fleming, Thomas. *The Man from Monticello: An Intimate Life of Thomas Jefferson.* New York: Morrow, 1969.

Langhorne, Elizabeth. *Monticello: A Family Story.* New York: Workman, 1989.

Malone, Dumas. *Jefferson the Virginian.* Boston: Little, Brown, 1948.

Appendix 6

Rachel Donelson Jackson

Born: June 15, 1767; Halifax County, Virginia
Died: December 22, 1828, several weeks prior to her husband's presidency; Nashville, Tennessee
President: Andrew Jackson (1767–1845), Seventh President
Husband's Presidential Term: 1829–1837 (Democrat)
Marriage: First: March 1, 1784 or 1785, to Lewis Robards (divorced 1790/1793). Second: August 1791; remarried January 17, 1794
Children: First marriage: None. Second marriage: None (adopted nephew Andrew Jr.)

Early Years

Rachel Donelson was born into a family of moderate affluence. Her father, John Donelson, was originally from Maryland and, after establishing himself in Virginia, served in the state legislature. Her mother, Rachel Stockley, was also from Virginia. Although Rachel was born there in 1767, she spent much of her adolescence in Tennessee. When she was twelve years old, her father became the leader of an adventurous group of 40 men and 110 women and children from Virginia who sought a better life on the rugged frontier of Tennessee. Rachel's father sent a few men in advance to begin clearing land and building homes for the settlers, then the main group followed in a dangerous trip that he chronicled in *Journal of a Voyage Intended by God's Permission.* The voyage down the Cumberland River was fraught with challenges, as the pioneers survived an epidemic of smallpox, confrontations with Indians, and treacherous waters that claimed some of their belongings.

Donelson's pioneers were among the first whites to inhabit the area. Although the Donelsons and others in the group prospered, the restless John Donelson moved again, this time to Kentucky. But the hazards of the frontier soon took their toll: After the family moved back to Tennessee both Rachel's father and brother died fighting Indians, leaving the Donelson women to forge a life in the frontier.

At age seventeen Rachel married Lewis Robards, who was from a prominent family in Kentucky and several years her senior. Although it appears that it was Robards who was unfaithful in marriage, he forbade his wife even to talk to other men, and his jealousy resulted in much abuse toward Rachel. The two agreed on very little and argued constantly during their brief marriage. Even Robards's mother, with whom the couple lived, recognized her son's abusive ways and sided with Rachel in many of the family quarrels. In a fit of rage, Robards eventually ordered Rachel out of the house. She moved back to Tennessee with her family and, in what was a very bold move for a woman of that time, decided to leave Robards. In 1790 she requested a divorce, but in the eighteenth century only men could legally initiate divorce proceedings. Robards never finalized his agreement to do so.

Marriage to Andrew Jackson

While Rachel was living with her mother, helping her family run their plantation and boarding house, a self-taught attorney named Andrew Jackson was establishing himself in Tennessee, riding his county judicial circuit on horseback. Because Jackson's large jurisdiction encompassed the Donelson property, the young circuit judge periodically stayed there. The area was still frontier, and tensions between Indians and white settlers remained, so Rachel's mother enjoyed the security of having the young man with a military background stay at her home. Whether the widow was matchmaking for her heartbroken daughter is unclear, but a love affair soon blossomed between Jackson and Rachel, and his visits to the Donelson home became more frequent.

The specifics of the story are unclear, but apparently Rachel and Jackson believed that at Andrew's insistence Lewis Robards had carried out divorce proceedings in Virginia. The couple wasted no time, marrying in October 1791. But they learned in December 1793 that Rachel's divorce had not been officially completed: Robards had never acted on the agreement to end the marriage and apparently the limited communications of the frontier prevented word of this from reaching the Jacksons. Why Robards failed to complete the divorce is uncertain, but the illegal marriage between Rachel and Jackson created a scandal that deeply wounded her. Moreover, the vindictive Robards then decided he would sue the couple on grounds of adultery and nullify their marriage. He also threatened to come to the Donelson home and take Rachel back with him. Predictably, the volatile Jackson exchanged words with Robards, threatening to cut off the man's ears if he attempted to make any further issue of the marriage. The stories of Jackson's temper and propensity for violence were legendary, and Robards wisely backed down. The divorce was granted.

Although Jackson initially opposed remarrying Rachel because he worried it would lend validity to Robards's arguments, he changed his mind, and the two were married a second time and legally in January 1794. The scandal of adultery and bigamy haunted them thereafter, however, and even threatened to undermine his political career. For the rest of her life, Rachel suffered emotionally from the accusations and apparently lost much of her youthful enthusiasm for life under the strain of public scandal. For his part, Jackson was always quick to anger and to defend his wife. On several occasions he fought a duel, once killing a man over the matter.

Family Life

"Old Hickory," as Andrew Jackson came to be known, built a cotton plantation near Nashville; the Hermitage would be their home for much of their life together. It was generally a happy union, although they were continually confronted with the scandal surrounding their marriage and were troubled that they never had children of their own. In 1809 the Jacksons adopted one of their nephews and named him for Andrew Jackson. They also helped raise several other nieces and nephews and entertained a steady flow of relatives and visitors to the Hermitage. Later in life Rachel especially enjoyed the company of her niece Emily, who had married her cousin, Andrew Jackson Donelson.

Rachel and Jackson were opposites in many ways, with Rachel private and religious and Andrew outgoing and rambunctious. Rachel's religious convictions contributed further pain to her marital scandal and seemed to intensify with each additional accusation. Rachel regularly attended church, observed the Sabbath, and was an avid reader of the Bible, but she was very judgmental of others, especially those who did not meet her expectations or hold the same religious views. When the couple traveled to New Orleans to celebrate Jackson's victory over the British in the Battle of New Orleans, she was repulsed by the city and its people, referring to it as "the great Babylon." But she did visit injured soldiers in the hospital during her visit. After the celebration they traveled to Washington and found the city eager to bestow honor upon the hero of the War of 1812, but Rachel did not care for the capital either. Upon Jackson's appointment as military governor of Florida after the Seminole Indian wars, Rachel was offended by the city of Pensacola, referring to the residents as "cast-off Americans" who were "no better than Spaniards." Because of her pious, narrow views, she was further upset by the lack of Protestant clergy in the Gulf region and the prevailing Catholicism of the populace. Rachel complained about the prevalence of gambling and was disturbed to find people enjoying dancing. The final straw seems to have been when she encountered stores and shops that were open on the Sabbath.

Part of her hostility toward Florida and New Orleans was the result of encountering a sizable nonwhite population in both regions. Rachel and Jackson owned twenty slaves and were harsh masters, threatening them with beatings. Rachel had a definite calming effect on him, and he even deferred to her on a range of matters. She also managed their plantation when "Mr. Jackson" or "the General," as she called him, was away at war or fulfilling the obligations of public office.

Jackson's political star was rising; he had become a national hero after the Battle of New Orleans at the close of the War of 1812. Rachel Jackson was not, however, pleased with his decision to enter public life, largely because of the prospect of the attacks both would inevitably experience. But he was very ambitious, and she could not dissuade him. Rachel never developed an interest in politics; although she played a visible, central role in their home, Rachel neither attempted nor accomplished much in public life. When her husband served as a delegate to Congress, Rachel chose not to accompany him to Washington (in fact, few political wives from the frontier ever made such trips to the capital).

Presidency

Both Jackson's first and second campaigns (in 1824 and 1828) for the presidency upset Rachel, as they brought intense scrutiny of their marriage. Moreover, she had not aged well. Now in her late fifties, she had gained an unhealthy amount of weight, suffered from poor health and a weak heart, and was bitter, solitary, judgmental, and depressed. Rachel worried about how she would hold up during the presidency. Likewise, the eastern press and public speculated about her ability to fulfill the social duties of the president's spouse, suggesting that Rachel, a hick from the frontier, would certainly be no Dolley Madison. Rachel entertained the idea of not attending the inaugural if Jackson were elected and had asked her favorite niece Emily in advance to preside over most White House duties for her.

Throughout the first campaign Rachel often stayed in her room rather than assist in or appear at social events on her husband's behalf. The campaign attacks were, as anticipated, brutal, and her fears that the supporters of John Quincy Adams, Jackson's rival, would use the divorce as a major campaign weapon were realized. She was devastated by the attacks on her, as well as those aimed at her husband, including rumors of his excessive gambling and pamphlets circulated about their divorce. A few newspapers picked up on the story and carried it, despite Jackson's efforts to contain it by providing a formal document stating his version of their marriage.

After Jackson's first but unsuccessful campaign for the White House—he won the popular vote but lost in the electoral college—the couple returned to Tennessee for a much-needed period of rest for Rachel. Her health had been in decline throughout the campaign, but she became quite ill after the race. After the second campaign four years later she was proud that her husband won the presidency, even though it meant she would face the pressures and responsibilities of the White House.

This was not to be. Rachel died just weeks before the start of her husband's presidency. Jackson, who wept openly at the funeral, was heartbroken over her death. He began wearing and keeping by his bedside a miniature portrait of her.

Legacy

Rachel Jackson was one of the most maligned presidential spouses, even though she never lived in the White House. Although she influenced her husband's personal and home life, which of course may have shaped his professional life, she had little interest in public life and achieved no significant accomplishments as a political spouse. Perhaps the only identifiable role she fulfilled in Andrew's political career was a negative one, as the cause of the claims that Jackson was a bigamist. Had she lived, it is doubtful she would have attempted or achieved much as a hostess at the White House, but she may have been a comfort to her husband, whose two terms are remembered as one of the more influential presidencies in the history of the office.

Rachel was buried at the Hermitage on Christmas Eve 1828, in the white dress she had purchased for her husband's inauguration.

Bibliography

Bassett, John Spencer. *Correspondence of Andrew Jackson.* 7 volumes. Washington, D.C.: Carnegie Institution, 1925–1935.

Burke, Pauline Wilcox. *Emily Donelson of Tennessee.* 2 volumes. Richmond: Garrett and Massie, 1941.

Caldwell, Mary French. *Andrew Jackson's Hermitage.* Nashville: Ladies Hermitage Association, 1933.

———. *General Jackson's Lady.* Nashville: Ladies Hermitage Association and Kingsport Press, 1936.

Heiskell, S. G. *Andrew Jackson and Early Tennessee History.* 2 volumes. Nashville: Ambrose Printing, 1918.

Remini, Robert Vincent. *Andrew Jackson and the Cause of the American Empire.* New York: Harper & Row, 1977.

Appendix 7

Hannah Hoes
Van Buren

Born: March 8, 1783; Kinderhook, New York
Died: February 5, 1819, eighteen years prior to her husband's presiden-
cy; Albany, New York
President: Martin Van Buren (1772–1862), Eighth President
Husband's Presidential Term: 1837–1841 (Democrat)
Marriage: February 21, 1807; Catskill, New York
Children: Abraham (1807–1873); John (1810–1866); Martin (1812–
1855); infant son (?); Smith Thompson (1817–1876)

Early Years
Both Hannah Hoes and her future husband, Martin Van Buren, grew
up in the same hometown of Kinderhook in New York. In fact, the
two were cousins, went to school together, and were even childhood
sweethearts. Kinderhook was a close-knit Dutch community, and
both Hannah and Martin were raised speaking the Dutch language at
home.

Hannah was born in Kinderhook on March 8, 1783. Both her family
and Van Buren's were somewhat prominent farmers and had recently
emigrated to the United States. Little is known about Hannah's upbringing except that she was not formally educated. Nevertheless, she would
later show herself to be a quick learner and capable partner in her husband's early legal and political careers.

Marriage

Van Buren courted Hannah while he began his law practice, but he wanted to establish himself professionally and financially before marrying. Both were in their mid-twenties when they wed in 1807, with Hannah a few months younger than her husband. The two seem to have been a good match and shared more than their family backgrounds and upbringing—they were both honest and good-natured, and had the same childhood friends. It appears that a pleasing physical appearance was one of the few things they did not have in common: Although "Jannetje," as Martin called Hannah, was described as attractive, Martin was reportedly quite the opposite.

Family Life

Very little is known about the family and home life of Hannah Van Buren; she is one of the least-known presidential wives, although she appears to have been happy in her marriage. A pleasant individual, she was described by a relative as a "loving" person with a "gentle disposition" and "modest, even timid manner." It is clear that she was warm and well liked, a simple, unassuming woman who lived the same type of life.

One of her passions was religion. From church archives we know that she regularly attended services and was involved in church programs and activities; her obituary in the Albany, New York, newspaper mentioned her strong Christian faith. Hannah was raised in the Dutch Reformed Church but was unable to find this denomination once they moved from the Kinderhook community. She attended the First Presbyterian Church in Albany while Martin was serving in office in the New York state capital and was also a member of the Presbyterian church in Hudson, New York, when they lived there. Church services at both were in English, in which she was fluent, although she continued to use Dutch at home all her life.

Hannah gave birth to their first child, Abraham, in 1807 while still living in Kinderhook and later had three sons in Hudson, while Van Buren held a minor political position there. He was a state senator from 1813 to 1820 and was made state attorney general in 1815, when his political career took the family to the state capital. Hannah managed a busy household in Albany: Martin's law partner and three law apprentices lived with the Van Burens. The couple entertained state politicians as well as visiting relatives from Kinderhook. Hannah occasionally got away from the demands of her life to return to Kinderhook for a visit, but not because of unhappiness with her husband, the city of Albany, or displeasure with entertaining political guests. Indeed, Hannah enjoyed the social side of politics, even though she had been somewhat shy growing up.

Presidency

After giving birth to a fifth son in January 1817, Hannah became very weak and never fully recovered. The following winter her health seriously began to fail. The record states that she was stoic to the end, supposedly giving a touching farewell to her loved ones on her deathbed. She died on February 5, 1819, apparently of tuberculosis. She was only thirty-five.

Martin Van Buren never remarried. He assumed the presidency in 1837, eighteen years after his wife's death, as a widower with four bachelor sons.

Legacy

Van Buren lived another four decades after Hannah died. Although he does not mention his wife by name in his autobiography, such omissions were not uncommon in the day: Before the nineteenth century a lady's name was not to appear in such records, and a gentleman would not violate this rule of etiquette. (He also scarcely mentioned his parents or children.) Not only was Hannah a very private woman, but a woman's personal life in the nineteenth century was also that: private.

Hannah was the first wife of a future president to be born a citizen of the United States. Yet she possibly can be credited for more than this. Van Buren was certainly an unlikely presidential candidate: He was the consummate political underdog throughout his career, not well educated, not very charismatic, and he spoke with a Dutch accent and seemed to have marginal political instincts. As such, his success could be explained as an anomaly, luck, the result of hard work and persistence, and as the result of the weakness of the presidency in the years following Andrew Jackson. But it is possible that Hannah played a role in supporting and assisting her husband at the outset of his career. The little information that exists suggests she was a caring, unselfish individual. One story provides an example: John Chester, the minister of the Albany church Hannah attended, developed a program to teach the city's poor to read. Reverend Chester ran into opposition from many in the community and even some in his congregation, but Hannah fully supported the project and even contributed to it financially. With the support of Hannah and a few others, the minister was able to initiate this worthwhile endeavor. On her deathbed Hannah continued her charitable and conscientious ways, requesting that the money for her funeral be spent instead on the poor.

Bibliography

Irelan, John Robert. *History of the Life, Administration and Times of Martin Van Buren*. 2 volumes. New York: Fairbanks and Palmer, 1886–1889.

Lynch, Dennis Tilden. *An Epoch and a Man: Martin Van Buren and His Times*. New York: Horace Liveright, 1929.

Niven, John. *Martin Van Buren: The Romantic Age of American Politics*. New York: Oxford University Press, 1983.

Shepherd, Edward M. *Martin Van Buren*. Boston: Houghton Mifflin, 1888.

Whitton, Mary Ormsbee. *First First Ladies, 1789–1865: A Study of the Wives of the Early Presidents*. New York: Hastings House, 1948.

Appendix 8

Ellen Lewis
Herndon Arthur

Born: August 30, 1837; Culpeper Court House, Virginia
Died: January 12, 1880, twenty months prior to her husband's presidency; Washington, D.C.
President: Chester A. Arthur (1829–1886), Twenty-first President
Husband's Presidential Term: 1881–1885 (Republican)
Marriage: October 25, 1859; New York, New York
Children: William Lewis (1860–1863); Chester Alan (1864–1937);
Ellen Herndon (1871–1915)

Early Years

Ellen Herndon was born in August 1837 at Culpeper Court House,
Virginia. She was the only child of a prominent Virginia family that was
well acquainted with Washington society. Her mother was Elizabeth
Hansbrough; her father, William Lewis Herndon, achieved minor fame
as a naval hero and was also known for his exploits leading an expedition down the Amazon River in 1851.

As a young girl Ellen moved with her family to Washington, where
her father had received a new posting: working with Matthew Fontaine
Maury, a relative, to establish the U.S. Naval Observatory. Ellen later
moved to New York when her father became commander of a mail
steamer based there.

Ellen seems to have been a well-adjusted young woman who
enjoyed a comfortable upbringing. A physically attractive girl with a

beautiful voice, she was a somewhat well-known and successful singer. At one point she was a featured vocalist at St. John's Episcopal Church on Lafayette Square in Washington.

Marriage

While living in New York, Ellen met Chester Arthur, a young lawyer setting up his practice in the state. The two were introduced in 1856 by Ellen's cousin Dabney Herndon. Apparently, the two fell for each other shortly after their initial meeting. A year later they became engaged but did not marry until October 25, 1859, perhaps because Arthur first wanted to establish a successful career. Their wedding was in New York City. Arthur, seven years Ellen's senior, called his bride "Nell," and she called him "Chet."

Ellen's romance with Chester was scarred by the death of her father. Herndon's ship encountered rough waters near Cape Hatteras, and after making sure his passengers and crew were safely removed, he went down with his vessel. Chester Arthur took over the family financial matters for the Herndons. Ellen's mother seems to have approved of her daughter's choice and was close to Arthur.

Family Life

Ellen had three children, the first born a year after her marriage and named for Ellen's father. Sadly, young William died at age two. A year later, in 1864, Ellen gave birth to another son, named Chester Alan, and a daughter, Ellen Herndon, was born in 1871; both children survived to adulthood.

Chester Arthur's legal practice continued to grow, and the Arthurs became very wealthy. They employed servants, their children were educated by the best private tutors, and the couple traveled extensively. They spent many days vacationing at Lake George in New York, one of their favorite places. Ellen decorated their home with elaborate, expensive furnishings and shopped for the latest fashions and jewelry in New York City's best stores. Her husband enjoyed buying clothing for Ellen, and much of her wardrobe came from London. Ellen's hostessing was equally impressive. She entertained frequently, and her events were attended by many of the leading members of the community. She was an outgoing, warm individual, and her style, described as southern and hospitable, matched her personality. Ellen apparently regarded herself as southern gentry.

Ellen's heritage caused minor tension between the Arthurs. Her family was from old Virginia and continued to identify with their past. The Herndon family owned slaves, and some would fight for the Confederacy. In contrast, Arthur's father, a Baptist preacher, was an ardent supporter of abolition, and Arthur himself, although not as passionate about abolition as his father, was nevertheless solidly behind the North. As a young lawyer before the outbreak of the Civil War, Arthur helped and defended former slaves who had escaped to New York from the South. In fact, one of his legal victories led to the racial integration of New York's streetcars. Their differences on the matter of the Civil War were not enough to threaten the marriage, however, as Ellen's family remained close to Arthur, and on occasion Arthur even teased Ellen, referring to her as his "little rebel wife."

Arthur's support of abolition and the Union continued when war broke out between the North and South, two years after his marriage. Although he was at times critical of Lincoln and a moderate on the slavery issue, he was pro-Union. During the war he served as inspector general and quartermaster general for the state of New York, working in support of the state's troops and overseeing the army's supplies and finances. When a few of Ellen's relatives who were fighting for the Confederacy were captured, Arthur used his influence to secure their release.

After the war the Arthur marriage became lukewarm at times. Arthur spent time away from home, often leaving Ellen feeling lonely. She was quite traditional and religious and disapproved of Arthur's fondness for drinking and smoking with his political cronies. Arthur was also hindered by his ties to the New York political machine. In fact, at one point his relations with less-than-upstanding politicians caused President Rutherford B. Hayes, a reformer, to remove Arthur from public office. Arthur's lifestyle also resulted in his gaining an unhealthy amount of weight. Even though the marriage was strained and they even contemplated separating occasionally, Ellen was bothered by the political attacks on her husband and allegations of his corruption.

She kept up her singing, performing in church, at the society affairs they attended, and during political fundraisers and events. In January 1880, while her husband was working in Albany, she attended a benefit concert in New York City. While awaiting her carriage in the crisp air after the event, she caught a cold, which quickly led to pneumonia. She died suddenly and unexpectedly the next day, January 12, 1880, only forty-two years old. Arthur rushed back to his wife's bedside, arriving just before she died, but she was already unconscious.

At the time of this tragedy, Arthur was considering a run for national office, and his political star was ascending rapidly. Ellen's death deeply affected him, however; he seems to have regretted his lifestyle and his inattentiveness to her, carrying this burden with him the rest of his life. He was never as motivated by politics again.

Presidency

He did not know it, but Chester Arthur was only twenty months away from assuming the presidency at the time of his wife's death. He would shortly become the vice presidential candidate on James Garfield's ticket. Yet both the vice presidency and, after the assassination of President Garfield, his succession to the presidency were somewhat anticlimatic for him. In his own words, because of Ellen's death, "honors to me are not what they once were." In memory of her, Arthur purchased a stained-glass window for St. John's Episcopal Church, where Ellen used to sing, and had it set in the south side of the church so that he could see it from the White House. Arthur also kept her picture in his room at the White House and regularly placed roses, a favorite of his late wife, beside it.

During his presidency, Arthur asked his youngest sister, Mary Arthur McElroy, to serve as mistress of the White House. In part because of the weight he had gained and also his grieving, his health declined during his term. His administration was marked by mediocrity and accomplished little.

Legacy

There was public speculation about whether Arthur would remarry after leaving the White House. Although he planned to return to his successful career in law, his health forced him to retire from both politics and law. Arthur died only a year after his term, from a cerebral hemorrhage in 1886.

Ellen Arthur was not a well-known presidential spouse. Chester Arthur burned most of their personal letters, and after her death rarely spoke of her again. She appears to have been a gifted hostess and was, like her husband, quite ambitious. Had she lived, she would likely have been a hospitable first lady. As to her influence either socially or politically over her husband, it is less probable she would have had much impact. Because she was not active in political affairs, and her marriage was not strong at the time of her death, it is doubtful she would have salvaged a weak presidency.

Bibliography

Howe, George F. *Chester A. Arthur: A Quarter-Century of Machine Politics.* Norwalk, CT: Easton Press, 1987.

McConnell, Burt, and Jane McConnell. *Our First Ladies.* New York: Crowell, 1969.

Reeves, Thomas C. *Gentleman Boss: The Life of Chester Alan Arthur.* New York: Knopf, 1975.

Sadler, Christine. *Children in the White House.* New York: Putnam's, 1967.

Selected Bibliography

Anthony, Carl Sferrazza. *First Ladies: The Saga of the Presidents' Wives and Their Power.* New York: William Morrow, 1991.

Boller, Paul F., Jr. *Presidential Wives: An Anecdotal History.* New York: Oxford University Press, 1988.

Caroli, Betty Boyd. *First Ladies.* New York: Oxford University Press, 1987.

Gould, Lewis L., ed. *American First Ladies: Their Lives and Their Legacy.* New York: Garland Publishing, 1996.

Gutin, Myra. *The President's Partner: The First Lady in the Twentieth Century.* New York: Greenwood Press, 1989.

Klapthor, Margaret Brown. *The First Ladies.* Washington, D.C.: White House Historical Association, 1994.

Rosebush, James S. *First Lady, Public Wife: A Behind-the-Scenes History of the Evolving Role of First Ladies in American Political Life.* New York: Madison Books, 1987.

Troy, Gil. *Affairs of State: The Rise and Rejection of the Presidential Couple Since World War II.* New York: Free Press, 1997.

Truman, Margaret. *The First Ladies: An Intimate Group Portrait of White House Wives.* New York: Random House, 1995.

Watson, Robert P. *The Presidents' Wives: Reassessing the Office of First Lady.* Boulder, CO: Lynne Rienner Publishers, 1999.

Index of First Ladies and Presidents

Subject Index

Abolition, 71
Adams, Abigail Amelia, 19, 21–22
Adams, Catherine Nuth, 42
Adams, Charles, 19, 22
Adams, Charles Francis, 42, 45
Adams, George Washington, 42, 45, 47
Adams, John Quincy II, 42, 45
Adams, Joshua Johnson, 42
Adams, Louisa II, 42
Adams, Susanna, 19, 22
Adams, Thomas, 19, 22
Adoption and Safe Family Act, 281
African American, 5, 125, 215, 223
Agnes Scott College, 266
Agnew, Spiro, 258
Alabama, 215, 224, 247
Albert, Edward, Prince of Wales, 104
Alexander, Czar, 45
Alexander, Minnie, 148
Alien and Sedition Act, 23
Allenwood Academy, 219, 289
American Association to Promote the
    Teaching of Speech to the Deaf,
    207
American Bible Society, 100
American Cancer Society, 241, 258, 260
American Colonization Society, 100
American Indian, 56–57, 104, 167, 193
American Legion, 209
American Lung Association, 209
Americans for Democratic Action,
    224–225

American Society for Foreign Missions,
    100
American Women's Voluntary Services,
    233
Amherst College, 209
Anderson, Marian, 223
Antietam, 132
Anti-Masons, 57, 89
Appalachia, 224
Appleton, Elizabeth Means, 95
Appleton, Jesse, 95
Appomattox, 127
Archbishop of Canterbury, 23, 102
Arkansas, 278–281
Arkansas Advocates for Children and
    Families, 280
Arlington National Cemetery, 181
Arthur, Chester Alan II, 307–308
Arthur, Ellen, 2, 142, 289–292,
    307–311; birth of, 307; childhood of,
    307–308; children of, 307; death of,
    307, 310; family life, 308–309; mar-
    riage, 307–309
Arthur, William, 307–308
Articles of Confederation, 37, 55
Ashley Hall boarding school, 274,
    289
Atlanta, 184, 186
Atomic bomb, 228
Auchincloss, Hugh D., 238
Axson, Margaret Jane Hoyt, 183
Axson, Rev. Samuel E., 183

317

About the Book

Whether editing speeches and appearing on the campaign trail, presiding over White House renovations and social events, championing important causes, or functioning as the president's most trusted adviser, first ladies have made significant contributions to the careers of the chief executives and to the nation. Yet, the accomplishments of those who have acted as the power behind the presidency have been largely unreported and underappreciated. Systematically profiling each first lady from Martha Washington to Laura Bush, Watson offers the reader an intimate look at these women who have served the United States.

The chronologically arranged biographies examine each first lady's early years and education, her family life, her presidential years, and her legacy. A short bibliography for each entry provides a selected list of additional sources. *First Ladies of the United States* is a convenient, thoroughly indexed reference, as well as an insightful account of the lives of forty-six women who have helped shape the course of U.S. history as first ladies.

Robert Watson is associate professor of political science at the University of Hawai'i–Hilo. His publications include *The Presidents' Wives: Reassessing the Office of First Lady.*